Praise for *Tomorrow's High School*

Gene Bottoms is unapologetically relentless in his work to help create tomorrow's high school. He offers unconditional determination and support for schools to make a greater difference in the lives of more students. And he has more than a plan—he has experience and results.

>—**Mark Musick,** President Emeritus, Southern Regional Education Board

Gene Bottoms issues a timely and relevant call to action in *Tomorrow's High School*. The book begins with a clear, concise assessment of the current educational context that prepares high percentages of students for low-wage jobs. A bold yet practical framework gleaned from decades of research and practice within the High Schools That Work consortium yields strategies for transforming the high school experience and outcomes for students. The focus on powerful assignments and redesigning transitions as students enter and exit high school are examples of specific tools for preparing career- and college-ready students. This book holds the potential to revolutionize high school education.

>—**Karen Bryant,** Department Head
>Lifelong Education, Administration, and Policy
>Mary Frances Early College of Education
>University of Georgia

Gene Bottoms distills a career's worth of wisdom and perspective to provide a framework that addresses the challenges of preparing *all young people* for a successful, happy, and productive future in the 21st century. He makes a compelling case for a student-centered, continuous improvement approach to examining school practices and blurring the lines between students' senior year and postsecondary education. In this, he draws on authentic, real-world efforts to improve education for all and offers recommendations likely to make a difference in the lives of America's students. *Tomorrow's High School* is a must read for forward-thinking state, district, and school leaders.

>—**James R. Stone III,** EdD
>Professor Emeritus, University of Minnesota
>Director, National Research Center for Career & Technical Education,
>Southern Regional Education Board

Education is a right. Our nation must move the current abysmal 60 percent college- and career-ready rate to an achievable 95 percent. Gene Bottoms's researched and prescribed model makes this a reality. Every learning institution and educator should assume the responsibility to immerse in a genuine self-study, and to develop a vision and plan that ensure that all students have the platform to reach career- and college-readiness standards.

—**Rebecca M. Dedmond,** PhD, LPC
NCDA Fellow
Associate Professor, George Washington University

TOMORROW'S HIGH SCHOOL

GENE BOTTOMS

TOMORROW'S HIGH SCHOOL

Creating Student Pathways for Both College and Career

Alexandria, Virginia USA

Southern Regional
Education Board

Atlanta, Georgia USA

1703 N. Beauregard St. • Alexandria, VA 22311-1714 USA
Phone: 800-933-2723 or 703-578-9600 • Fax: 703-575-5400
Website: www.ascd.org • Email: member@ascd.org
Author guidelines: www.ascd.org/write

SREB | Southern Regional
Education Board

Southern Regional Education Board
592 10th St. N.W.
Atlanta, GA 30318-5776
Website: www.sreb.org

Ranjit Sidhu, *CEO & Executive Director;* Penny Reinart, *Chief Impact Officer;* Genny Ostertag, *Managing Director, Book Acquisitions & Editing;* Susan Hills, *Senior Acquisitions Editor;* Julie Houtz, *Director, Book Editing;* Liz Wegner, *Editor;* Thomas Lytle, *Creative Director;* Donald Ely, *Art Director;* Samantha Wood & Derrick Douglass, *Graphic Designers;* Cynthia Stock, *Typesetter;* Kelly Marshall, *Production Manager;* Shajuan Martin, *E-Publishing Specialist;* Christopher Logan, *Senior Production Specialist*

The appendixes are available online at at www.ascd.org/CareerTechEdTools.

All web links in this book are correct as of the publication date below but may have become inactive or otherwise modified since that time. If you notice a deactivated or changed link, please email books@ascd.org with the words "Link Update" in the subject line. In your message, please specify the web link, the book title, and the page number on which the link appears.

PAPERBACK ISBN: 978-1-4166-3087-6   ASCD product #122017   n3/22
PDF E-BOOK ISBN: 978-1-4166-3088-3; see Books in Print for other formats.
Quantity discounts are available: email programteam@ascd.org or call 800-933-2723, ext. 5773, or 703-575-5773. For desk copies, go to www.ascd.org/deskcopy.

Library of Congress Cataloging-in-Publication Data

Names: Bottoms, Gene, author.
Title: Tomorrow's high school : creating student pathways for both college and career / Gene Bottoms.
Description: Alexandria, Virginia : ASCD, [2022] | Includes bibliographical references and index.
Identifiers: LCCN 2021047265 (print) | LCCN 2021047266 (ebook) | ISBN 9781416630876 (paperback) | ISBN 9781416630883 (pdf)
Subjects: LCSH: High school teaching. | College preparation programs. | School-to-work transition. | Education, Secondary—Aims and objectives.
Classification: LCC LB1607 .B62 2022 (print) | LCC LB1607 (ebook) | DDC 373.1102—dc23/eng/20211103
LC record available at https://lccn.loc.gov/2021047265
LC ebook record available at https://lccn.loc.gov/2021047266

TOMORROW'S HIGH SCHOOL

Creating Student Pathways for Both College and Career

Introduction: Tomorrow's High School 1

1. Setting Bold Goals 9

2. Building District Buy-In to Give All Students a Career Focus........................23

3. Sharing Leadership to Achieve Continuous Improvement............................ 42

4. Powerful Assignments: A Critical Component of CTE Classes 70

5. Developing Powerful Mathematics Assignments 91

6. Developing Powerful Literacy-Based Assignments......................................107

7. Building Successful Transitions into High School 124

8. Rethinking Senior Year: A Launching Pad, Not a Rest Stop 141

9. Empowering Counselors and Teachers to Help
   Students Find Their Path to Success...159

10. Acting on Our Beliefs to Achieve Bold Goals and
    Transform Our Schools... 176

Acknowledgments 197

Downloadable Appendixes...199

Notes...200

Index 214

About the Author...219

Introduction:
Tomorrow's High School

Decades into the new millennium—after years of talk about preparing students for a job market requiring higher levels of cognitive, academic, technical, and personal skills—high schools today are still consigning many graduates to a lifetime in the margins of the U.S. economy. In 1972, 72 percent of jobs were filled by people who had a high school diploma or less. By 2016, that figure had dropped to 34 percent, whereas 66 percent of jobs were held by employees who had a bachelor's degree, an associate's degree, or some college coursework.[1] Compare these facts with data consistently showing that the typical high school prepares *too many students* for the one-third of jobs that require the most basic high school education (or less), and *too few students* for the two-thirds that require an advanced certification or postsecondary degree. Figuratively speaking, we need to move more students to the deeper end of the pool (see Figure I.1).

Figure I.1

Moving Learning to the Deeper End of the Pool

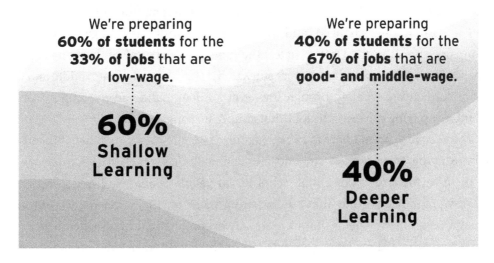

We're preparing **60% of students** for the **33% of jobs** that are low-wage.

We're preparing **40% of students** for the **67% of jobs** that are good- and middle-wage.

60%
Shallow
Learning

40%
Deeper
Learning

The result? An oversupply of young adults competing for lower-level jobs has contributed to the rising youth unemployment rate—especially among minority individuals under the age of 25.[2] The consequences of high youth unemployment are all around us, as young adults struggle to find direction, purpose, and a sense of civic ownership and responsibility.

The impact of the COVID-19 global pandemic has only increased the urgency for educators—and for business and political leaders—to address the problems of a national high school system failing to serve many students well. In the wake of a pandemic in which the U.S. workforce destabilized and employers increasingly turned to technological solutions, the demand for new workers to fill jobs requiring advanced certifications or college degrees is expected to grow at a rate *twice* that predicted before the pandemic.[3]

A Closer Look at Where We Are

As COVID-19's ripple effects continue—eliminating outdated jobs and expanding the demand for employees with the skills to adapt to automation, artificial intelligence, smart devices, and virtual reality environments—where do high schools in the United States find themselves? Before the pandemic began, high schools were producing far too many graduates who weren't well prepared for the rapidly transforming 21st century workplace. That bleak assessment hasn't changed and is likely to worsen after COVID-19 without deep reform. Among the next generation of workers still in school are far too many students with the aptitude for new and emerging career opportunities but without the necessary interest, understanding, or preparation.

The economy has changed, and the way we do work has changed, but in most secondary schools in the United States, the practice of labeling and sorting students remains. As a result, many students are stuck in the shallow end of the middle and high school curriculum, wading through low-level academic and career pathway courses toward low-paying careers or to jobs that simply no longer exist.

This mismatch doesn't have to be their destiny. As some progressive high schools are demonstrating, most of these students are capable of doing higher-level work.

In these forward-looking high schools, "average" students are mastering career pathway programs of study that are preparing them for higher-paying jobs in high-demand career fields—fields that were already experiencing shortages before the pandemic, and where labor market experts tell us there will be an even greater need for employees in the future.[4]

These high schools are not still mired in 20th century sorting practices. They are flexible, student-centered, and goal-oriented, led by bold and creative educators—divergent thinkers who understand the world outside school.

If you are reading this book, you likely agree that yesterday's approach to teaching and learning is not preparing high school students for the employment options they face today, or the fluid job market they will confront in the coming years. You may also believe, as I do, that district, school, and teacher leaders have the power to change this trajectory. This book considers *how* we can make those changes.

Tomorrow's High School sets forth a vision of what high schools and classroom practices must look like if we are to flip the current system. In this vision, 95 percent of students are engaged and challenged to move out of the shallow end of the curriculum and into deeper learning experiences they find compelling and rewarding.

This vision imagines high schools that join a rigorous college-ready core with intellectually demanding career pathway courses, places where teachers provide higher-level cognitive assignments and deeper learning in both career pathway and academic classes. It describes an overarching model that tears down the silos and empowers the vast majority of students to complete high school and to graduate college-ready, career-ready, or both.

The good news is this: these aren't just pipe dreams. The models are out there, waiting to be emulated by determined educators who are motivated to learn and to grow themselves.

One School's Story[5]

Camden County High School (CCHS) is the only secondary school in Kingsland, Georgia, a town of about 16,000 residents, approximately 35 miles north of Jacksonville, Florida. This school draws 45 percent of its 2,400 students from low-income families. Yet, through its efforts as a long-time member of High Schools That Work (HSTW), a school-improvement initiative of the Southern Regional Education Board (SREB), it has become one of the state's highest-performing schools, with graduation rates comparable to those of schools in Atlanta's wealthy suburbs.

The overall graduation rate at Camden County High School in 2018 was 92.5 percent and trending upward. That high rate was consistent across demographic groups: 89 percent among economically disadvantaged students, and 94 percent, 92 percent, and 92 percent among Black, Hispanic, and white students, respectively. The rate for students with disabilities is not far behind, at 83 percent.

When John Tucker became CCHS principal in 2007, the graduation picture was much different. The overall graduation rate of 74 percent that year was above average for the time in Georgia, but the rates for economically disadvantaged students (59 percent), Hispanic students (62 percent), and students with disabilities (31 percent) indicated the school's lack of success in serving all of its students equally well.

Tucker, who began a new leadership role as county superintendent in 2019, attributes the dramatic rise in the graduation rate and the equally dramatic narrowing of gaps among demographic groups to seven "keys to success" that evolved and strengthened during his 13-year tenure:

- Hold students to very high graduation standards.

- Help students see connections between core academics and their career interests.

- Provide a strong support system that pushes students to pass at least one end-of-course exam in the four academic areas at the Developmental level set by the state. (Although the state no longer requires passing an exam for graduation, CCHS has maintained this requirement.)

- Continually strive for students to meet the higher Proficient and Distinguished levels on the exams.

- Require every student to take a solid core of academic classes—no exceptions.

- Encourage every student to select a career focus relevant to his or her future.

- Enroll students in career academies based on their area of interest, not their ability level. Career pathway classes include AP, honors, and regular college prep classes.

Camden County High School reflects many elements of a vision for tomorrow's high schools. Students aren't just graduating from this school—they are graduating ready for college and careers. Sixty percent of graduates meet readiness standards to pursue an associate or bachelor's degree, with almost all of the remaining 40 percent achieving the level of academic readiness to progress into the workplace or enter an advanced certification program of study.

What happened at CCHS to bring about this remarkable result? With the support and involvement of district, school, and teacher leaders, CCHS established benchmarks for academic readiness for college and careers. Academic college readiness was defined as meeting the state's Proficient or Distinguished levels on four of six different end-of-course exams in literacy, mathematics, science, and social studies. Academic career readiness was defined as achieving the Developmental level on at least one exam in each of the core subjects: mathematics, science, social studies, and English language arts.

To achieve the bold goal of college and career readiness for all, CCHS required all students to complete college preparatory academic courses. Lower-level tracks of academic courses were eliminated. Through dual-credit and advanced placement offerings, 70 percent of the school's class of 2018 graduated with some postsecondary credit. All students were also required to complete at least three courses in one of the school's career pathways, to help them see the connection between academics and future careers.

The school was reorganized around six career-themed academies, designed to ensure that every student could identify a career interest and focus. Importantly, through collaborative planning, academic and career pathway teachers developed *connected lessons* that allow students to apply academic skills to complete rigorous assignments in career pathway classes.

The school and teacher leaders at CCHS are relentless in their efforts to provide extra time and academic support to enable students to achieve college and career readiness. "It is fruitless," Tucker says, "to set high expectations for students if our call for rigor is not backed up with intensive support for both students and teachers." Using federal Title I funding, the school engages 15 certified teachers on an hourly basis to provide tutoring to students who are not on track to pass the end-of-course exam and meet either the college- or career-readiness benchmarks.

In addition to academic support, the school provides a career counseling and advisement system that connects each student with a teacher-advisor. Whenever possible, each student keeps the same teacher-advisor throughout high school and has weekly advisement sessions. The advisement system is focused on helping students link their career and educational goals with a program of study that spans both high school and postsecondary education.

This ambitious agenda could not be achieved without a close-knit faculty and administration committed to professional growth. School and teacher leaders have a collaborative approach in creating a culture of continuous improvement at CCHS.

Leadership is shared among distributed leadership teams of teachers from different disciplines who are responsible for identifying school challenges and working to find solutions. A data team helps identify problem areas for the teams to address. Other distributed leadership teams include a counseling and advisement team, a policy team to focus on schoolwide issues, and a team for improving achievement for students with disabilities.

Each team's chairperson (and at least one teacher from every career academy) serves on a schoolwide steering committee that advises the principal. A full-time graduation coach knows every CCHS student's status toward earning a diploma and shares that information so that every teacher has a list of students and the steps required for graduation.

When a visitor asked a faculty member to describe what it's like to teach at CCHS, the answer was straightforward: "Intense. But I wouldn't have it any other way."

Working on Tomorrow's High School Today

I offer this brief synopsis of the Camden County High School story as a stage-setter. I hope it achieves two purposes: first, to put forward a proof-of-concept that what you will read in *Tomorrow's High School* is not "pie-in-the-sky" theorizing, divorced from the reality of today's U.S. public school system. As you read on, you will learn more about CCHS and other diverse high schools where many or all of the practices described here are in play. Second, although CCHS still needs to strengthen areas of its program, it is doing a lot of things right. It encompasses most of the components identified throughout this book. The educators at Camden County High School would be the first to say each component is a work in progress. "Continuous improvement" is their hallmark. That said, their impressive achievement offers a context for setting out the essential ingredients of true high school reform.

Chapter Overview: How This Book Can Help

The vision put forth in this book draws on more than 30 years of research and practice inside the largest high school improvement network in the United States. It presents solutions that are both proven and practical—solutions that promise to finally make high schools a rich and rewarding experience for all students, whatever their future college and career goals may be—along with real-world examples of what these solutions look like in action.

Chapter 1 calls for local school districts to *set forth bold goals,* with an accountability system that unlocks both the middle and high school from the low expectations held for too many students.

Chapter 2 guides school districts to take the lead in *building districtwide buy-in* for achieving the bold goals through the creation of four district-level teams that build momentum and help shape supportive policies and practices.

Chapter 3 examines an approach for *strengthening the shared leadership structure* in middle and high schools to plan, launch, and sustain continuous improvement, using a team strategy of distributed leadership.

Chapters 4, 5, and 6 focus on powerful assignments—career pathway, mathematics, and literacy-based assignments that result in more students achieving college *and* career readiness through *higher-level learning.*

Chapters 7 and 8 address the need to *redesign the transitions into and out of high school* so that more students graduate from high school college-ready, career-ready, or both.

Chapter 9 explains how schools can use *a diffused system of counseling, exploring, and advising* to affect students' readiness for their future.

Chapter 10 explores the major shifts in attitude and beliefs that are essential for *career pathway programs of study to become a catalytic force* for transforming today's low-performing high schools into successful high schools of tomorrow. Finally, the appendixes are available online at www.ascd.org/CareerTechEdTools.

District, school, and teacher leader teams who read this book and embrace its message will learn how to

- Join with community and parent leaders to develop and articulate a shared vision for school transformation that includes achievable goals and an aligned accountability system.

- Take ownership of a high school improvement plan that addresses the unique features of their school(s).

- Replace weak career/technical programs with high-quality career pathway programs leading to postsecondary studies and good jobs.

- Design programs that blend rigorous career pathways and a college-ready core, ensuring students can find greater meaning and purpose in their high school studies.

- Support teachers as they engage more students in deeper learning to successfully complete complex assignments linked to college- and career-readiness standards.

- Employ transitional improvement strategies (including special literacy and math courses) that get and keep students on track and enable those who are ready at the end of grades 8 and 11 to pursue accelerated learning experiences.

- Ensure that many more students complete high school and graduate college-ready, career-ready, or both.

Creating a Culture of Continuous Improvement

This book describes personalized learning techniques that—once they become an integral part of professional practice—will drive a school culture of continuous improvement, connecting learning to student interests and personal goals. The result: each student has the capacity and support to master the cognitive, academic, technical, and technology standards—and the habits of behavior and mind—that lead to success in postsecondary studies, career aspirations, and adult life.

To alleviate concern that these are unrealistic or unachievable ideas, this book will illustrate successful ways that diverse schools have created the culture of continuous improvement necessary to launch such initiatives and achieve such results. You will learn how schools are already advancing students' readiness for college and careers through a range of strategies and practices that penetrate the "business as usual" mindset that is characteristic of too many high schools.

If you are ready to embrace *bold goals* and build tomorrow's high school, this book can be your springboard into the deep end of the learning pool.

Setting Bold Goals

High school teachers and leaders in the United States are understandably proud when they can point to a rising curve in the percentage of graduates who enter higher education. School boards, business and community leaders, parents and families, and members of the local media typically echo that pride. Sending more young people off to college feels like community progress. Yet, when we look a little deeper, we find that although the number of high school graduates heading to college has increased modestly in recent years, these increases have not been matched with a comparable gain in attaining a college degree or other credential.[6]

Looking at the U.S. high school graduating class of 2012—the latest for which the National Center for Education Statistics (NCES) has long-range data—about three-fifths of those who enrolled in four-year institutions earned a degree within six years, and about one-third who enrolled in two-year degree or credentialing programs earned the certificate within three years. About one-third of the graduating class of 2012 did not enter postsecondary education within a year of graduation.

When we consider those students who did not graduate from high school, those who did not pursue a postsecondary education, and those who did not earn a post-secondary credential, we see that well over half of the high school class of 2012 did not hold a credible post–high school credential by the year 2018. This data snapshot invites the question: *Have high schools in general changed their practices sufficiently since 2012 such that these discouraging outcomes are no longer valid?* I argue that they have not—and that these data reveal the consequences of curriculum and instructional practices that still prevail in the majority of today's high schools.

Unprepared for Success—Now and in the Future

Data from the U.S. Census Bureau shows that 59 percent of Americans over 25 have a high school diploma or less, while about 20 percent of high school graduates attended college for a while. Only about 41 percent of Americans over 25 have an associate's degree or higher (8.5 percent have an associate's degree; 19.8 percent have a bachelor's degree; 12.4 percent have a postgraduate degree).[7] Meanwhile, 8 out of 10 good jobs created today require some type of postsecondary credential or degree. These jobs typically require some complex analysis and decision making as well as advanced communications and administration skills.[8]

What's the takeaway? The United States faces a shortage of persons prepared for critical high-skill and high-wage jobs who hold an advanced credential, an associate's degree, a bachelor's degree, or higher.

The "college for all" movement has led many students to express an interest in attending a four-year college, not necessarily because they want to earn a specific degree required for a specific career but because they lack exposure to or understanding of the specifics—including career paths that can lead to advanced credentials and good jobs aligned with their interests and skills.

The challenge is not simply that we have too few people with a bachelor's or master's degree; we have too many young adults who do not hold a credible credential or postsecondary degree leading to a high-demand, high-paying job. At the same time, in the world of work, critical career fields have major gaps that could be filled by employees with an associate's degree or advanced credential.

The problem is compounded by the reality that we have too many students coming through our middle and high schools who fail to meet the academic-readiness standards for success in college and other postsecondary options. (Of students in the class of 2019 who took the ACT exams, for example, only 37 percent met college-readiness benchmarks in all four subject areas—English, reading, math, and science.[9]) These challenges have roots deeper than high schools and extend into the middle grades, school district offices, and even the broader community.

Part of the challenge is about recalibrating our vision and mission. A 2010 survey by the Southern Regional Education Board of more than 10,000 middle school teachers underscored a lingering attitudinal issue faced by policy and education leaders: only 53 percent of respondents reported that preparing almost all students with the academic knowledge and skills needed for college preparatory courses in high school was a "very important goal." Even fewer (34 percent) reported that preparing all students to be ready for college preparatory high school courses without remediation is "a primary mission of the middle schools."[10] Just as startling, only 8 percent of local school board members rank creating college-ready students as a priority for their schools. The same low percentage say preparing students for careers should be the top priority, according to a National School Boards Association survey.[11]

Why this weak emphasis on preparing young people for a productive future? Perhaps it's because future workplace needs are so unclear to many families and in many schools. Parents, students, and educators continue to receive mixed messages about what it means to be college-ready because the readiness benchmarks are not widely advertised and may differ greatly among regional two- and four-year institutions. And when it comes to career paths other than college, little is done to educate students, parents, high school leaders, teachers, and counselors about the level of academic readiness needed to pursue an advanced career credential.[12]

Failing to sort out this tangle of confusing and often contradictory messaging affects the nation's long-term economic competitiveness, which depends on success in closing skill gaps and accelerating the attainment of critical credentials. With the rapid influx of new jobs that require some type of postsecondary education, by 2025 a high school diploma will be adequate preparation for only one out of every three available jobs in the United States. In addition, the demand for individuals with an advanced credential or degree at the associate level or higher may outstrip supply by as many as 11 million people.[13]

From a high school perspective, our failure to reduce the flow of poorly prepared graduates will hamper many young people for the rest of their lives and hurt their chances of attaining good jobs. Already today, a high percentage of recent graduates and a growing number of older adults, particularly persons of color and men, are chronically unemployed or underemployed because they lack the preparation necessary to obtain a good job.[14]

What Does a "Good Job" Look Like?

According to the Georgetown University Center on Education and the Workforce, in 2015 a "good job" meant that a worker earned a median salary of $65,000 or higher by age 45. The center stated that "most good jobs are full time . . . and twice as likely to provide health insurance . . . and retirement plans."[15] Importantly, the percentage of persons holding a good job increased as a function of the amount of postsecondary education and the major completed.

These statistics paint an alarming picture, *but schools have the power to set and meet bold goals that can reverse these trends.* We must begin by convincing parents, students, and the broader public that we can no longer settle for the status quo in high school education.

A big part of the problem is pace. High school education is improving, but the pace of improvement has not kept up with the emerging demands for workers with higher levels of education and cognitive skills. We also need better alignment between educational outcomes, the opportunities in the economy, and rising workplace expectations; and we must increase the percentage of students completing high school and graduating with the foundational skills needed to access good jobs and pursue advanced studies.

The heart of this book's message is this: rapidly improving students' preparation for college and careers will require *setting higher expectations* for students and then *relentlessly providing unconditional support* for each student to meet those higher standards and to graduate from high school truly equipped for success after graduation.

Decision makers must support a rapid transition away from a system focused on teaching students how to answer test items on low-level exams, without a deeper understanding of the subject. Teachers need support to design assignments and lessons that engage all students in critical thinking and deeper learning, always moving toward *credentials that matter*—whether they are university, technical, or career-based.

Who will do this work? The burden of achieving bold goals for high schools cannot be borne by high schools alone. Goal-setting initiatives must extend in every direction. One critical goal, for example, will be to fully align middle school and high school instruction to greatly increase the percentage of students who leave the 8th grade ready for challenging high school studies.

This undertaking cannot be simply a paperwork enterprise, to be sketched out and filed away. Educators in middle schools and high schools must break with tradition and collaborate to develop innovative classroom practices that enable students to master high standards—what I describe in this book as the academic, cognitive, technical, technological, personal, and interpersonal *power standards*—that are essential for success in the new economy.

How We Can Achieve Bold Goals

Setting bold goals is not a matter of telling districts and school leaders they must change. We have ample evidence that that approach has never worked, and it never will. Instead, change agents must actively help principals and teachers understand what change means—to perceive with their own eyes, ears, minds, and hearts why and how innovative school and classroom practices can prepare more students to graduate ready for postsecondary studies, careers, or both.

Our bold goals must be two-tiered, affecting both high schools and middle schools. They must be ambitious, set at a level that demands that we search for solutions that at first may seem beyond our capacity but that have been accomplished by schools facing multiple challenges.

The bold goals for connected learning I have proposed (see Figure 1.1) are designed to challenge both high school and middle school educators to ensure an accelerated and connected college and career pathway for every student from 6th grade through high school graduation. Setting such bold goals is the first essential step to markedly increase the percentage of students acquiring advanced credentials or degrees that can lead to a middle-class income or higher.

Figure 1.1
Bold Goals for Connected Learning

Bold Goals for High Schools to Accelerate Career and College Readiness

- At least 95 percent of students who enter 9th grade graduate from high school on time.
- At least 95 percent of students complete a college-ready core aligned with an academic or career-pathway program of study.
- At least 90 percent of high school students graduate college-ready, career-ready, or both, having mastered the power standards in literacy and mathematics so critical to future success.
- At least 80 percent of students earn a credential or degree of value by age 25.

Bold Goals for Middle Grades to Accelerate High School Readiness

- At least 70 percent of students enter 9th grade ready to succeed in college preparatory academic courses and in challenging career pathway courses.
- At least 70 percent of students enter 9th grade with demonstrated literacy skills needed to read, analyze, and comprehend a range of grade-level texts and materials in all subject areas.
- At least 70 percent of students enter 9th grade having successfully completed Algebra I to a validated performance level or demonstrate readiness for Algebra I.
- At least 90 percent of students exit grade 8 with a stated tentative career goal and a planned program of high school studies that includes rigorous academics and either an academic or a career focus connected to a good job and postsecondary studies.

Essential Actions for Setting and Achieving Bold Goals

Bold goals cannot be achieved by local schools acting in isolation. District leaders, school board leaders, business leaders, community members, and parents must be invested. They must understand the consequences of failing to set such goals, and then they must act strategically and with intensity to achieve them. Only such an effort can energize local leaders to create the necessary conditions. Simply stated, reaching bold goals will require bold leadership from across the community, focused on the essential actions described in the following sections.

Base Local Accountability Systems on the Principle of Valuing College Readiness and Career Readiness Equally

Progressive local school districts must create a sufficiently rigorous accountability system that gives equal value to college readiness and career readiness. The system must include benchmarks that will truly prepare graduates to meet the bold goals of one or the other—or both. Increasing local accountability sometimes requires a disruptive event, as Superintendent James Flynn of Simpson County, Kentucky, discovered when his district realized change was essential:

> In December 2012, Franklin-Simpson High School was identified for state intervention due to low test scores and failing to make adequate yearly progress for three consecutive years according to NCLB. That single event energized the school board, district leaders, faculty and school leaders, parents, business and community leaders, and higher education partners to take bold actions and make major needed changes in school and classroom practices.[16]

Today, Franklin-Simpson High appears in the top tier of Kentucky's academic rankings year after year.

As Simpson County leaders discovered, local schools and community leaders must examine how they value college *and* career readiness and how to take student engagement and rigor to the next level. Do the connections between middle schools and high schools support critical pathways toward postgraduation success in college, careers, or both? Do local definitions of "readiness" place enough weight on *career* readiness?

Undervaluing the career component of "college and career readiness" hampers our ability to envision and implement career pathway programs of study that motivate students and lead to both good jobs and postsecondary studies. Local accountability systems should define college readiness and career readiness in ways that value both equally, with the greatest value placed on ensuring that, with few exceptions, every student will meet the challenging goal of becoming *both* college- and career-ready.

Researchers have concluded that all high school students—whether they plan to attend college or immediately enter the workforce—need to be educated to a comparable level of readiness in reading and mathematics in order to compete for higher-earning jobs.[17] Thus, district, school, and classroom practices need to hold students to the same high standards, regardless of their postgraduation plans.

Set Accountability Standards for Graduation and for College and Career Readiness Higher Than Those Set by the State

Local accountability systems should build on and expand the state's framework, using additional indicators for assessing readiness. When Simpson County leaders, for example, decided to take bold actions to improve students' post–high school outcomes, they set their standards for high school graduation even higher than the state's requirements. To graduate from high school, students must meet readiness for either college or careers, and they are provided incentives to meet both. (Similar readiness standards had been set by the state but were not required for high school graduation.) In addition, Simpson County requires students to complete 32 credits for graduation—10 more than mandated by the state.

Over years of research, SREB's High Schools That Work program found that higher-performing school districts and schools set targets that exceeded state expectations; and these higher expectations resulted in changes in how students were taught, what they were taught, and the types of assessments they were given.

Do Not Undervalue Students by Holding Them to Lower Readiness Standards

We undervalue students when we fail to set rigorous, across-the-board readiness indicators for college and careers. Low standards send the message that the school does not see a compelling need to change, does not believe most students can meet higher standards, and has not seriously thought about—or been willing to embrace—the breakthrough changes in school and classroom practices needed to help more students meet standards.

District leaders, school leaders, and teachers must rethink their beliefs about students' ability and fully buy into a growth mindset—a mindset that ability and capacity can be greatly increased when students have opportunities to participate in higher-level learning experiences often reserved for the "best" students. School and teacher leaders must show that they value students by championing the changes necessary to move away from a system that allows more than half of students to leave high school without the literacy and mathematical knowledge and skills needed to succeed in college and careers.

Recognize the Role of Middle School Education in Achieving Bold Goals

The connection between middle school and high school is a critical piece of any district's ability to meet bold graduation goals. An attitude prevails in some systems that the mission of middle school falls outside the realm of rigorous academic preparation—that academic learning is a responsibility best left to the high schools, while educators in the middle focus on the transition through adolescence.[18] The most successful middle schools understand that their emerging adults need to be fully equipped for a successful life and that students cannot take a detour around serious studies for three or four critical years.

No one argues that adolescence is a challenging time, and middle school educators have an important role in supporting young people through this stage of development. But, as highly successful middle-level teachers have demonstrated, that role can be fulfilled while also supporting and preparing students in grades 6 through 8 for rigorous high school studies that lead to most students graduating ready for some level of postsecondary education.

Breaking down traditional barriers and stereotypes that make middle/high school collaboration so difficult is essential. It will require an intensive effort—with all "eyes on the prize"—to align the middle school curriculum to high school readiness standards for literacy, mathematics, and science, and to create rigorous pathways toward success.

Based on data from the 2019 National Assessment of Educational Progress (NAEP), only a third of students leaving 8th grade demonstrated literacy (34 percent) and mathematics (33 percent) achievement at the Proficient or Advanced level—the levels that predict success in challenging high school studies.[19] These current deficits in 8th grade student achievement are too great to overcome in four years of high school. Any major reimagining of high school in the United States will require a stronger emphasis on academic success in grades 6 to 8 to begin closing this readiness gap before students enter 9th grade.

Work with Postsecondary Institutions and Employers to Bring New Depth to Curriculum and Course Design

In establishing accountability systems to achieve bold goals, local school systems also need to work with two- and four-year colleges and employers to define true academic readiness for students' next steps. Local school districts can work with postsecondary partners using state and other assessments and indicators to determine literacy and mathematics performance levels and school experiences that would indicate academic readiness for college and careers.

Engagement with employers is essential. In its work with states, SREB has convened panels of employers to learn more about the skills gaps they observed in graduates who had completed career pathway programs of study. One of the biggest gaps was in critical-thinking and problem-solving skills. Although almost all high school and career/technical leaders felt their graduates met the necessary problem-solving standards, fewer than half of employers found the graduates to have adequate problem-solving skills *to meet their workplace needs.* Employers were quite clear that developing critical-thinking and problem-solving skills also requires students to seek out and acquire deep content knowledge—to look below the surface and understand how facts fit together and why things work the way they do.

Their feedback on literacy and mathematics readiness was also illuminating. Employers consistently reported that most graduates could not read technical materials, comprehend them, or express their understanding of the materials either orally or in writing. Many complained that they couldn't find employees who could solve multistep math problems and that too many young graduates lacked a sense of mathematics. Recent hires typically did not have the ability to know when numbers are wrong, they said, or to apply and reason with mathematics in the context of the work setting.

To bridge these "expectation gaps" among educators and employers, local school systems must engage both human resource professionals and postsecondary educational leaders in deep discussions that help reach a common understanding of what we mean by academic career readiness, technical readiness, and personal readiness for good jobs.

Hold Teachers at Every Grade Level Accountable for Keeping Students on Track for College and Career Readiness—and Fully Support Those Teachers to Meet Bold Goals

Both teachers and students need to know that the school community is committed—unconditionally—to giving them whatever support is necessary to meet rigorous expectations. Teachers need resources to learn new methods and approaches, and some students need extra time and support to meet higher standards.

For many years the SREB staff conducted technical-review visits to schools. Focus groups of students were often asked to name the classrooms in which they learned the most or always worked hard to succeed. Students tended to name the same three or four teachers, citing reasons such as "these teachers care," or "they believe we can do the work," or "they respect me as an individual." Similarly, at an ASCD national conference, 2016 Minnesota Teacher of the Year Abdul Wright discussed his educational experiences growing up in an underserved area within a major U.S. city. He emphasized that the unconditional support he received from key teachers was what ultimately convinced him that he was worthy of success and could succeed at higher levels. What the focus group students found in their teachers must become pervasive if we are to have hundreds of thousands more students completing high school each year ready for college and careers.

Improved Accountability: Measuring Progress Toward Achieving Bold Goals

How will we know our essential actions are having the desired effects? It is through a well-designed and implemented accountability system that we learn whether proven practices in schools and classrooms have become *everyday* practices and whether they are advancing students' readiness for future success.

Achieving bold goals requires not only agreeing upon the desired level of achievement but also frequently and accurately measuring progress toward those desired outcomes. And the success of such measurements depends on a well-developed local accountability system that includes every group, role, and individual responsible for success.

One lesson we should have learned by now is that we can never get students to meet higher standards by teaching them to lower standards. The local accountability system should propel instruction toward deeper and more demanding levels of learning for all students—*and should hold all teachers accountable for teaching students to those higher-level standards that advance the cognitive skills necessary to achieve college and career readiness.*

A well-designed local accountability system provides incentives to both students and teachers to ensure graduates meet readiness standards. It encourages high school academic teachers to help students see the connection between academic knowledge and rigorous project assignments in their career pathway classes; and it encourages career pathway teachers to develop authentic and intellectually demanding assignments that require students to apply higher-level academic and technical knowledge and skills.

To incentivize students and teachers, the accountability system cannot measure just one type of data. The local school system must track *annually* and *over time* the growth in the percentages of students who graduate college-ready, career-ready, or both. Just as important, it must track the changes in the percentages of students experiencing higher-level, engaging assignments in academic *and* career pathway classes.

The accountability system should be designed to recognize students who

- Demonstrate readiness for both college and careers.

- Complete at least a three- or four-course career pathway sequence in a priority, high-demand, high-paying career field, and earn a passing score on an approved end-of-course exam or industry certification exam.

- Complete at least a three- or four-course sequence in a focused area of advanced placement, International Baccalaureate, or advanced career courses (such as those developed by SREB), and score at the Proficient level or above on approved end-of-course exams.

- Earn a college- and career-readiness endorsement for completing a true college-ready academic core and a rigorous career pathway program of study. (See Chapter 2 for more information on career pathway programs.)

- Earn an advanced credential or a significant number of dual credits toward a credential or degree in a priority STEM (science, technology, engineering, and math) or other career field.

What "Academic and Technical Readiness" Means

An essential feature of an effective local accountability system involves identifying what it means to be academically college-ready, academically career-ready, and technically ready for college and careers.

Academic college readiness means students can enter credit-bearing postsecondary courses leading to an associate or a bachelor's degree without having to take remedial courses. Local systems and their partner postsecondary institutions may select from a mix of valid measures for determining academic postsecondary readiness, including the following:

- Empirically derived benchmarks on ACT, SAT, or state assessments or other placement exams to determine college readiness, starting in 11th grade so that the senior year can be used to close readiness gaps. (For more on this, see Chapter 8.)

- Empirically derived benchmarks on state literacy and mathematics exams in at least grades 5, 8, 9, and 10, signaling to teachers at all levels that they have a role in getting more students on track to be college-ready and career-ready.

- Performance in high school as measured by, for example, grade point averages in selected courses that predict success in college, the number and level of mathematics and English courses taken, the number of courses failed, and the total number of secondary credits earned.[20]

- Achievement on select end-of-course exams, such as advanced placement, International Baccalaureate, and academic dual-credit course exams.

Academic career readiness refers to the need to ensure that more career-oriented students are academically prepared for careers. As schools move toward holding all students to the same standards—whether they plan to pursue postsecondary studies or careers immediately after graduation—they can take steps to address this need. Defining academic readiness for the workplace and for the pursuit of an advanced credential sends a message that both academic teachers and career/technical teachers are responsible for improving students' academic achievement.

An academically career-ready student has the foundational literacy and mathematical skills needed to succeed in advanced-training programs and to adapt to rising workplace requirements. It may be some time before high schools can have most or all students meeting the threshold benchmarks for academic college readiness. Given this reality, it is imperative that the district establish with employers and certificate programs the foundational academic skills that students need to be academically career-ready.

Defining and measuring academic career readiness must be addressed by ensuring the local accountability system tracks progress within pathways and within schools. The accountability system can use the following measures to determine which career pathway students are academically career-ready:

- The percentage of career pathway students who meet academic college-readiness benchmarks at the end of 11th grade.
- The percentage of students who demonstrate academic career-readiness benchmarks through, for example,
    o Scoring at the silver level or higher on the ACT WorkKeys exam.
    o Meeting cut scores on placement exams, particularly in reading and mathematics.
    o Meeting cut scores on the Armed Services Vocational Aptitude Battery, which aligns with military careers and high-demand public-sector jobs.
    o Completing at least two academic and two technical dual-credit courses that qualify as credit-bearing courses and shorten the time needed to earn an advanced certification or a degree at postsecondary institutions.

Such assessment of academic career readiness sends a strong message to career/technical teachers and academic teachers that *both have an obligation to advance the academic readiness of career-oriented students*—and it will encourage academic and career pathway teachers to identify academic-readiness gaps and implement strategies for closing them.

Technical readiness is not included in most state accountability systems but represents an important range of skills and knowledge that contribute to success in both college and careers. Students who demonstrate technical readiness have (1) job- and industry-specific skills; (2) cognitive skills to think critically in the context of their career field; (3) research and literacy skills necessary to find and use information to improve a product, service, or process; (4) personal habits that make them good employees and help them advance in their careers; (5) the abilities to effectively work on a team and adapt to new technology and software; and (6) the habits of mind that enable them to tackle challenging tasks.

Local accountability systems can assess technical readiness through a range of valid and reliable measures, including the following:

- Passing an industry certification exam that has been vetted by employers; carries transferable postsecondary credit in a field recognized as being of value to the state, regional, or local economy; provides students an advantage in the hiring process; and can lead to good jobs.

- Passing a state license exam.

- Completing at least two technical dual-credit courses that shorten students' time to complete a credential or degree.[21]

- Passing valid end-of-course exams in career pathway courses at a level that postsecondary institutions agree would carry college credit, such as the exams associated with SREB's 36 Advanced Career (AC) courses.[22]

- Participating in a high-quality, structured, work-based learning experience or completing a complex long-term capstone project that integrates academic, technical, cognitive, and workplace-readiness skills and may involve work in the community or on a jobsite.[23]

Evaluating School and Classroom Experiences

Any effective accountability system not only tracks changes in students' level of academic and technical readiness but also assesses the extent to which students are experiencing school and classroom practices that have been proven to lead to improved student readiness and, ultimately, achievement of bold goals. Schools will know they are on the path toward meeting their goals when students

- Take more academic courses that prepare them for postsecondary studies.

- Receive counseling for careers and postsecondary studies that enable them to make informed educational and career decisions.

- Experience work-based learning that exposes them to real-world work settings and provides opportunities to develop personal and professional skills.

- Receive the intensive, unconditional support necessary to achieve college and career readiness.

Data on experiences that lead to higher student learning can be collected from well-developed student surveys. To work toward meeting bold goals, schools will need to analyze data and ensure all students—across the school's demographic and socioeconomic groups—are seeing similar growth in achievement and having similar school and classroom experiences.

What should a student survey measure? Through decades of data collection at its High Schools That Work sites, SREB has identified student experiences that are connected to higher achievement and improved college and career readiness. In high-performing schools, students report, for example,

- Taking more college preparatory classes (advanced placement, honors, dual-credit).
- Completing four years of mathematics, science, and English language arts courses.
- Earning at least 16 academic credits.
- Receiving career counseling and advisement from counselors and teacher-advisors on topics important to their future plans (e.g., the right core academic courses needed to be prepared for both careers and college, how to choose a college or postsecondary technical school, the type of training necessary to prepare for a given career).
- Completing a career concentration of three or four courses in a high-demand, high-wage career field.
- Frequently using literacy strategies and mathematics knowledge to complete challenging assignments in both academic and technical courses.
- Completing work-based experiences to learn about careers and the habits of mind and behavior that enable professional success.

Summing Up and Looking Ahead

A thoughtful set of well-established, agreed-upon *bold goals* can inspire educators to prepare all students for success in their next steps forward. The need for such goals is urgent, as is the need for effective accountability systems that accurately measure progress toward those goals and enable schools to make thoughtful and continuous improvement in school and classroom practices.

Many of the key indicators of success and central strategies for achieving bold goals rely on schools' establishing career pathway programs of study. Chapter 2 will examine how districts, schools, and community leaders and parents can design a high school around rigorous career pathways connected to a college-ready core—providing students with greater equity of opportunity and more satisfaction in their work, personal, community, and civic life.

Building District Buy-In to Give All Students a Career Focus

Many of Steubenville High School's 700 students lacked access to career pathways leading to postsecondary studies and a good job. Beginning in 2014, the district decided to ensure all students in this Ohio school had the opportunity for post–high school success. The principal of the district's only high school, Ted Gorman, explains how they addressed the problem:

> We had many students who planned to attend college but did not have a career goal. As we consulted with families, we found most of our parents wanted their students prepared both for college and a career. After considerable study by district and school leaders and consultation with business, industry, and postsecondary leaders, we selected four of the STEM Advanced Curriculum (AC) curricula developed by the Southern Regional Education Board: aerospace engineering, innovations in science and technology, health informatics, and global logistics and supply chain management.

Each of the industry and postsecondary partners who consulted with the district on the selection of the curricula agreed to review and provide feedback on students' projects and to help organize field trips and other worksite observational experiences for students. Representatives from partner companies also agreed to serve on the school advisory board to offer advice, resources, and assistance as needed.

"The AC curricula has energized and motivated more students to complete coursework for postsecondary studies," Gorman says. The school has also developed guided pathways around the four AC curricula with Eastern Gateway Community College, Ohio State University, and Kent State University. "These four curricula align perfectly with one of our primary goals—to provide every student with access to a career pathway connected to a college-ready core, to a good job, and to postsecondary studies," Gorman reports.

After building districtwide buy-in and reorganizing around rigorous career pathways, the district now has almost 200 students enrolled in these four programs of study. School leaders and teachers have been pleasantly surprised to see that students are excited to take on and complete the tough assignments in the AC courses, says the district's STEM coordinator, Shana Wydra.

In 2019, Steubenville High School had a 99 percent graduation rate and a 95.4 percent daily attendance rate. That year, 34 students graduated from high school with both a high school diploma and an associate's degree.

Nationwide, the United States has a misalignment between the curriculum that students are completing and their post–high school plans. An analysis of more than 23,000 high school graduates in 2013 offers a revealing picture of this misalignment (see Figure 2.1).[24] Only 39 percent of high school students completed a genuine college-ready core, and only 8 percent of high school graduates connected that core with a career and technical education (CTE) pathway, whereas nearly half of students completed neither a college-ready core nor a career pathway *despite* their plans to pursue an associate's, bachelor's, or advanced degree. Six years later, many of these underguided and undersupported students will not have earned the degree they set out to obtain, resulting in a lost resource of many thousands of talented young people. Simply put, these data tell us that school districts—through policies or actions—are not encouraging their high school students to enroll in college-ready academic courses connected with either an advanced career or advanced academic focus.

Figure 2.1
National Transcript Outcomes of 2013 High School Graduates

Pathway/Curriculum Completed	% Who Completed	% Who Planned Bachelor's Degree or Higher	% Who Planned Associate's Degree or Higher
College- and career-ready	8%	77%	11%
College-ready	31%	78%	12%
Career-ready	13%	52%	22%
No cohesive curriculum	47%	61%	17%

Source: From "Meandering Toward Graduation: Transcript Outcomes of High School Graduates," by M. Bromberg and C. Theokas, 2016, *The Education Trust.* Reprinted with permission.

Here's the root of the problem: too many high schools are still stuck in the 1960s and 1970s, sorting students into one of three silos—college, workplace, and everyone else—and then assuming nature will somehow take its course and everyone with a high school diploma will find their way to a fruitful career. *We need to flip the current system to help more students pursue and earn an advanced credential or an associate's degree in a career field with emerging opportunities.*

As the transcript study suggests, this outcome will not happen automatically. It's a rare 8th or 9th grader who is capable of making a meaningful career plan without help. Students need well-designed high schools that lead and engage them to make thoughtful choices along a pathway of career-oriented programs of study. The result: we graduate many more students who are prepared for both postsecondary studies *and* careers and many fewer who are likely to find themselves adrift.

Seven Design Features of Rigorous and Relevant Career Pathways

Simply implementing more career pathways will not necessarily result in school districts meeting bold goals. Many existing pathways, in fact, connect students with jobs that may be locally plentiful but are relatively low-paying by industry standards.[25] Reaching bold goals requires school districts and their high schools to provide more students with access to multiple intellectually demanding programs of study that include these seven design features:

1. They connect at least three (and preferably four or more) coherent career pathway courses with a college-ready curriculum of English, mathematics, science, and social studies, designed to engage students in deeper learning and advance their readiness for careers and post–high school education. Additionally, career pathway programs of study should be broadened to include an option for advanced academic focus in which students can complete three AP courses in mathematics and science, three AP courses in the humanities or fine arts, or three International Baccalaureate career diploma courses.

Recommended Requirements for High School Graduation

- Students pursuing credentials and degrees in STEM career fields complete Algebra II and two additional higher-level math courses.
- Students in non-STEM fields complete Algebra I, geometry, and two career-related math courses (such as statistics and other specialized math courses linked directly to a career field of study).
- All career pathway students complete
  - Four years of college preparatory English language arts courses, in which they read complex literary texts, conduct research, prepare written reports, and make presentations to internal and external audiences.
  - At least four college preparatory lab science courses and three social studies courses.

2. They ensure students complete at least three (preferably four or more) coherent career pathway courses—with a high percentage reporting completing rigorous assignments (based on the indicators for powerful assignments listed in Chapter 4).

3. They connect three stages of learning—high school, post–high school education, and the workplace—by including dual-enrollment courses and work-based learning opportunities.

4. They connect to high-skill, high-wage, high-demand careers that help students secure a good job.

5. They are organized into career-themed academies or are grouped with other career pathways in which academic and career/technical teachers who share a cohort of students have common planning time to work together on developing connected learning assignments.

6. They connect grade-level college-readiness standards with rigorous assignments in career pathway and academic courses so graduates can adjust to rising and changing job requirements.

7. They ensure all graduates can meet computer science, information technology, and digital-fluency standards, demonstrated through a cumulative portfolio that begins no later than 7th grade and follows the student through academic and career pathway classes.

The COVID-19 pandemic experience further underscores the following conclusions by national education and political leaders regarding the last design feature:

> Computer science can no longer be considered an optional component of K–12, or offered only to students considering careers in science, technology, engineering, and math (STEM) fields. Computer science offers students much more than the knowledge of how computers work or the skills needed to build a device, write code, or manage data. It builds lifelong learning skills that hold value in every academic discipline, industry, and profession.[26]

We will examine each of these features later in the chapter. But before schools and districts can implement these actions, they must rally all stakeholders around the need for change. To do that, they will need strategic actions to build buy-in across the district, the schools, and the community.

Using District Study Groups to Engage Internal and External Stakeholders

To help schools make the changes required to pursue bold goals, district leaders need more than a clear vision of what constitutes a good school. They also must have buy-in from district staff, school and teacher leaders, and community movers and shakers who grasp the "why" behind the need to conjoin higher-level academic and CTE studies.

The role of district leaders is to create a shared ownership of both the problem and the proposed solutions at the school, district, and community levels, so all stakeholders understand why we need to move more students from the shallow end of learning into deeper educational experiences. Key internal and external stakeholders need to recognize the gaps between desired goals and current results so they can support the changes in expectations and level of learning needed to prepare more students for new and emerging opportunities in the community and beyond.

One of the most effective ways to get buy-in is through *district-level study groups* composed of a cross-section of school, district, community, and external partners. As members of study groups grasp the consequences of failing to act strategically and with intensity, they become energized to support and create the conditions for achieving bold goals. They can then help other district educators and community members come to understand that strengthening the bond between higher-level academic and CTE studies will not dumb down the curriculum. Rather, it will motivate many more students to acquire the higher-level knowledge and habits that make for successful students and successful careers.

We have found that four district study groups—one each for assessment, career pathways, high school organization and scheduling, and strategic planning—are essential for getting buy-in and building momentum (see the top row of Figure 2.2). Each of these widely representative teams includes one or more members from the school board, district leadership, middle and high school teachers and leaders, local CTE leadership, engaged parents, community influencers, business leaders, postsecondary leaders from two- and four-year colleges, and a teacher from fine and performing arts.

Here are brief descriptions of the four groups:

- The *district assessment study group* determines the gaps between current practices and the bold goals of ensuring 8th grade students are ready for 9th grade and high school graduates are ready for college and careers. An honest appraisal by such a team is a good way to raise awareness among key groups about the misalignment between current student readiness levels for high school, college, and careers and the rising education levels required for a good job. This appraisal is essential if more students from historically marginalized groups are to be prepared for the projected growth in good jobs that will require studies beyond high school.[27]

- The *district career pathway study group* analyzes gaps between the seven design features of career pathways and current school practices across all schools within a district and makes recommendations for closing the gaps. We have observed that schools making the most improvement

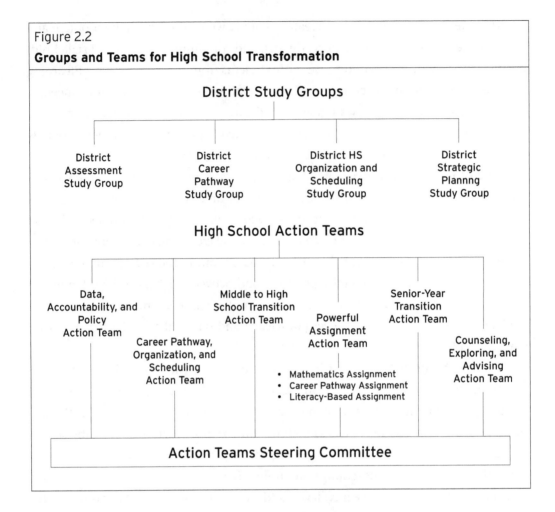

Figure 2.2

Groups and Teams for High School Transformation

District Study Groups

- District Assessment Study Group
- District Career Pathway Study Group
- District HS Organization and Scheduling Study Group
- District Strategic Plannng Study Group

High School Action Teams

- Data, Accountability, and Policy Action Team
- Career Pathway, Organization, and Scheduling Action Team
- Middle to High School Transition Action Team
- Powerful Assignment Action Team
  - Mathematics Assignment
  - Career Pathway Assignment
  - Literacy-Based Assignment
- Senior-Year Transition Action Team
- Counseling, Exploring, and Advising Action Team

Action Teams Steering Committee

have greatly increased the percentage of students who have access to career pathways that are linked to good jobs, that address the full range of students' interests and aptitudes, and that are connected to worksite experiences, postsecondary studies, and rigorous academics.

- The *district high school organization and scheduling study group* analyzes best practices for increasing student motivation through connected academic and career studies. This group presents options and guiding principles for organizing the high school around students' career interests connected to a college-ready core—and develops a scheduling system that allows academic and career pathway teachers to coplan connected learning experiences for shared cohorts of students.

- The *district strategic-planning study group,* composed of representatives from the other study groups, helps ensure communication and coordination across all the groups' work. Ultimately, this group will take the results of all the study groups and develop a comprehensive district plan. A successful strategic plan addresses the necessary policies, professional development needs, and projected costs associated with the transformation initiative. The strategic planning group develops a framework of best practices, a communication plan for internal and external audiences, a process for supporting continuous improvements at the district and school levels, and guidance on how district staff and outside providers will support individual schools in designing their own customized improvement plan.

The remainder of this chapter will examine the responsibilities of each of these district-level groups and their roles in using the seven design features for achieving bold goals. (Chapter 3 describes the responsibilities and roles of the high school action teams shown in Figure 2.2.)

The District Assessment Study Group

The district assessment study group determines the district's and school's current readiness to graduate 95 percent of students who enter 9th grade, with 90 percent graduating college-ready, career-ready, or both. This group develops a set of indicators and definitions to evaluate the current readiness status overall and across specific student groups (e.g., by gender, race/ethnicity, socioeconomic status, special needs). The group assesses both the district as a whole and individual schools for their progress on the bold goals outlined in Chapter 1.

This study group also examines the district's current performance on many of the readiness indicators described in Chapter 1 as it builds a case for necessary changes to district, school, and classroom practices. Because the group examines data across the district, it will need access to district office personnel with special knowledge and skills to help establish reliable indicators and analyze available data.

The group can begin by assessing the percentage of the district's students entering 9th grade who are ready to succeed in college preparatory academic courses and challenging career pathway courses, looking at both the overall data and the data for specific subgroups. In particular, the assessment study group should analyze

- Achievement levels on indicators that predict at least a 50 percent chance of succeeding in true college preparatory-level English language arts, social studies, and science courses in 9th grade.
- How many more students could likely succeed in college preparatory courses on schedule, if given extensive support.

- The percentages of students leaving 8th grade unprepared for college preparatory courses in 9th grade.

- The percentages of 8th grade students who have successfully completed or demonstrate readiness for true college preparatory Algebra I.

Moving on through the transition into high school, the group members need to examine the success of 9th grade students. They should determine the percentage of 9th graders during the previous three years who earned enough credits to be classified as sophomores, and determine what percent succeeded in the true college-ready track: four years of college preparatory math, four years of college preparatory English, at least four lab science courses, and at least three social studies courses.

Once the literacy- and mathematics-readiness gaps are identified for entering 9th grade students, the assessment study group can consider changes needed in the middle grades and in grade 9 regarding how students are taught, what is expected of them, and which group of students needs greater assistance to successfully complete college preparatory academic courses. *The goal here is to ensure that 95 percent of students progress into college preparatory 10th grade courses on time.* This outcome will require special professional development and support as teachers improve enough to successfully engage all students in rigorous grade-level assignments in grades 6 through 9.

Next, the team should examine students' success in transitioning from high school into postsecondary studies and careers. Leaders from industry and postsecondary institutions that enroll a large proportion of the district's graduates can work with the assessment study group to determine academic-readiness indicators for college, as well as academic- and technical-readiness indicators for advanced certification programs leading to a good job. (See Chapter 1 for sample indicators and Chapter 9 for percent of students meeting college- and career-readiness standards.) The team should analyze data, across all students and by specific subgroups, related to

- Graduation rates compared with the 95 percent goal (see Chapter 9 for calculations of graduation rates).

- The percentage of graduates who graduated college-ready, career-ready, or both, over the past three years.

- The percentage of past graduates who earned a credible credential or degree by age 25 (see Chapter 9). A credible credential is one that employers recognize and would give a person an edge for a job or for which postsecondary institutions would award credit toward an associate's degree or advanced credential.

- The percentage of students who completed a coherent sequence of three or more career pathway courses and who met academic-readiness indicators for college and met technical-readiness indicators.

- The percentage of the district's graduates who met math- and literacy-readiness indicators on the SAT, ACT, or other valid exam.

- The percentage of career pathway graduates who did not complete a true college-ready curriculum but elected further study.

- The percentage of graduates completing one year of postsecondary studies over the previous three years.

- The percentage of students entering college who completed a true college-ready core as defined in this chapter or by the college.

- The percentage of students who neither met academic-readiness indicators nor completed a true college-ready core but successfully completed the first year of college. (The team should also identify what was unique about these students' high school experiences.)

Assessing the current status on these indicators will help the study group build a case for the need to expand access for historically disenfranchised students to the true college-ready academic core. Too often the process used to place students in the accelerated curriculum in middle and high schools results in sorting students by socio-economic levels.[28] Examining districtwide data for all students and within student subgroups will help the study group determine if such an inequitable sorting system exists in their district.

Districts quite likely will find substantial gaps between the percentage of students who plan to attend college and the percentage who actually attend and complete an advanced credential, associate's degree, or higher. *These results will create buy-in among internal and external stakeholders to support actions needed to close the postsecondary and career-readiness gaps.*

The District Career Pathway Study Group

The career pathway study group evaluates gaps between current school practices and the seven essential design features for career pathways—and then develops recommendations for closing them. True career pathways are still the exception in middle and high schools in the United States. Districts that are serious about using career pathways for improving high schools must recognize the need for pathways that have a different look. Leaders in these districts will carefully select internal and external study group members who understand that today's economy is driven by high-level service and technology industries, and it is *this* economy for which we need to prepare graduates. Members of the career pathway study group evaluate best practices and build the case for the district to

- Discontinue or redesign legacy CTE career pathway courses aligned to yesterday's jobs and replace them with pathways in emerging career fields.
- Engage students in rigorous assignments in both career pathway and core academic classes to advance students' readiness to succeed in a career and in postsecondary studies.
- Connect career pathway classes to work-based learning experiences that motivate students to persist in meeting career- and academic-readiness standards.

The career pathway study group's first task is to analyze district data regarding students' completion of either an advanced academic or a career pathway focus. The group will answer critical questions not just about pathway completion but also about the scope and quality of students' experiences in existing career pathway programs of technical and academic study. It will need to address these targeted questions:

- How many students complete a coherent sequence of three or more courses in career pathways?
- How is career pathway enrollment distributed among pathways, schools, and student subgroups?
- How many career pathway students are also completing a true college-ready academic curriculum?
- How many students completed at least three courses with an advanced academic focus (beyond the college-ready academic core) in STEM, the humanities, or fine arts?
- How many students completed a true college preparatory curriculum but did not complete three coherent career pathway courses or courses with an advanced academic focus?
- Looking at success rates in the first year of college, how do students who completed a coherent sequence of at least three career pathway courses and a true college preparatory academic core compare with
  - o Students who completed only the traditional college preparatory program?
  - o Students who completed neither a college-ready curriculum nor a career pathway?
- What percentage of students completing three or more coherent courses in a career pathway program were required to complete powerful assignments? (See Chapter 4 for criteria of powerful assignments.)

- What percentage of career pathway students experienced at least three of the following work-based learning experiences?
    - o A career fair
    - o An organized tour of at least one business
    - o Structured job shadowing
    - o A structured internship lasting for several weeks
    - o A one-year on-the-job learning experience planned collaboratively by the employer and educators
    - o A capstone project with an employer and a teacher advisor (SREB's research on Advanced Career [AC] courses reveals that students who have such real-world experiences are two-and-a-half times more likely to persist in successfully completing a coherent sequence of three or four rigorous AC pathway courses.)

- Which career pathways are formally connected to an advanced credential, to an associate's degree or higher, and to a good job in high-demand and high-wage career fields?

- What percentage of students completing three or more courses by pathways pursued at least one year of postsecondary studies toward an advanced credential, an associate's degree, or a bachelor's degree?

- Do current CTE and academic teachers have common times to coplan lessons that connect academics to assignments in career pathway classes and to embed real-world problems into academic classes?

- Do both academic and career pathway teachers frequently engage students in applying higher-level academic standards in literacy (reading, writing, and speaking) and mathematics to complete real-world projects in their classes?

● Concepts and Applications: A Power Couple

Recalling a highlight of her career, one-time Algebra II teacher Donna Johnson said this:

> One of my great learning experiences was when I was a math teacher at Sussex Technical High School in Delaware, where I met weekly with teachers from the trades to plan how we could connect Algebra II concepts to students' assignments in their career/technical courses. I found that the contextual base of trade courses provided a way for students to grasp algebra concepts and apply them to complete their assignments. I was successful in teaching a group of students who many high school teachers would assume couldn't learn Algebra II. As a consequence, we had students go on to two- and four-year colleges where they did not have to take remedial math courses.

Donna went on to become a staff member for the Delaware State Board of Education and more recently joined the staff of the Board of Education in Washington, DC.

Why pursue these penetrating questions? Determining how many students in the district have a focus and are completing a program of study leading to a goal—and how many are just hanging out in high school—can help build the case for designing high schools in which every student has a career or an advanced academic focus. It also guides the career pathway study group's decisions regarding which pathways should be replaced or redesigned to increase students' chances of leaving high school prepared to enter postsecondary studies or the workplace and eventually get a good job.

The career pathway study group recommends ways to modernize existing pathways and select new career pathways to prepare students for a double purpose, leading to flexible career choices. To open more doors to good jobs, existing CTE pathways must be modernized to provide students with

- Deeper and broader knowledge of a career field.
- Solid literacy and mathematics knowledge and skills.
- Good work ethics and relationship skills.

When evaluating existing career pathways, the study group can begin by identifying CTE courses currently offered across the district and within specific schools that can be organized into a coherent sequence of three or more courses connected to a career field and to postsecondary studies. As part of this process, the study group should pay attention both to what is taught in these courses and to the learning environment in which the courses are taught. Many existing high school CTE labs are cluttered with outdated technology.

● Sending the Message

A superintendent in a Georgia school district who wanted to implement SREB's High Schools That Work improvement strategies became so concerned about the state of the school's automotive lab that she engaged two custodial workers and the automotive teacher to help clean out the shop one Saturday. Then, during the summer, the shop was modernized with up-to-date technology, new classroom furniture, and new paint, making it a showcase for the school. This effort sent a message that CTE studies were a valued and essential part of this and other high schools in the district.

We know that high school graduates can still enter lower-paying jobs and work their way up to managerial or other senior positions across a variety of fields, such as construction, manufacturing, retail, food service, and office support. However, members of the career pathway study group should understand the need not only to retain existing quality pathways but also to develop pathways that lead to new career opportunities in the 21st century economy. They should include recommendations for new pathways in high-demand and high-wage fields that connect to the full range of students' interests and aptitudes (careers that students might not otherwise know about) and that may require some postsecondary education.

● Planting Dreams

A math teacher and a business teacher at one of South Carolina's lowest-performing high schools shared a story of a graduate from their high school who went on to earn a bachelor's degree in business at the University of South Carolina and now works as an investment analyst on Wall Street. The business teacher had received $25,000 from a bank to establish an investment club as part of the school's business pathway, in which students each year would analyze the market and buy and sell stocks. This assignment enabled the student to discover a career area that was not prevalent in his immediate community but that he realized he had the aptitude and passion to pursue.

Districts often make the mistake of retaining existing pathways and adding a couple of new ones without thoughtfully identifying emerging career opportunities in the local, regional, state, and even national economies. The career pathway study group should analyze labor market trends to align pathways with career fields that have projected employee shortages, especially those that will provide good jobs and may require a credible credential and preparation beyond high school. The study group can also engage industry and postsecondary leaders to identify career pathways that fit the region's needs. For example, it is projected that 4 million workers will be needed over the next decade in the broad field of computer science. Seventy percent of these jobs will require a bachelor's degree, and the remainder can be filled by employees with high school education, some college, or an associate's degree.[29]

Healthcare, financial services, and technology-focused manufacturing are other growing fields that require cognitive skills, applied mathematics, broad-based understanding of technology, and the ability to learn and use new software. They can lead more students to high-wage careers.

After developing a set of recommended pathways, the study group's next step is to determine whether the multiple career pathways proposed—both existing and new—address the full range of student interests and aptitudes. One way to do this is to consider how the pathways align with various personality types and interests, using a tool such as Holland's Six Personality Types: realistic, investigative, artistic, social, enterprising, and conventional.[30] (See Appendix A at www.ascd.org/CareerTechEdTools for information about career areas fitting these various personality types.) The intent is to

ensure that all students can explore fields that connect with their interests and aptitudes while preparing them for successful careers.

Because the career pathway study group's goal is to strengthen the connection
between high schools, employers, and postsecondary institutions, it is uniquely posi-
tioned to develop a process and conditions for guided pathways of study that connect
students to positive outcomes after high school. Such pathways blur the line between
grade 12 and "grade 13" so that qualified students can graduate from high school having completed one year toward an advanced certificate or degree—reducing the cost of
postsecondary education for them and their families. Developing these pathways will
require at least a year of planning and working with secondary schools and two- and
four-year colleges to overcome their traditional ways of doing business. (See Chapter 8
for details on redesigning the senior year.)

Finally, the career pathway study group will need to develop cost estimates to
modernize existing and new pathways and to connect them to a college-ready academic core, advanced credentials, and postsecondary studies. And just as important
(if not more so), the group needs to ensure that stakeholders clearly understand the
return on this investment. The bold goal of rigorous pathways aligned to future opportunities will not be achieved unless district leaders, school leaders, teachers, students,
and parents can see clearly where the cost and effort are leading.

The District High School Organization and Scheduling Study Group

*The high school organization and scheduling study group ensures schools can effectively
organize around career pathways connected to college preparatory academics.* Career pathway programs cannot turn a district around unless core academic teachers (English
language arts, mathematics, science) and career pathway CTE teachers have the time,
professional development, and support needed to connect academic knowledge and
skills to powerful assignments in career pathway classes. The organization and scheduling study group can ensure those resources are in place.

This study group develops a district-level plan to tear down the silos that isolate
academic and career pathway teachers, with the goal of enabling students to see reasons for mastering three sets of skills: academic, technical, and personal. One way to
do this is to allow teachers to share a common cohort of students and have a common planning time to connect learning experiences and develop rigorous assignments
in career pathways as a catalyst to inspire students to master higher-level academic
knowledge and skills. Such an applied approach to learning is something that both
internal and external stakeholders are likely to buy into.

This district study team—and ultimately, the system leadership team—will need to consider the size of the high school(s) as it determines strategies for connecting a college-ready core to career pathways. Large high schools of 1,000 or more students can be organized around career-theme academies, each operating as a small learning community of 300 to 500 students and offering two or more career pathways. Students in each academy would be taught by the same career pathway and core academic teachers. These academies work best when led by a leadership team composed of an assistant principal, an academic and a career pathway teacher, and a counselor. In high schools with fewer than 1,000 students, where separate academies may not be feasible, the design works best when it is organized around four or more career pathways. Each career pathway teacher should have academic partners in English language arts, mathematics, and science to develop learning experiences that require students to apply academic knowledge and skills to complete complex assignments.

Christina Kerns, curriculum and instructional supervisor at the Penta Career Center in Perrysburg, Ohio, offers this account of pairing career pathway and academic instruction:

> As we planned to implement SREB's Advanced Career curriculum in automated materials joining, we found that the assigned CTE teacher could not engage students in applying the mathematical knowledge and skills required to complete the assignments. We assigned a math teacher to co-teach with the career pathway teacher, to work directly with students to understand and apply the math necessary to complete each of the major project assignments. We doubled the time in this class so students could earn a credit in automated materials joining and a credit in mathematics. The lesson we learned is that students are motivated to learn and apply math to complete a project in which they have an interest.

For career pathways to work, teams of academic and career pathway CTE teachers must commit to coplanning deeper and more connected learning experiences for their cohort of students. Whether in a large or a small school, it takes time for academic and CTE teachers to learn how to talk to each other, to respect each other's knowledge and skills, and to work together.

The high school organization and scheduling study group can recommend policies and strategies that provide time for such planning. For example, districts can provide a one-week summer institute to support academic and CTE pathway teachers in planning connected learning experiences around at least one major project students would complete during the first nine weeks of school. (See Chapter 4 for details on developing such projects.) In addition, districts can provide at least four hours of monthly coplanning time. Researchers have found that students enrolled in an organizational structure in which CTE teachers and academic teachers share the same cohort of students and coplan connected lessons have significantly higher grades and perform better than comparative students in the same high school.[31] (See Chapter 3 for more information on scheduling.)

The District Strategic Planning Study Group

The strategic planning study group can set forth practical district-level actions, policies, procedures, and conditions for school success. Districts cannot expect schools to change on their own. They should be willing to provide policies and resources to support schools, and to develop both a communication plan about expected changes and an accountability plan to track progress. Unless school board and district leaders set forth board policies and other actions—including steps that will empower school and teacher leaders at the building level to make informed professional decisions—the educators and other stakeholders involved are unlikely to believe that change will take place.

The district strategic planning study group demonstrates that the district and school board are seriously committed to achieving bold goals and implementing career pathways. This group uses the work of the other district study groups to develop a strategic plan that includes school board policies, financial resources, and district support for the schools.

Members of the strategic planning study group are chosen from members of the three other study groups. These should be individuals who have demonstrated an understanding of the need to greatly increase the percentage of students graduating college-ready, career-ready, or both. Membership should also include several leaders at the highest levels of the system with sufficient authority to make change happen.

A first action of this study group will be to recommend a reward system for achieving the bold goals of 95 percent of students graduating and 90 percent graduating college-ready, career-ready, or both—and a companion reporting system for tracking school- and district-level progress. This pairing of rewards and accountability sends a message to all that the status quo is no longer acceptable.

Next, the group should consider a wide range of specific policies, practices, and investments that will enable schools to make the necessary changes. The first step involves setting districtwide graduation requirements *above those set by the state.*

Camden County School District in Georgia provides a noteworthy example of this step. The district set graduation requirements significantly higher than those of the state, requiring students to pass four end-of-course exams in the four core academic areas (mathematics, English language arts, science, and social studies) at the Basic level or above, to earn 32 credits, and to complete a career focus in one of several career pathways. Even with the demanding requirements, Camden County's graduation rate continues to reach the mid-90s across almost all student populations.

After setting districtwide graduation requirements, the strategic planning study group establishes a framework of best practices for achieving the bold goals and for implementing career pathways (as recommended by the career pathway study group). The framework allows each high school to customize its strategic plan.

To show that redesigning schools is worthwhile—and to inspire buy-in from schools, parents, and community leaders—the school board and district will need to commit resources and invest in improvement efforts. The district strategic planning group should provide recommendations for areas needing investment, such as

- Modernizing existing career pathways and expanding access to new career pathways aligned to good jobs and postsecondary studies.

- Expanding access to a true college-ready core.

- Recruiting academic and career pathway teachers who understand how the abstract nature of mathematics and science can be applied through well-designed project-based assignments and who feel comfortable coplanning connected learning experiences with other teachers.

- Having specialized outside coaching assistance and professional development experiences, including conferences, to help teachers design connected-learning experiences for both academic and CTE-pathway teachers.

- Expanding support for students needing assistance to succeed in an accelerated college-ready academic core and in challenging career pathway studies.

When a district makes strategic investments and goes the extra mile, it increases the buy-in of students, teachers, and parents because the action indicates a district-level commitment to each student's success.

Investing in What Matters Most

Gwinnett County Schools in Georgia made considerable investments in seven high schools that implemented a wall-to-wall career pathway organizational structure. These investments included adding several new career pathways at each participating high school, renovating CTE labs, adding new staff, and purchasing new technology appropriate for each pathway. The district also invested in extended professional development for three years for core academic teachers and career pathway teachers that focused on literacy-based assignments, a balanced approach for teaching mathematics, and designing project-based assignments. These investments sent a message to school leaders, teachers, students, and parents about the commitment to making high school meaningful and rigorous. As a result, high schools are witnessing a rising graduation rate, a decline in discipline problems, and improved student readiness for both college and careers.

The strategic planning study group must also consider what is needed to enable schools to work with local business and industry and make these key external stakeholders full partners in graduating students who are both college-ready and career-ready. In Georgia, Gwinnett County district leaders, for example, learned that they needed a dedicated staff member at the central office to work as a liaison with business and industry partners in ensuring that all students are prepared for post–high school success.

Teachers and leaders need to know how district staff and external providers will work collaboratively with them to further implement several key features of the pathway design. The strategic-planning group can set forth recommendations and a process for the district and outside providers to support each school in taking the essential actions for achieving bold goals. As we've noted before, these goals cannot be achieved by each school operating independently.

Large-scale buy-in depends on common messaging from both internal and external stakeholders. It is important that the strategic planning study group develop a statement for communicating the changes proposed and the benefits of these changes in terms of improved student readiness.

The study group will want to develop a plan to communicate the impact that quality career pathways can have on improving outcomes for students, including students who are not motivated by traditional academic courses, students from low-socioeconomic backgrounds, students of color, English learners, and students with special needs. Effectively communicating these benefits will increase support for implementing the seven essential design features of career pathways.

The strategic planning study group should consider structuring effective communications around these themes:

- Career pathways are the complete educational package: they provide all the elements students need to learn high-level academic, cognitive, personal, social, technical, and civic skills and responsibilities.

- Students are more likely to work harder and have bigger dreams if their education is meaningful to them, if they enjoy the extra effort, and if their opportunities expand beyond the school building to experience learning in business, industry, and the helping professions.

Summing Up and Looking Ahead

District study groups and district strategies are essential for engaging and getting buy-in from key district, school, community, and other stakeholders around the goal of transforming high schools. The goal is to organize high schools around rigorous career pathways connected to a college-ready curriculum and to postsecondary learning experiences in high-demand, high-wage career fields.

Chapter 3 will focus on school-level strategies for engaging cross-discipline high school action teams in developing a customized, continuous school-improvement process unique to their school. Their work will be informed by a framework of bold goals, pathway design features, and essential conditions set forth in the district strategic plan.

3

Sharing Leadership to Achieve Continuous Improvement

Creating a high school that maximizes opportunity for all students is a several-year enterprise—it's not about quick fixes or "flavor of the month" inservice training. After several years of partnering with high schools, my colleagues and I became convinced that the use of *distributed leadership teams* are the best—and perhaps the only—strategy that will deepen and sustain ownership of the work of school transformation. Formally structured leadership teams also play key roles in initial planning and raising awareness, in supporting the launch phase, and in growing a continuous improvement culture that's necessary to stay on course.

Effective distributed leadership teams engage all school stakeholders in the improvement process. They enable teachers to discover they have power to make middle and high schools more rigorous and relevant. These teams help students accept greater responsibility for their own learning, and they strengthen relationships among students, teachers, counselors, and parents.

The 4Rs of Continuous Improvement

School leaders must use the findings of current research to guide their implementation of distributed leadership teams and keep them focused on the 4Rs of continuous improvement: rigor, relevance, relationships, and responsibility. We know that

- Students learn more when they are engaged in *rigorous* assignments that require them to think, reflect, analyze, do background research, synthesize information, and produce a product demonstrating their learning. In status quo schools, these learning tasks often are reserved for only the so-called best students.[32]

- Students are more motivated when they are engaged with *relevant* learning experiences that are connected to familiar contexts and involve complex problems important to achieving their personal goals.[33]

- Students learn more when they have a personal *relationship* with adults who see them as worthy and who care about and persist in helping them master complex learning tasks. Students also learn more when they have opportunities to interact with peers in small groups to complete open-ended, challenging assignments that enable them to learn from others and to contribute to the learning of others.[34]

- Students take greater *responsibility* for and ownership of their own learning when they believe the content they are being asked to master is important to them—and when the task allows them some autonomy in selecting methods for completing the assignment.[35]

Effective teams that truly distribute leadership among all teachers do not form overnight. School leaders should plan to spend a full year engaged in teamwork with the entire faculty to develop a transformative plan that is clearly focused on reorganizing the school around rigorous and relevant career pathways connected to a college-ready core curriculum. Once a plan is in place, team roles will shift as they begin to lead implementation and evaluate progress in optimizing curriculum and instruction and establishing a smooth-running process of continuous improvement.

Action Teams: Focus and Composition

To achieve bold goals over time, schools need at least six distributed leadership teams that are keenly focused on a variety of challenges and strategies. Each action-oriented team will address one of the following:

- Data, accountability, and policy
- Career pathways, school organization, and scheduling
- Powerful assignments (with three subteams focused on CTE, math, and literacy)
- Transition from middle to high school
- Transition from senior year of high school to careers and postsecondary studies
- Counseling, exploring, and advising for careers and postsecondary studies

Each action team should include high school academic, career/technical education, special education, fine and performing arts, and other elective teachers. Each team should have a person with counseling experience, a school principal or assistant principal, and a parent.

The teams focused on the transition into high school and counseling for careers and postsecondary studies should also include representation from the middle school, such as academic and career exploratory teachers, a counselor, a principal or assistant principal, and a parent. The other four teams may want to include a school board member, business and postsecondary educational leaders, and a district leader specializing in academic and CTE curricula or in data analysis (for the data and accountability team). A well-supported steering committee composed of the chairs of each team keeps faculty informed about and connected to the progress in developing the school-specific transformation plan.

One School's Teaming Model

Each month, chairs of the distributed leadership teams at Camden County High School in Georgia meet to discuss written reports about the work of their teams and possible recommended actions. The monthly written reports keep other teams and school leaders informed about their work and facilitate collaboration across teams.

Camden schedules one day each month for a faculty meeting led by the principal to review progress on implementation of the transformative plan, to share emerging issues and recommend actions, and to receive faculty feedback. "Distributed leadership teams are a way to keep everybody involved and informed. It's worked exceedingly well for us," says former principal John Tucker. "For 10 years, this process has kept everyone engaged and committed to the 4Rs of a continuous improvement culture, with dramatic results in graduation rates and graduating students college-ready, career-ready, or both."

PDSA: A Process to Achieve a Continuous Improvement Culture

Distributed leadership teams need a common process to use in developing a transformative plan and adjusting action plans as needed. One highly effective method is the Plan, Do, Study, Act (PDSA) process. Using this approach, middle and high schools work through four cyclical stages to build a culture of continuous improvement and to develop and implement a transformative plan for achieving their bold goals. The process consists of the following four action steps:

1. **Plan:**
   a. *Identify and describe the problem and state why it is important* that it be addressed.
   b. *Identify the root causes* contributing to the problem.
   c. *Set goals describing the desired student outcomes;* then outline desired changes in school and classroom practices and how each could be measured.
   d. *Assess and identify the major shifts in school and classroom practices* that would best fit the school's situation.
   e. *Describe the specific actions needed,* including those related to resources, professional development, administrative support, and classroom

coaching, and the amount of effort necessary to reliably implement the shifts in school and instructional practices to achieve the desired results. Consider *theory of action* "if/then" statements to identify the conditions that must occur to achieve the changes needed in school and classroom practices. For example,

- *If* we provide teachers with professional development on X, *then* . . .

- *If* we use certified professional development trainers, *then* . . .

- *If* we provide collaborative follow-up coaching by the trainers, designated district staff, and principals, *then* . . .

- *If* the teacher engages students in higher-level learning experiences, *then* . . .

    f. *Identify indicators for assessing results*, who will be responsible for monitoring the results, and who will prepare a report each 45 days to evaluate progress in achieving goals.

2. **Do:** Take action to implement the changes in school and classroom practices, including those related to professional development, organizational structure, scheduling, implementation of classroom strategies, and support from school and district leaders for the shifts.

3. **Study:** Ask these questions: Were the desired outcomes obtained? Was the intervention implemented as envisioned? What refinement needs to be made in the intervention to achieve greater results?

4. **Act:** Using results from the study, begin the process again. Make necessary changes in the plan and the theory of action. Repeat implementation and continue to monitor the results every 45 days.

"With PDSA, you can validate for teachers that proven practices work when implemented with fidelity," says Susan Allred, author and experienced school and district administrator.[36] "For chronically low-performing schools, PDSA breaks the cycle of expecting to fail by taking away excuses and by validating that the new practices work."

Plan, Do, Study, Act: "All the Pieces Come Together"

The following is an excerpt from an interview with Susan Allred, author of Without Trumpets: Continuous Educational Improvement, Journey to Sustainability. *Susan has worked with schools in Kentucky and other Southern states to use the PDSA process effectively.*

Why use the PDSA process?

Through this process, all the pieces come together as part of a specific set of written actions and timelines. Teachers can discover they have the power to change things that make a difference in the lives of students today and in their future. Educators working in most low-performing schools have good intentions but seldom get the important work done because they lack a defined set of practices for fixing the problems. Having a common approach to addressing problems makes it easier to transfer knowledge from one classroom to another and inform the overall work.

What conditions are essential for successful implementation of the PDSA process?

District and school leaders must be committed to using PDSA tools to design, analyze issues, develop systems, develop an action plan, and monitor plan implementation. Monitoring is crucial, because it creates new actions for continuous improvement. It's important that each PDSA team member understands the goal and problem they are to address and what is expected of them, how they will be supported in acquiring new knowledge and skills, and how long it might take to become successful.

Team Support from Four Perspectives

To achieve a culture of continuous improvement using distributed leadership teams, collaboration and support must come from four perspectives: top-down, bottom-up, peer-to-peer, and outside-in.

Districts must provide the *top-down perspective* by setting bold goals that communicate a vision of high expectations for all students and supporting schools as they customize their transformative plan (as outlined in Chapter 2). Both internal and external stakeholders begin to believe bold goals are achievable when districts adopt a framework of bold actions, including (1) an accountability system for tracking progress; (2) support for school and teacher leaders to change school and classroom practices; and (3) the dogged pursuit of rigorous and relevant curriculum and instruction.

Districts set the stage for transformative actions by selecting and developing skilled and knowledgeable school leaders who can foster the right *bottom-up perspective*—leaders who understand what it means to engage all faculty in creating a middle school and a high school where teachers believe that, with support, almost all students can achieve at high levels.[37] Launching and sustaining transformative change depends on a bottom-up perspective that uses feedback from principals and teachers to create a customized plan unique to the school and community.

Peer-to-peer perspectives enable teachers to take ownership of the continuous improvement process through communication and collaboration within and among distributed teams as they identify and solve problems. By participating in decision-making teams, teachers will become the advocates for connecting academic knowledge and skills to career pathway assignments, for engaging students in relearning, and for working with middle schools, postsecondary institutions, and employers to plan transitions.

An *outside-in perspective* is needed to ensure schools have the necessary support from school improvement specialists to identify the root causes of their challenges and to adopt proven improvement practices. An outside perspective can help reduce the risk of schools implementing a fragmented and disconnected set of independent projects, workshops, contracted consultants, and products that never add up to a coherent vision for a transformative school plan.

Distributed leadership teams provide the framework that pulls these four perspectives together to create and enact a shared, scalable vision for improvement. The remainder of this chapter provides an overview of the various teams schools should consider forming and the work each team will need to accomplish. The remaining chapters of this book will provide an in-depth look at how the various teams can bring about the changes needed to help schools achieve their bold goals.

The overarching goal of this work is to create a spirit of collaboration, an eagerness to learn from each other, and a shared commitment to ensuring all students are well-served. As that goal begins to crystallize, the seemingly impossible becomes possible.

The Data, Accountability, and Policy Action Team

The data, accountability, and policy action team has the following goals and objectives.

Primary team goals:

- Collect and analyze data regarding the percentage of students meeting high school readiness standards (upon entering 9th grade) and college- and career-readiness standards (upon graduation), and regarding current school and classroom practices experienced by different groups of students in middle and high school.

- Identify possible school and classroom root causes of students' failure to meet the readiness standards.

- Recommend policies for increasing the percentage of students meeting readiness goals.

- Develop an accountability and tracking system for monitoring progress toward achieving bold goals.

Team objectives:

- Choose indicators from Chapter 1, or use state or local indicators, to establish baseline data on the percentage of current students who meet readiness goals for high school, college, and careers.

- Identify questions that will frame data collection and analysis and will enable the team to determine which gaps in school and classroom practices may be preventing students from meeting readiness goals. (See Chapter 2 for additional questions.)

- Share data with other action teams and ask them to share their ideas on district policies and support needed to implement the transformative plan.

Analyzing data. In the Plan stage of the PDSA process, the data, accountability, and policy action team should analyze student data overall, and by subgroups, related to several key questions:

1. What problems has the team been asked to address?

2. What do the data say about which subgroups of students receive rigorous and engaging instruction in academic and career pathway classes and which do not?

3. What percentage of students meet high school readiness goals and indicators?

4. What percentage of students graduate from high school college-ready, career-ready, or both?

5. What is missing in the experiences of students who fail to meet the readiness goals?

6. What percentage of students entering 9th grade fail to graduate from high school?

7. What are the root causes of some students' failure to meet readiness goals for 9th grade?

8. What changes are needed in what is expected of students, how they are taught, and how they are supported to meet higher expectations?

9. What proven school and classroom practices could increase the percentage of our students who enter high school ready for challenging studies and who graduate college- and career-ready?

10. What changes are needed in school and classroom practices to achieve the bold goals?

(Also review areas of analysis for the district assessment study group in Chapter 2.)

Once student outcomes and necessary changes in school and classroom practices are identified, the team can develop *theory of action* statements.

Conducting a survey and review. In the planning year, this team should consider surveying a random sample of students in grades 8, 10, and 12 regarding their perceptions of their school experiences. The voices of students can help pinpoint the extent to which students from different racial and socioeconomic backgrounds are experiencing different expectations.

Linking survey results to student performance on external exams will illustrate how achievement is linked to students' experiences in school and to what was expected of them. To conduct such a survey, the team can request district funding or contract with organizations that have experience in implementing such surveys and providing results linked to student achievement, such as My Student Survey.

An external school improvement coach can help conduct a review of curriculum and instruction to identify differences in assignments given to different subgroups of students and the level of learning expected from each subgroup. This process could include a desktop review of key data, stakeholder interviews, and an on-site review by an external team that includes members from high schools with similar students but with significantly higher performance levels, along with representatives from postsecondary institutions and businesses who are familiar with local high school graduates and can highlight actions needed to close readiness gaps.

Both the student survey and the on-site external review can provide eye-opening perspectives on school data and highlight actions needed to close readiness gaps.

Reporting on priority goals and objectives. After it collects and analyzes the necessary information, the data, accountability, and policy action team prepares a report of their findings, including the following:

- Current status of students' readiness for high school and post–high school and the status of school and classroom practices for different subgroups of students.

- A root-cause analysis of the major factors preventing many students from meeting readiness goals, with emphasis on factors within the district's and school's ability to address.

- Proposed policies for the school board and actions that other teams can take to change the quality of curriculum and instructional experiences, to engage students in higher-level learning, and to provide students and teachers with the support needed to advance student readiness.

Following the planning year, this team shifts its focus to becoming proactive for continuous improvement, tracking progress on key indicators regarding high school, career, and postsecondary readiness, and measuring whether expected school and classroom practices are being implemented at the desired levels. The team continues to provide school and district leaders and other established action teams with annual reports based on its analysis of their work—reports that include potential actions and policy changes that are needed.

The Career Pathway, Organization, and Scheduling Action Team

The career pathway, organization, and scheduling action team has the following goal and objectives.

Primary team goal:

- Provide all students with access to career pathway courses that prepare them for both postsecondary studies and careers leading to a middle-class income.

Team objectives:

- Align existing and new pathways to good jobs and postsecondary studies.
- Organize the high school around students' career interests, connected to a college-ready academic core.
- Design a schedule that enables career pathway teachers and academic teachers (at least English language arts, mathematics, and science) who share a cohort of students to have frequent common planning time to design rigorous connected-learning experiences for students.
- Broaden the concept of career pathway programs of study to include at least three coherent advanced academic courses linked to a career and educational goal.
- **Provide leadership support to career pathway teachers as they prepare students for careers and postsecondary studies through rigorous academic and pathway studies.**

These objectives are essential elements for connecting rigorous and relevant career pathways to a college-ready academic core for the purpose of engaging students in deeper learning. A failure to address these objectives is a failure to recognize the essence of the bold goals that transform high schools.

The career pathway, organization, and scheduling action team should study the student survey data and the report prepared by the data and accountability team. Within the Plan stage of the PDSA process, this team should ask the following questions:

1. What percentage of graduates earn a bachelor's degree within six years of high school graduation, or complete either an advanced credential or an associate's degree within three years of high school graduation in a high-demand, high-wage career field?

2. What percentage of graduates who did not attend college are employed by the age of 25 in a job leading to a middle-class income?

3. In which existing career pathways are 90 percent of completers prepared academically and technically for postsecondary studies and a career leading to a good job?

4. Which existing career pathway courses engage students in rigorous assignments (based on the criteria in Chapter 4)?

5. What root causes are preventing some career pathway courses from making the maximum contributions to advancing students' readiness for careers and postsecondary studies?

6. How frequently do academic and career pathway teachers plan connected assignments aimed at advancing students' academic readiness?

7. What additional career pathways are needed to provide students with access to new and emerging career opportunities in the community and beyond, leading to postsecondary study and a good job?

8. What actions are needed in existing career pathways to connect the curriculum and instruction to good jobs and postsecondary studies?

9. Who is responsible for providing leadership to support CTE pathway teachers in designing rigorous assignments?

Remember: improvement cannot begin if school leaders and teachers believe they are already perfect. To allow for meaningful improvement, begin with an honest, data-informed appraisal of the quality of existing career pathways. (See Chapter 2 for additional information on high-quality career pathways.)

Continuous Improvement Requires Committed Leaders

In the late 1990s, a west Tennessee high school with an outstanding principal and a team of teacher leaders implemented with fidelity many practices outlined in this book. Those practices included enrolling all students in a college-ready academic core and making it possible for academic and CTE teachers to plan connected-learning experiences. The school provided extensive support to both teachers and students as needed, and it created a counseling system in which teachers became advisors so that every student had a mentor throughout high school. Special efforts were made to engage parents in the process.

Over a period of five years, student performance and graduation rates increased greatly, and discipline problems became virtually nonexistent. When the principal moved on to another job, however, the district employed a new principal who, in one year's time, divided the students into three different curriculum tracks: college prep, general, and basic. Within three years, the school had returned to its previous low-performance levels.

The lesson? Without district and school leaders who have the courage and commitment to continue support for *what is hard but what is working*, even the most successful schools will spiral down into mediocrity once more.

The career pathway action team is responsible for developing several key pieces of the transformative plan. It will decide which existing pathways should be retained and improved, and which new career pathways should be added to prepare students for rising workplace requirements and for postsecondary studies. As part of this effort, the team should *broaden the definition of career pathways* to include academic concentrations in STEM (science, technology, engineering, and math) fields, the humanities, and fine and performing arts.

The team's transformative plan should make recommendations for organizing the high school around students' interests by creating career-themed academies that each include three or four career pathways. For example, a STEM academy could include one pathway of three or more AP-level college preparatory math and science courses, one pathway of four advanced career CTE courses in the field of energy and power, and one pathway of four courses related to electrical trades. Each of these pathways has the potential for connected-learning experiences involving literacy, mathematics, and science.

The team should recommend a position to be filled by a qualified person who will help and support career pathway and academic teachers as they align their assignments to middle-class career opportunities and postsecondary studies. The team's plan also should define professional expectations for the person providing support to academic and CTE teachers, criteria for measuring the level of rigor achieved in both career pathway and academic courses, and specific actions to be taken to support career pathway and academic teachers in codesigning and implementing rigorous connected-learning experiences in their classes.

Design Feature 7 (Chapter 2, p. 26) requires all graduates to meet computer science, information technology, and digital fluency standards, demonstrated and documented through a cumulative portfolio that begins in middle school and follows the student through academic, career exploratory, and career pathway classes. Working with the middle to high school transition action team, the career pathway action team is well-positioned to take the lead in instigating a process that will turn this important cross-grade learning goal into a viable driver for ensuring that all students gain the critical digital technology skills required for 21st century jobs.

Finally, in the planning year, the career pathway action team will need to design a schedule that enables CTE and academic teachers to share common cohorts of students and to coplan connected-learning assignments. The schedule design will likely be different for small and larger high schools. For example, large high schools with students organized in three or more academies may consider assigning nonteaching professional staff to take over classes for a half-day once a month to free up time for coplanning.

Lessons Learned About Cross-Disciplinary Planning

Jennifer Frentress is a school improvement specialist who often works with high schools and districts to develop cross-disciplinary instructional planning. She is currently associate superintendent of instructional services in San Mateo County, California. The following interview, edited for length and clarity, highlights some of the lessons she's learned about creating a schedule that enables academic and CTE teachers to coplan connected-learning experiences. What implications do her experiences have for designing a schedule for your high school?

What conditions are essential for enabling academic and CTE teachers to successfully coplan rigorous lessons that connect academics with assignments in CTE classes?

First, they must understand the reason for breaking down the silos between academic and career/technical education. One reason we have a shortage of people prepared for good jobs is because many graduates leave high school lacking the foundational academic, cognitive, technical, technology, and 21st century skills to qualify. This understanding is best acquired when principals, teachers, and counselors are engaged in a study process to determine how connected-learning experiences advance students' motivation and learning.

Second, schools need a principal who *truly* believes all students can learn at high levels. It helps if the principal has been a teacher who engaged all students to learn at a high level. And creating structures for coplanning requires the principal to take time to get into the classroom and look at the kind of connected assignments students are being given and the cognitive level required to complete them. The principal needs an *investigative curiosity* to see the impact that such assignments have on student achievement compared with classrooms where such assignments are not prevalent.

How can schools design a schedule to facilitate connected learning between academic and CTE teachers?

Have a team composed of academic and CTE teachers, along with the scheduling person from the high school, explore a variety of options. Members of this team must buy into the vision that connected learning will increase student motivation and readiness for postsecondary studies. If that is the case, it has been my experience that they will figure out how to find four or five hours each month for teachers to do coplanning. A well-chosen team will seldom fail in this regard.

What factors often prevent schools from being successful in planning connected-learning experiences?

First, the staff often do not understand what they are being asked to do. Second, they do not understand what it looks like when it is done well. Third, school leaders often ask all teachers to do it all at once, rather than starting with those who are willing and enthusiastic, and then letting the others see the results. It can't be hurried.

Beyond these elements of the career pathway team's plan, this team will work closely with the career-counseling team and the middle to high school transition action team in planning how to enroll all students in college preparatory English and Algebra I in 9th grade. This effort includes enrolling those students who did not satisfactorily complete these courses in 8th grade and those needing intensive support and increased time to meet college-ready academic standards in the courses by the end of 9th grade.

After the planning year, this team remains responsible for tracking the school's progress in implementing with fidelity the following three conditions that research has shown will result in more students meeting college- and career-readiness goals:

- Providing rigorous and relevant assignments in pathway classes that engage students in taking responsibility for using higher-level academic, cognitive, technical and technological, and 21st century skills to complete such assignments (see Chapter 4).
- Ensuring students complete a college-ready academic core that engages them in higher-level learning experiences using literacy-based assignments in all classes and multistep abstract and real-world assignments in mathematics classes.
- Providing academic and career pathway teachers time to coplan learning experiences that require connecting academic knowledge and skills to complete rigorous projects in CTE classes.

These three conditions are nonnegotiable. If they are not implemented systematically and intensively, the career pathway team needs to identify the root causes preventing successful implementation and develop a set of actions with designated responsibilities, timelines, checkpoints, and support necessary to implement their plan with fidelity.

The Powerful Assignment Action Team

The powerful assignment action team has the following goal.

Primary team goal:

- Connect assignments for students in all courses to college- and career-readiness standards and to instructional strategies that engage them in higher-level learning experiences that are *rigorous, relevant, and necessary to graduate from high school college-ready, career-ready, or both.*

The powerful assignment action team is organized around three subteams focused on powerful CTE, mathematics, and literacy assignments. Chapters 4, 5, and 6 discuss powerful assignments in greater detail, including criteria and instructional shifts needed to implement such assignments in all classes, and recommended membership of the three subteams.

The subteams analyze reports from the data, accountability, and policy action team and other information from student surveys, interviews, assignments, and artifacts of student work to determine the extent to which all students are experiencing rigorous and relevant assignments. Based on this analysis, each subteam should ask the following questions during the Plan stage of the PDSA process:

1. To what extent are assignments given in academic and career pathway classes preparing students to be both college- and career-ready?

2. Which subgroups of students are receiving rigorous, relevant, and engaging assignments in academic and career pathway classes, and which are not?

3. What does the information reveal about opportunities for improvement?

4. What major instructional shifts are needed in both academic and career pathway classes to prepare all students—including historically underserved students—to earn a middle-class income and become informed citizens?

In the planning year, each subteam develops a plan of action to close the gap between the current level of assignments and the level necessary to achieve the bold goals in its area of focus. This undertaking involves identifying gaps in student performance and probable root causes for why students are not engaged in instructional practices that lead to higher levels of learning. Each subteam will also need to provide a clear vision of such assignments by developing a set of indicators for determining when assignments are sufficiently rigorous to prepare students for postsecondary studies and a career.

The powerful assignment action team's effort will be crucial for ensuring that middle and high schools work successfully for all students. Challenging and engaging assignments are the springboard to higher levels of achievement.

Many of the necessary instructional shifts will go against what has become acceptable practice in many low- and average-performing middle and high schools. In too many schools, students other than the highest achievers experience instruction that is teacher-centered and test-driven, providing them with low-level, repetitive tasks that do not motivate them to engage in higher-level learning. School leaders and teachers misinterpret this lack of effort as a lack of ability to do demanding work.

The powerful assignment subteams will need to carefully analyze the current status of assignments in their focus area and build a strong case for the need to provide all students with higher-level learning experiences in academic and CTE courses and with a clear vision of what those experiences must look like. As a whole, the powerful assignment action team will lead the effort to ensure that students' ability is no longer perceived to be fixed but rather can be greatly increased by having opportunities to engage in higher-level learning experiences.

The powerful assignment action team should meet both as an overall team and as subteams. At the whole-team level, members review the work of each subteam to ensure assignments are aligned to college- and career-readiness standards.

In creating its plan of action, each subteam should develop

- A statement of need for engaging more students in higher-level learning assignments.
- A root-cause analysis resulting in a statement of why the current need exists.
- A list of indicators for assessing progress in achieving targeted goals.
- A statement of proven best practices that can result in more students meeting college- and career-readiness standards.
- A theory of specific actions that result in instructional shifts that motivate students to complete powerful assignments.

The powerful assignment action team may recommend intensive professional development to support academic and CTE teachers and principals in making the instructional shifts outlined in Chapters 4, 5, and 6.

After the planning year, the whole team and subteams function as a continuous improvement team, studying and analyzing data on the extent to which the plans have been implemented and the desired student outcomes have been achieved. This function will involve making modifications in professional development and other support needed to spread the shift in instructional strategies to more classrooms, until all teachers are engaged and all students are performing at expected levels.

The Middle to High School Transition Action Team

The middle to high school transition action team has the following goals.

Primary team goals:

- Enroll all middle school students in an accelerated curriculum, and enroll all students entering 9th grade into a college-ready core.

- Design a modified schedule to provide extended time and assistance to those students needing extra support to succeed.

A key principle that the middle to high school transition action team must keep in mind is that *students will not meet grade-level standards through remediation*. Students in grades 6 through 9 must be assigned grade-level work and then supported until they master the content and skills to complete assignments at grade level.

This action team begins by answering many of the same questions listed for the data and accountability team. This effort includes looking at 8th grade assessment data for rising 9th graders, as well as data for 6th and 7th grade students to determine the level of extra support some will need in grades 8 and 9 to succeed in a college-ready core.

The team then develops an action plan to work toward the bold goal of ensuring *at least 95 percent of entering 9th grade students successfully complete college preparatory classes by the end of 9th grade*. As part of this plan, the team will identify the root causes that are currently preventing the high school from redesigning the 9th grade to provide intensive time and support to ensure most students complete college preparatory courses in English language arts, mathematics, and science. This team works with the career pathway, organization, and scheduling action team to arrange for the added time needed in 9th grade for students to complete grade-level assignments and to revisit the learning experiences until they demonstrate successful completion of assignments at a *B* grade level.

Beyond the planning phase, this team regularly tracks both student outcomes and changes in school and classroom practices to assess the progress being made to advance students' high school readiness, to measure the extent to which the desired shifts in school and classroom practices are occurring, and to identify existing challenges and develop potential solutions.

The Senior-Year Transition Action Team

The senior-year transition action team has the following goal.

Primary team goal:

- Design the senior year so students who are ready can earn one year of postsecondary credit toward a degree or an advanced credential and other students can meet readiness standards for postsecondary studies and careers. (See Chapter 8 for the primary charge to the senior-year transition action team to develop a three-part action plan to transform the senior year.)

Team objectives:

- Ensure all students have a plan for their next step, and for the school to assist them in carrying out that plan. To achieve this objective, this team will create an action plan for redesigning the senior year so that graduates leave high school ready for postsecondary studies, careers, or both. (See Chapter 8 for more information on transforming the senior year.)

Within the Plan stage of the PDSA process, the senior-year transition action team should analyze data overall and by student subgroups and ask the following questions:

- On average, how many dual credits are students earning while in high school?
- Are dual credits resulting in a shortened time to attain a degree or credential? If not, why?
- What percentage of students meet college-readiness standards by the end of 11th grade, as defined by the appropriate state board or by the primary postsecondary institutions enrolling most of the school's graduates? (If such indicators have not been developed, review Chapters 1 and 2 and define indicators to identify students who meet readiness standards.)
- What percentage of students plan to pursue postsecondary studies after high school? What proportion of these students did not meet postsecondary academic readiness or academic- and technical career-readiness standards by the end of 11th grade?
- Of students who said they were going to college, what percentage over the past three years enrolled in and completed one year of postsecondary studies? Why are others choosing not to pursue postsecondary studies?

After the planning year, the senior-year transition action team will continue to function as a continuous improvement team by tracking the school's progress in using the senior year to get more students ready to pursue advanced studies and jobs leading to future growth and development. The senior-year transition action team will need to continually use the PDSA process to find, implement, and advocate for solutions to emerging problems.

The Counseling, Exploring, and Advising Action Team

The counseling, exploring, and advising action team has the following goal.

Primary team goal:

- Develop a counseling, exploring, and advising program that engages all faculty in cultivating a relationship with assigned students to support, motivate, and assist them and their parents in making informed decisions and plans in middle and high school to achieve college- and career-readiness goals.

Team objectives:

- Help students make good choices.
- Recognize that all students can benefit from rigorous career pathways and academic studies in preparing to access opportunities for postsecondary studies and careers that lead to a middle-class income.

Addressing these objectives is essential if the school is going to achieve its bold goal of ensuring that 95 percent of students graduate from high school, with 90 percent graduating college-ready, career-ready, or both.

The information in Chapter 9, along with data collected by the accountability and other action teams, will inform the work of the counseling, exploring, and advising action team. The team should use the following questions in the Plan stage of their PDSA process to collect and analyze additional data about their students overall and by subgroup:

1. What percentage of students entering 9th grade are prepared for challenging high school studies?

2. What percentage of students are enrolled in a true college preparatory curriculum?

3. What do the student survey results reveal about which students receive intensive assistance in planning a guided pathway of academic and career studies to prepare them for both careers and postsecondary studies?

4. What percentage of parents and students meet at least annually with either a counselor or a teacher-advisor to review the student's plan of academic and career studies leading to a post–high school goal?

5. What percentage of seniors reported having opportunities to learn about careers and related educational opportunities?

6. What percentage of students reported having a range of job-shadowing experiences in career fields of interest to them?

7. What implications do the data from these and other questions have for making revisions in the counseling, exploring, and advising opportunities being offered to all students and to specific groups of students?

The National Student Clearinghouse is one potential source of information for answering some of these questions.

As team members review data regarding the strengths and weaknesses of the current counseling system, they may find that counselor-student ratios make it impossible to provide personalized support to each student. If so, a diffused counseling program with several components will be needed to achieve the goal and objectives. (See Chapter 9 for best practices.)

Whatever plan the team develops, it will need to carefully define the role that counselors and teacher-advisors play in placing all students in a college-ready academic core, in providing timely support for students to succeed, and in identifying students who can succeed in an accelerated curriculum with special support. This effort will require close coordination with the middle to high school transition team and the career pathways team. The counseling team also should outline how this plan would be communicated to students and parents.

Three Ways to Build Strong Student Connections

When asked what accounted for the high graduation rates at a high school in Kentucky, the principal at the time responded:

We work hard to connect each student in three different ways. First, we connect each student to a teacher who remains their advisor throughout high school and meets regularly with them with planned lessons. Second, we work with students and their parents to connect each student and their parent with a post-high school goal and a planned program of study to prepare them to achieve their goal. Third, we connect each student to a peer group within the school—athletics, school clubs, vocational student organization—or an adult mentor in the community. We believe these three connections build important relationships with the students and have contributed to a graduation rate in the mid-90s.

After the planning year, this team contributes to continuous improvement by tracking and reporting on progress in implementing a counseling, exploring, and advising program. Designated team members prepare reports at regular time intervals with recommendations for adjusting and improving the components of the program. This team's approach to continuous improvement should be built around one central question: to what extent are all students experiencing the intensive career counseling and support (including extra support for marginalized students) needed to make informed decisions, graduate from high school ready for college and careers, and make successful transitions to their next step?

Sharing Leadership: Practical Steps Schools Can Take Now

Schools that are unable to use the framework of the six action teams outlined in this chapter (due to school size or other factors) can still take steps now to raise the rigor of CTE and academic courses in high school, so that most students experience higher levels of learning.

Start by developing a single school-level action leadership team composed of counselors, academic teachers from each of the four major disciplines, at least two career pathway teachers, an elective teacher, and at least three external members who can bring the perspectives of higher education, parents, and local employers. Charge this team to do the following:

1. Identify school and classroom practices that are preventing many students from leaving high school college-ready, career-ready, or both.

2. Collect data using the questions in this and other chapters, and identify which students are not engaged in higher-level learning—the type of learning that team members would want for children in their own families.

3. Determine the root causes that are keeping some students from receiving the same rigorous and relevant learning experiences that are given to the best students.

4. Develop a set of actions to provide all students with the quality of learning experiences traditionally reserved for the "best" students, so that at least 95 percent graduate from high school and 90 percent graduate college-ready, career-ready, or both.

5. Create a plan for implementing the proposed actions and a system of indicators for regularly assessing changes in the rigor and relevance of learning experiences, as well as changes in student achievement, and make adjustments as needed.

Summing Up and Looking Ahead

Distributed leadership in the form of action teams with specific goals is an essential component of successful high school transformation. These teams can use strategies to design high schools that are *relevant*, that are *rigorous*, and that strengthen *relationships* among students, teachers, counselors, and parents, resulting in students accepting greater *responsibility* for their own learning—using invigorated career pathways as the catalyst. The approach engages the faculty in owning the problems and the solutions for achieving a culture of continuous improvement, with collaboration and support from four perspectives: top-down, bottom-up, outside-in, and peer-to-peer.

The first three chapters of this book expressed what may seem to be a radical idea: using high-quality career pathways to redesign schools for tomorrow. I understand that before leaders are willing to take the dramatic steps described in these chapters, they will want some proof of concept. The following "Spotlight" story of Delaware's Polytech High School illustrates what this framework of bold goals and actions might produce in practice, when a school implements a transformative plan with fidelity.

The following six chapters then offer a detailed "how-to"—*how* to take the steps I've advocated in the first three chapters of this book and exemplified by Polytech High School. These chapters offer practical implementation strategies, research on their effectiveness, and stories of how real schools have benefited from these practices.

Spotlight: Polytech High School's Story

In my decades leading the High Schools That Work initiative, I've been fortunate to visit and work with schools in just about every state. Many stand out in specific areas of improvement, but only a few have truly devoted themselves to the complete portfolio of strategies that lead to greater student success.

Polytech High School in Woodside, Delaware, is one of the best examples of a school that covers all the bases in creating success strategies for all students. The best thing about Polytech's portfolio is that these are the kinds of strategies that virtually any high school can use. Many are not expensive, but they do require planning, organization, and an unwavering staff-wide dedication to helping *every student* meet high standards and find success after high school.

Polytech High School masterfully connects its 20 career and technical education pathway courses with rigorous academic courses and high expectations. Most students understand why they're learning certain skills in core academic classes; and because academic and CTE teachers often coordinate their lessons, students can apply that knowledge in their CTE courses.

First and foremost, Polytech requires *every* student to complete *a college-ready academic core.*

If you think your school or some of your students cannot meet such academic standards or college and career goals, consider this: when Polytech joined the SREB High Schools That Work network in 1992, it had *the lowest scores of any high school among the hundreds of schools in our network*. If Polytech can do it, just about any school can do it.

Polytech High School's Portfolio for Success

At Polytech High School, attendance had declined, students were not held to high academic standards in their home high schools, and there was no common vision to connect academics with the courses at the area vocational center.

Polytech school leaders made the transition from a shared-time vocational center to a full-time high school in 1992 and became an active member of the SREB High Schools That Work initiative. School leaders worked with distributed leadership teams of CTE and new academic faculty to improve curriculum and instruction—and eventually, Polytech became one of the higher-achieving high schools in the network.

Polytech's leaders are worth emulating. They are never satisfied. They are continually exploring ways they can improve students' experiences and preparation for college and career. Over the past 25 years, Polytech has built a continuous improvement culture stressing the 4Rs—rigor, relevance, relationships, and responsibility—to engage students in high-level learning experiences and support them to meet their career or college goals.

In a remarkable accomplishment for a career-oriented high school, Polytech recently graduated 97 percent of its seniors and ranked 6th among Delaware's 45 high schools in reading achievement and 14th in mathematics. The graduation rate is even more impressive when you consider that Polytech High School voluntarily has *higher* graduation requirements for students than does the state. The school's standard is 28 credits, including 4 mathematics and 4 English credits, 3 science and 3 social studies credits, and 10.5 CTE credits. In short, Polytech graduates virtually all of its senior students—most of them college- or career-ready, and increasingly, both.

Today, Polytech enrolls about 1,200 students, roughly 60 percent of whom are white and 40 percent are students of color; 10 percent of its students are enrolled in special education. More than 650 students apply to attend Polytech each year, but the school can accept only 320. Only students with a sibling enrolled at the school or a parent who works at the school are given preference for admission; all others are accepted based on a lottery system.

Polytech begins building *relationships* with students and families before they even arrive for their first day. In the spring before students' first year, a Polytech faculty member personally visits each new student at home, if possible. The meetings introduce students to the school's high expectations in both academic and CTE courses. "We explain that this is a no-excuse high school, and students are expected to take responsibility for meeting classroom expectations and having respectful relationships with peers and faculty," principal Ryan Fuller said. Building these relationships from the beginning among teachers, students, and families is especially important, because students are drawn from five different school districts and charter schools. Typically, the same school counselor and assistant principal stay with each class throughout high school. This strong emphasis on *relationships* has made the school safer and has reduced student discipline issues. In the 2018–19 school year, only 3 percent of students were suspended, compared to a state average of 7.3 percent.

To be sure, Polytech High School is *a goal-driven high school*. All Polytech first-year students begin to set specific career and educational goals in their first semester, spending three to four days exploring the school's 20 different career pathways. Students complete a short hands-on lesson in each pathway to learn about each field of study. In the third nine-week session of school, every first-year student works with a counselor and CTE teachers to choose two career pathways for a deeper learning experience, lasting a total of four weeks each.

In this two months of exploration, students learn about the technology required and the career and postsecondary education opportunities in those two pathways. Academic and CTE teachers work together to design hands-on activities that introduce students to careers in each pathway. Students have opportunities to consider which pathway might best fit their interests, aptitudes, and vision for themselves. "These rotation exploratory experiences are important because students chose Polytech to start the journey toward an advanced credential, associate, or bachelor's degree in a career field of their choice," the principal said.

In the final nine-week session, counselors and CTE teachers help each student choose a career pathway. According to Principal Fuller, 95 percent of students enter a career pathway of their first choice at the end of their 9th grade exploratory experience.

A distributed leadership team of counselors and academic and CTE teachers develops and implements a plan to enroll all students in a *rigorous* college preparatory curriculum. There are no low-level courses at Polytech. After an analysis of each student's grades, state assessment results from the previous year, and other information, students who meet the high school–readiness standards advance to college preparatory academic courses.

Students who need more time to complete college prep Algebra I in 9th grade are enrolled in a yearlong, foundational, 82-minute-per-session class. Teachers of the course have intensive professional development in formative assessment–driven math lessons to help them engage students in multiple-step abstract and real-world problems aimed at advancing their understanding, reasoning, and use of mathematics in their career pathway labs. It's not about teaching students only math *procedures*, but how and why the math is used—and how logic and reasoning skills may apply to life and work. Students also can access digital lessons based on the formative assessment. By the end of the 9th grade, about 97 percent of these students are ready for the next college preparatory mathematics class.

The same strategy is used in language arts. Virtually all 9th graders take college preparatory English; but students who lack grade-level skills in reading, comprehension, and oral and written communication also take a foundational class that includes time management, organization, and study skills.

Finally, all 9th graders take a CTE foundations course focusing on citizenship, future careers, and postsecondary options, and the attributes and social skills necessary for the workplace and work-based learning.

"The 9th grade program is essential to our students' continued success," Principal Fuller said. The program's deep design ensures that most students will be well-prepared to advance through grades 10 through 12. Students who do still have academic deficiencies and learning challenges after grade 9 receive additional support through an enrichment class in grades 10 and 11.

Polytech provides 20 different career pathway programs of study grouped in four academies: industrial, professional services, health and medical services, and modern technology. Each career academy has a strong partnership with businesses and postsecondary institutions, with advanced studies in each career field. Advisory meetings are held with industry and postsecondary partners twice each year for advice on labor markets, new technology, industry certification, and possible deficits in students' academic, technical, and 21st century skills. Each program undergoes a review every four years by employers and postsecondary leaders to ensure the courses are up-to-date.

For graduation, Polytech students also must complete *a capstone senior project* that counts for a half credit. This project requires students to apply core academic knowledge and skills, to learn new technology, and to demonstrate skills in research and report writing and oral presentation. Teams of career pathway and English language arts teachers work with students on the projects. The projects are evaluated using specific rubrics, including a student presentation that business and college partners and students' families are invited to attend.

Polytech's results in one recent school year were impressive:

- Eighty-nine percent of seniors met the state's college- and/or career-readiness standards.

- One hundred thirty-two seniors earned dual-enrollment credit, and 164 earned state-approved industry certifications.

- One-third of seniors earned course credit for work-based learning.

- Eighty-two students passed one or more advanced placement exams.

- Seventy-six percent of graduates enrolled in college their first year after high school (44 percent in a four-year college and 32 percent in a two-year college), and 82 percent returned for the second year; only 16 percent needed postsecondary remedial college math and 11 percent needed remedial college English.

How Polytech Keeps Improving

Never satisfied, Polytech school leaders were pursuing improvements in several areas when I spoke with them in 2020. Here is a summary of their comments:

- **Redesigning the senior year.** Polytech was studying how to give ready seniors greater access to postsecondary credit and to assist other seniors to become postsecondary- and career-ready.

- **Continuous improvement culture.** Each academic department at Polytech meets weekly to discuss students' progress, analyze deficiencies, and develop steps to address them. When we talked, a team of math, science, and CTE faculty was developing strategies to improve students' preparation for college and workplace math. Polytech teachers and school leaders are always looking for ways to connect academics to project-based assignments in CTE courses. This direct connection between academics and technical studies is truly powerful—and as other high school educators know, not readily achieved.

Connected-Learning Framework: Six Bold Actions for Achieving Bold Goals

To meet or exceed Polytech High's success, your school district can launch a campaign to achieve bold goals tailored to meet your unique needs (see Chapter 1)—and then provide the support school leaders and teachers will need to implement the six bold actions that follow (see Chapter 2). For each of these actions, teams like those described in Chapter 3 will lead the charge to develop and implement a plan, and to foster a culture of continuous improvement using the Plan, Do, Study, Act (PDSA) improvement cycle. Here are the six bold actions:

- **Action 1:** Design career pathway courses around rigorous project-based assignments that engage students in using a mix of technical, technology, academic, cognitive, and 21st century skills.

- **Action 2:** Implement multistep abstract and real-world assignments in mathematics, career pathway, and science classes to engage students in solving problems designed to advance mathematical reasoning and understanding and develop the ability to use math in a variety of settings.

- **Action 3:** Embed literacy-based assignments in all core academic and career pathway classes, which advance both content knowledge and students' abilities to read, comprehend, and analyze grade-level text and documents and to express their understanding orally and in writing.

- **Action 4:** Provide accelerated learning experiences to all students in grades 6 through 9, so that 95 percent of entering 9th grade students successfully complete *true* college preparatory classes by the end of 9th grade.

- **Action 5:** Use the senior year to provide students who are academically ready for careers and post–high school studies with access to a full year of post–high school credit toward an advanced credential or degree, while preparing other seniors for postsecondary studies and work.

- **Action 6:** Empower counselors in middle and high schools to develop a diffused system of counseling, exploring, and advising for high school, career, and postsecondary readiness. Engage all students and parents in learning about their students' unique talents and aspirations and how these link to emerging career opportunities and to programs of study in high school and beyond.

To succeed, these actions must be implemented in ways that provide students with the personalized support and extra time needed to master foundational academic, technical, technological, cognitive, and personal skills—and that provide teachers with the ongoing professional development needed to engage students in higher-level learning that promotes success in the workplace and in post–high school education. The remaining chapters of this book offer detailed strategies for implementing each of these six bold actions.

4

Powerful Assignments: A Critical Component of CTE Classes

John Dewey wrote, "Give the pupils something to do, not something to learn. If the doing is of such a nature as to demand thinking, learning naturally results."[38] We know that jobs built around routine, repetitive tasks are on the decline. To obtain a good job in today's economy—in which customization of products and services is coupled with explosive use of technology—employees need a more complex combination of academic, technical, technological, and workplace skills. Business and industry leaders have made it clear that they also seek employees who can work on teams, communicate with colleagues, understand and analyze complicated data, and apply literacy and mathematics skills to solve complex problems.[39]

Many career/technical education programs have made progress in recent decades to adapt to a rapidly evolving economy. But changes are still needed to ensure CTE can provide students with the skills and knowledge necessary for success in postsecondary studies and in the jobs that will await them not just today, but 10 and 20 years from now.

Students know when they're experiencing the type of learning that helps them prepare for their future. Consider the data from two demographically similar groups of students, both enrolled in schools that are part of the High Schools That Work network.[40] Students in one group were enrolled in Advanced Career (AC) curricula intentionally designed to incorporate a mix of knowledge and skills valued by employers. Students in the second group were enrolled in traditional CTE classes. Their responses, shown in Figure 4.1, clearly demonstrate that far too few students in "old-school" CTE classes are engaged in experiences that allow them to learn and apply the mix of knowledge and skills needed to prepare for rising workplace requirements.

CTE students who report frequently experiencing the types of learning experiences specified in Figure 4.1 are more likely to meet college- and career-readiness benchmarks in reading, math, and science (see Figure 4.2).[41] What are the implications for CTE?

Figure 4.1

Students' Perceptions of Assignments: A Comparison of AC Students and Those in Other CTE Programs at HSTW Schools

Students reported completing assignments that required them to . . .	AC Students	HSTW CTE Students
Predict outcomes based on observations or information provided.	87%	29%
Develop a logical argument for their solution to problems or projects.	88%	26%
Do background research for problems or projects, such as reading technical articles, before developing a plan or solution.	89%	29%
Make inferences from information provided to develop a solution for a problem or project.	85%	25%
Use math to solve complex problems related to their course.	85%	24%
Apply academic knowledge and skills to their career courses.	89%	33%
Apply technical knowledge and skills to new situations.	92%	31%
Complete an extended project that requires planning, developing a solution or product, and presenting the results orally or in writing.	88%	26%
Use computer software, other technology, digital skills related to their courses.	87%	13%
Make journal or lab manual entries that record their class work.	82%	25%

Source: SREB student surveys presented in 2014 at SREB Summer Staff Development Conference.

Figure 4.2

Correlation Between Powerful CTE Assignments and Higher Achievement

Subject Area Assessed	Percentage of Students Meeting College- and Career-Readiness Standards	
	CTE Students with Rigorous Assignments (n = 7,890)	CTE Students Without Rigorous Assignments (n = 7,890*)
Reading	69%	49%
Mathematics	66%	50%
Science	67%	48%

*For the group of students who did not experience rigorous assignments, SREB researchers developed a demographic match based on gender, race, and socioeconomic status (using parents' postsecondary education level as a proxy for SES).

Source: SREB, 2013.

The assignments that students complete in CTE courses have the potential to prepare them for greater success after high school. Specifically, rigorous and powerful CTE assignments that engage students in applying a mix of knowledge and skills make a significant difference in their readiness for college and careers. Yet many CTE students still lack access to the types of CTE assignments that engage them in higher-level learning.[42]

If we want more graduates to have a broader mix of higher-level skills, then some CTE teachers will have to increase the rigor of their assignments. But many do not know how to move from procedural-based assignments, which ask students to follow certain steps, to higher-level assignments that require students to conduct background research, develop a work plan, and use a range of technical, academic, technology, and employability skills.[43] And some CTE and academic teachers may need to realign not just their instructional practices, but also their beliefs about students' abilities to complete more challenging work. Designing career pathways around powerful, higher-level assignments connected to rigorous academics—and encouraging students to complete those assignments successfully—is essential if we are to advance students' readiness for careers and postsecondary studies and achieve bold goals.

Connecting CTE and Academic Assignments

The rigorous CTE assignments described in this chapter require coordination and collaboration between academic and CTE teachers. (Appendix B at www.ascd.org/CareerTechEd Tools offers an example of what an assignment looks like when teachers meet this challenge to better connect academic and CTE assignments.) This approach works best when schedule structures break down traditional discipline-focused silos and allow CTE and academic teachers from English language arts, mathematics, and science adequate time to coplan connected-learning experiences for a common cohort of students. Schools that create such structures will witness increased student motivation and higher percentages of students graduating from high school both college- and career-ready.

The challenge is for school leaders to encourage CTE and core academic teachers to work together in shaping authentic project assignments that answer the often-asked question "How will I ever use this in the real world?" Building a connected assignment involves the following steps:

1. The CTE teacher provides information regarding the project.
2. The CTE and the academic teachers discuss the project overview to ensure understanding.

3. The supporting academic teachers determine how the standards are used in the project.

4. The math, English language arts, and science teachers recommend how the CTE teacher may support struggling students during the CTE class.

5. The math, English language arts, and science teachers determine how to support students during the academic class time and record the plan in the graphic organizer.

6. The team discusses opportunities for working with subject-matter experts from business, industry, and postsecondary partners.

Here is how a teacher of a Global Logistics course (part of the Advanced Careers curriculum) described the experience of working with an academic teacher:

> The algebra teacher asked me what kind of math problems I was giving in my class, because students in the Algebra I class were saying they had already learned these concepts in their Global Logistics class. This conversation started what became a close working relationship between myself and the math teacher to further connect Algebra I concepts to real-world problems.

What Makes Assignments Powerful?

Powerful assignments engage students in *a productive struggle* that they find interesting and worthwhile, motivating them to persist in solving a problem or completing a major task. Powerful assignments help both students and teachers develop a different mindset about students' ability to learn. When teachers can show students evidence of their personal progress, students make the connection between effort and learning, which in turn motivates them to make greater effort to achieve at higher levels. Here's how a teacher describes meaningful math assignments in an Aerospace Engineering course in the AC curriculum:

> Assignments in this class have motivated students to learn and apply mathematical skills and knowledge to solve problems in the aerospace field of study. This deepens their understanding of mathematics and increases their effort in their academic math class.

In addition to enhancing motivation, powerful assignments have other positive effects. These include significant improvement in students' higher-order abilities, skills (foundational, academic, technical, technological, problem-solving, teamwork, and more), self-reflection, and readiness for post–high school options.

Powerful Assignments Advance Students' Ability to Research, Analyze, Plan, and Evaluate

Because powerful assignments are comprehensive and complex, they require students to conduct background research and develop a foundation of knowledge before finishing the assignment. Students study, analyze, and reflect on the information they acquire before developing a plan of action for completing the project. At each step, students evaluate their progress and make needed adjustments.

Students learn how to conduct background research by reading technical materials and documents, interviewing highly skilled workers, and determining what information is most essential for developing a project plan and management process. A teacher described how students go deeper into learning in a Clean Energy Technology class:

> The rigorous assignments in the AC Clean Energy Technology class made them better students and prepared them for success in postsecondary studies. Many come back and tell me that it was in this class that they learned how to do background research and develop a plan for completing projects, take ownership of their own learning, write a project report, prepare and make a presentation, and so on. They realize that this class prepared them for the success they are now experiencing.

Powerful Assignments Advance Students' Technical and Technological Skills

Such assignments enhance students' skills with familiar hardware, software, and technology tools, while also engaging them in developing new technological and digital skills. A good project management plan requires students to consider how they will acquire and use all the technical, technological, and academic standards needed to complete the project. Powerful assignments often motivate students to work on projects outside normal school hours, and they often require learning how to use new technology or software.

Powerful Assignments Encourage Student Self-Reflection on Personal Goals

A challenging and authentic assignment will engage students in exploring and reflecting on how well their current learning experiences fit their interests, aptitudes, and career goals. Each assignment enables students to gain insights into different career and educational options and provides opportunities to practice various tasks they will encounter in real-world jobs in that field. Such assignments often require students to keep a journal in which they reflect on what they have learned, identify gaps in their learning, and plan steps to close these gaps. The journals can have an unanticipated effect, as described by a teacher of an Integration Production Technology course: "I've been surprised how having students keep a notebook to reflect on what they've learned really inspires students' pride in recognizing how much they are learning."

Powerful Assignments Advance Students' Academic Readiness for Postsecondary Studies and Careers

Studies correlating students' achievement with their educational experiences have shown that the most powerful factor in advancing students' readiness for postsecondary studies and careers is the completion of a college preparatory core of English, math, and science courses. The second most powerful factor is rigorous, relevant, real-world assignments.[44] A teacher of an Energy and Power course shared this observation: "Many of my students are discovering future opportunities they had never envisioned, and surprisingly, many are going on for further study, pursuing advanced credentials and degrees in some aspect of the field of energy and power."

Criteria for Powerful Assignments

The criteria in Figure 4.3 can help teachers, school leaders, and parents determine whether assignments are rigorous enough to advance students' academic, technical, and workplace knowledge and skills. They reflect employers' views on the knowledge and skills necessary for obtaining a good job, and they incorporate learning experiences that have been tied to higher student achievement. These criteria can serve as a guide to assess and power up existing assignments and to develop new challenges for students.

For its Advanced Careers curricula, the Southern Regional Education Board worked with partner states to develop more than 190 project-based assignments that meet the criteria in Figure 4.3 and then used those assignments as the foundation for the creation of 36 courses in nine high-demand, high-wage career fields.[45] Teachers who lead Advanced Careers classes have seen how assignments that meet the criteria for being "powerful" can change student outcomes and advance student achievement. Here's how one of those teachers describes students' reactions:

> The excitement, depth of engagement, and level of effort I see students making in AC Clean Energy Technology classes is something I never saw in my first 10 years of teaching chemistry. When students come to class early and stay late, and you see the level of engagement they have in their work, you are doing something right. And I never experienced that before.

Figure 4.3

Criteria for Powerful Assignments

Assignments That Advance Readiness for Researching, Analyzing, Planning, and Evaluating

1. Students conduct background research and develop options for completing the assignment, drawing from technical documents and knowledge of highly skilled workers in the field.

2. Students follow a problem-solving process used by experts in the career field.

3. Students reflect, problem solve, analyze, plan, and experience a productive struggle.

Assignments That Address Technical Readiness

1. Students use existing knowledge and skills with familiar software to advance their knowledge and skills in learning new software in completing a challenging assignment.

2. Students learn and use work-related technology and technical skills to complete assignments.

3. Students learn to work as a team to successfully address the project or problem.

4. Students work both independently and as a team to contribute to the learning of others, to learn from other students and teachers, and to learn from adult mentors in the field.

Assignments That Allow Students to Self-Reflect on Personal Goals

1. Students explore and reflect on their interests, aptitudes, and educational and career options based on new insights gained from the learning experience.

2. Students keep a journal that documents their work, contains their reflections about the new knowledge and skills they have developed, and identifies gaps to be addressed in their readiness for both career and postsecondary studies.

Assignments That Address Academic and Career Readiness

1. Students apply grade-level literacy, mathematics, and science knowledge and skills to complete the work.

2. Each student prepares a written final report, and each team develops a team report based on individual student reports.

3. Students present a final oral report to an authentic audience consisting of business, industry, and postsecondary partners who review students' work.

An Example of a Powerful Assignment

What do the criteria in Figure 4.3 look like in practice? The following project, which comes from the first course in the AC Integrated Production Technology curriculum, illustrates how the various elements of powerful assignments come together to advance student knowledge and skills in a variety of areas. Assignments such as this spread students' learning over several days. Each assignment is a new experience that requires students to transfer what they've learned so far into a new context, thus deepening their understanding and retention. Each assignment also offers students an opportunity to test their interests, aptitudes, and aspirations in the context of the field they are studying.

> **Course 1:** Advanced Technology for Design and Production[46]
>
> **Project Title:** Tank Volume Control—Automated Decision Making
>
> **Essential Question:** How can we design an automated system to maintain proper volumes of liquids in tanks before shipping and storage?
>
> **Project Description:** You are a project engineer working for Liquimax Inc. Your company packages liquids for a variety of commercial and industrial firms. Managing tanks in your facility is a precision process. Liquid products are stored in closed tanks before shipping to market, and it is critical to ensure that the liquid volumes in those tanks are maintained at specific amounts for safe storage. Currently, a technician is responsible for checking these tank volumes daily. This manual task is time-consuming and not always accurate; technicians sometimes miss a tank check, incorrectly read a tank level, or fail to correctly add/remove liquid to maintain a constant volume. Your supervisor has asked your team to develop a control system that will automatically check the volume level of a tank and add or remove liquid as needed to maintain a constant volume as the temperature varies.
>
> - After reading informational texts on process control and thermodynamics and participating in enabling learning activities to help you design and build an automated process for maintaining a constant volume of liquid in an industrial tank, write an engineering report in which you describe your product development and analyze the effectiveness of your system. Conduct needed research and then develop a project management plan that will guide your process. Your team's design brief must include a labeled sketch, a prototyping strategy, and a method for collecting and analyzing data.
>
> - Construct a prototype of your design using sensors and software to control tank volume at various temperatures. Your program must consider the type of liquid and its properties, such as temperature and viscosity. You will test your prototype system and analyze your test data using statistical methods to determine if your solution will meet the needs of Liquimax Inc.
>
> - Develop a cost-benefit analysis detailing the annual cost of the current technician method versus your Automated Tank Volume Control system. Include a break-even analysis to find the time it will take to see a return on the investment. When you have determined that your design solution is viable and cost-effective, prepare an engineering report that includes recommendations for the new system, a cost-benefit analysis, and design documentation.
>
> - Demonstrate your prototype and present your engineering report to an authentic audience. As the audience will be composed of STEM and non-STEM experts, you must design and explain your results in a way that can be understood by a diverse group. As a representative of Liquimax Inc., you are expected to give a professional, polished presentation that speaks well for your company.

This project required a mix of knowledge and skills. Consider these key phrases:

- **Project engineer**—The project places students in a career role and helps them learn the way of thinking that a professional would use.

- **Liquid volume, soft storage, temperature varies**—Students must understand and apply grade-level physical science concepts to complete the assignment.

- **Read informational text**—Students are expected to read and analyze technical documents.
- **Designing and building an automated process using sensors and software**—Students are expected to design and create a prototype of an automated process using technology and technical skills.
- **Management plan**—Students develop a management plan for completing the assignment.
- **Analyze test data using statistical methods**—Students must collect and analyze data.
- **Develop a cost-benefit analysis**—Students detail the annual cost of the current technical method versus the automated tank volume control system.
- **Write an engineering report and give a professional, polished presentation**—Students must reflect on their work by keeping a daily journal, prepare a written report, and present that report to other students and external audiences.
- **Design team**—Students demonstrate 21st century skills in working with a team.

These terms, either directly or indirectly, indicate which criteria for powerful assignments are being met. As CTE teachers begin to evaluate the rigor of existing assignments or design new powerful assignments, these types of key words and phrases can serve as guideposts to ensure CTE assignments are leading toward improved student learning. A completed project unit has been designed for this project and illustrates how, by working with CTE teachers, the mathematics, English language arts, and science teachers can advance students' technical, mathematics, literacy, and science knowledge and skills (see Appendix B).

Preparing Teachers to Develop and Implement Powerful Assignments

The remainder of this chapter offers a 10-step process that a team of CTE and core academic teachers can use to design authentic, powerful assignments. The work is challenging and will require regular allotments of time, real commitment, and a shift in attitudes by both academic and CTE teachers about their instructional roles. In particular, CTE teachers will be asked to design assignments considerably more complex than many will have created in the past.

The goal will be to create five project assignments for each of three (and possibly four) courses. The process can be scaled over three to five years, as in this example:

- **Summer before year 1:** A powerful CTE assignment development team (see Step 1, below) spends a full week producing one fully developed project assignment, with an outline of engaging learning activities organized around the seven-step engineering process.

- **Year 1 (midyear):** The team develops a second project description and instructional outline over a three-day session.

- **Years 2 and 3:** The team builds on the year-one experiences to develop six additional projects each year, and the CTE teachers develop one assignment independently.

- **Year 4 (optional):** Schools may elect to develop five project-based units for a fourth course in the pathway, as students who complete four courses will have an edge in terms of advancement to a good job and postsecondary studies in the field.

Schools can also use the 12 criteria outlined in Figure 4.3 to improve *existing* CTE projects, where feasible.

Schools should consider investing in an experienced project facilitator who can coach CTE teachers and academic teachers to design and implement powerful assignments and to guide them as they become skilled at promoting learning by asking probing questions and using formative assessment to refine the curriculum. Additional costs of implementing this plan include stipends for participating CTE and academic teachers.

Step 1: Establish a Team to Develop Powerful CTE Assignments

Charge the team with the task of developing rigorous project-based assignments for career pathway courses. This team is described in Chapter 3 as a subteam of the powerful assignment action team. If need be, an adjunct powerful assignment development team might be created to focus specifically on this labor-intensive curriculum development aspect of the action team's work.

The CTE assignment team—composed of CTE, English language arts, mathematics, and science teachers—will lead the three- to five-year effort to design powerful project-based assignments, using the remaining steps described in this chapter. At the outset, this team should also include key representatives from postsecondary institutions, business, and industry. With time and support from the district, the team should aim to develop at least five major project assignments in each of three or four courses in a career pathway.

Step 2: Identify the Knowledge and Skills Students Will Need to Be Ready for Employment and Postsecondary Studies

The powerful CTE assignment development team begins by determining what students should know and be able to do after completing each career pathway. The team can consider attributes needed to obtain a good job, as well as state college- and career-readiness standards and unique technical and technology standards for the pathway(s) they will focus on. The team then organizes the relevant standards into the following categories for each career pathway:

- Technical, technology, software, and digital skills
- Literacy (reading, speaking, listening, and writing)
- Quantitative and analytical mathematics (advanced arithmetic, algebra, geometry, statistics, Algebra II and higher)
- Science and engineering skills (including the investigative process)
- 21st century knowledge and skills (teamwork, creativity, innovation, critical thinking, problem solving, work ethic)
- All aspects of business and industry that are particularly relevant to the career field or to a specific project

Once the team has completed the full list of knowledge and skill standards, they should organize these by courses and grade levels, and indicate when the standard might be first introduced and reinforced at deeper levels in future assignments. For example, courses designed for grades 9 and 10 may emphasize mathematics standards concerning advanced arithmetic, algebra, geometry, and statistics; later courses may draw on additional mathematics standards for Algebra II, trigonometry, and precalculus.

Step 3: Brainstorm a List of Potential Project Titles

Select project titles that would meet the criteria for powerful assignments and would spark students' interests and imagination.

In developing a list of potential projects, the powerful assignments team might want to select existing assignments in which students have shown a great deal of interest as a starting point for developing more rigorous project-based assignments. The business, industry, and postsecondary representatives on the team also can identify project titles that could engage students in relevant, deeper learning. (For more information on project titles, see Appendix C at www.ascd.org/CareerTechEdTools.)

Next, examine each project title and assess if the project can be sufficiently rigorous to engage students in learning and applying critical academic, technical, technology, digital, cognitive, and 21st century skills. To help narrow down the list, the team should consider which project titles best fit into a sequence of three or four courses in a career pathway—keeping in mind that the learning standards and skills will need to build upon previous learning as students advance through the pathway.

Step 4: Identify the Essential Academic, Technical, Technological, Cognitive, and 21st Century Skills Students Must Apply to Complete a Given Project Assignment

For each project assignment, the team identifies essential standards that must be met to complete the assignment (see the example in Appendix B). Each project should require students to apply a mix of knowledge and skills—not only CTE and academic knowledge, but also technological, cognitive, digital, and 21st century skills. Some skills should be incorporated into every project, with the expectation that students will continue to grow in their ability to use these important skills. For example, conducting background research and summarizing multiple sources relevant to a design or work plan is a skill set that will be applied in all projects and strengthen over time.

Step 5: Develop an Essential Question for Each Project

The essential question is the central question that students will answer to complete the project. It helps students focus their learning and identify what outcomes are expected of them. Good questions require background research and engage students in examining new concepts, exploring alternatives, and continuously reevaluating their strategies and solutions.

A good essential question places students at the edge of their comfort zone. This is not a question that students can simply answer upon first glance or after cursory research. Instead, this open-ended question allows for many possible correct responses and solutions and stimulates students to develop their own meaning of what is being asked. They must ask questions about what they'll need to know, conduct research, carry out investigations, and use the information to arrive at an answer. (See the example provided earlier in this chapter and in Appendix B and directions in Appendix C.)

Because the essential question can be answered in more than one way, it enables students to take multiple approaches to come up with the right solution. Effective essential questions give students opportunities to persist in solving difficult problems—and that type of persistence sparks deeper learning. As one student in a Clean Energy class recalled, after the initial solution failed, "Our solar hot water heater leaked like a sieve, and we had to go back to the drawing board. But I'll learn more by failing in this class than I will by passing in other classes."

Step 6: Determine What Career Role Students Will Take to Complete the Project

To strengthen the connection between learning and real-world applications, powerful assignments should place students in an authentic career role that has the potential to support a middle-class lifestyle and that helps students learn about future career options. This connection engages students in career exploration, enabling them to imagine themselves in a specific career role and to further reflect on their own career goals, as well. (See Appendix C for information on developing the project description with an authentic career role.)

Step 7: Develop a Project Description That Outlines Actions Students Must Take to Master Standards and Complete the Project

The project description provides students with the context of the project and its expected outcomes (see Appendix C). The description should include enough complexity and flexibility that each student team might arrive at a different solution. Although project descriptions will offer different contexts, and some flexibility within the descriptions is essential, each project description should either directly or indirectly require students to do the following:

- Form teams and collaborate to design an optimal solution for completing the project.
- Document the process they use to create a solution, using an engineering notebook or a journal (see Appendix D at www.ascd.org/CareerTechEdTools for sample instructions for using an engineering notebook).
- Apply academic knowledge and skills.
- Apply personal, workplace, technical, and technological skills.
- Apply technical literacy—the abilities to read, analyze, interpret, and communicate orally and in writing, using the appropriate vocabulary of the career field.

The project description will need to outline some of the enabling learning activities that students will complete to master new concepts and to learn new technology or tools as they work toward answering the essential question. *But teachers should avoid the temptation to provide too much guidance or instruction.* The description provides the context and some support for the assignment but never provides step-by-step instructions.

Powerful assignments ensure that enough work exists for each student on a team, without overwhelming the team. Students must understand that each team member is responsible for mastering the key learning knowledge and skills and process required to complete the project (no "siloing"). This mastering requires students to do work outside class and requires the team members to do their own assessment of each other.

Step 8: Develop the Full Project Unit

To begin building out the full project unit, the powerful CTE assignment development team will first need to create a project-pacing calendar (see Appendix E at www .ascd.org/CareerTechEdTools). The calendar includes a day-to-day plan for the lessons and other teacher-facilitated experiences—including field trips and contact with mentors—and time for students to work as a team.

Then, using the planning template and the pacing calendar, the team builds out a full project unit that follows the seven-step engineering design process shown in Figure 4.4.

Embedding Mathematics in the Project

Each project engages students in applying at least grade-level mathematics skills and knowledge. The National Research Center for Career and Technical Education has developed a math in CTE pedagogic framework that can guide teachers in ensuring that the mathematics embedded in the project is applied and understood by students. This research-based model has shown a significant positive impact. It provides an opportunity for math and CTE teacher teams to work together to identify where mathematics intersects with CTE concepts and applications, leading to the creation of embedded math lessons in CTE. Unless CTE teachers have a strong mathematical background, they will need to partner with math teachers who have an interest in contextual learning to both develop the math lessons and engage students in understanding how the math concepts apply to both abstract and real-world contexts. For more information, see **www.nrccte.org**.

Step 9: Determine What Evidence Will Be Used to Assess Whether Students Achieved the Learning Goals

Two types of assessments are crucial for determining powerful assignments' impact on student learning: formative and summative.[47] *Formative assessment* is used to help teachers and students identify the need for additional instruction and learning. Often

Figure 4.4

The Seven-Step Engineering Design Process Applied to Powerful Assignments

Step	Student Activities
1. Ask	• Read the essential question and project description. • Research technical and related documents, and read and reflect upon technical articles about the content area. • Identify criteria and constraints for the problem. • Define, in their own words, what the assignment is expecting them to do. • Refine the project statement. • Identify what they need to know to complete the assignment. • Consider why this assignment is important for building knowledge.
2. Imagine	• Create a project management plan. • Conduct research related to the problem statement. • Brainstorm possible solutions. • Create a design brief. • Identify what resources they can use. • Determine how they will evaluate information they find. • Ask, "What is my role in the process?"
3. Plan	• Research the viability of possible solutions. • Design testing methods for critical assumptions. • Create optimization charts for decision making and select a solution. • Seek additional information needed. • Apply the information acquired to the planning task.
4. Create	• Develop, refine, and document selected solutions. • Create a prototype.
5. Experiment and Evaluate	• Test and acquire data. • Analyze test data. • Identify what new questions they have and what new information they may need. Consider new insights they have acquired about the project design.
6. Improve	• Refine and iterate the design. • Finalize documentation of design. • Analyze results, summarize knowledge gained, and evaluate the proposed improvement.
7. Communicate	• Prepare a communication plan for an authentic audience. • Prepare reports, design documentation, and design proposals or presentations for the authentic audience, identifying what information they should explain about their work and how best to share that information with others. • Ask, "What have I learned from this project?" • Present/defend to an authentic audience and receive feedback.

students redo work after class hours or during special homework sessions to avoid slowing the pace of the team or the class. And teachers do not give grades for formative assessment until students demonstrate the desired level of mastery. *Summative assessments* measure progress students have made regarding academic, technical, technology, digital, and 21st century standards at the end of the project or through an end-of-course exam or project. Students ordinarily do not redo summative assessments.

To achieve a balance of formative and summative assessments, powerful assignments can draw from five sources of information to determine student progress: (1) an engineering notebook or journal (formative), (2) an assessment of 21st century skills (formative), (3) an end-of-project exam (summative), (4) a project grade (summative), and (5) an end-of-course exam (summative).

Engineering notebook or journal (formative). Students maintain an electronic portfolio or a written notebook for each project. Students use these to document their research, reflect (daily and weekly) on work accomplished and new insights, define new technical vocabulary, record math formulas used to complete assignments, and demonstrate organizational and information-management skills necessary for post–high school success. The notebook also serves as a study guide for the end-of-project exam and a resource for developing the final written product. Teachers can use these notebooks as formative assessment, reviewing them periodically to check for students' understanding and to reteach as needed. (See Appendix F at www.ascd.org/CareerTechEdTools for an example of a rubric to assess an engineering notebook or journal.)

Assessment of 21st century skills (formative). Teachers assess students' understanding and application of 21st century skills by observing how well they take on responsibilities, respect others, complete assigned tasks, organize work, contribute to the team, and learn from team members. When assignments require students to interact with community experts, academic teachers, or other adult mentors, the teacher observes and scores students' ability to communicate in a professional manner. (See Appendix G at www.ascd.org/CareerTechEdTools for an example of a rubric to assess 21st century skills.)

End-of-project exam (summative). The end-of-project exam is designed to ensure that each student on the team has developed his or her own academic and technical skills and knowledge, rather than relying on other team members to do the work. The assessment includes multiple-choice questions, mathematics problems, science questions, and constructed-response questions that require students to write clearly for a specific audience. The end-of-project exam is designed to assess whether each student made progress in reading and comprehending technical materials, understanding and applying grade-level mathematics concepts, understanding the science concepts under-pinning the project, and understanding the technical content knowledge and skills required for the project. When developing the exam questions, a good ratio to aim for is 50 percent focused on technical and technology knowledge and skills and 50 percent on academic and 21st century skills. Some questions may address multiple categories.

Project grade (summative). Teachers determine individual grades by assessing students' progress through a variety of measures: the project's technical and academic tasks, including the final product and written report (worth 30 percent of the project grade); the engineering notebook and demonstration of 21st century skills (worth 30 percent of the project grade); and the end-of-project exam (worth 40 percent of the project grade).

End-of-course exam (summative). At the end of each project, students complete a rigorous, comprehensive exam that assesses their progress on a mix of technical, academic, digital, and 21st century knowledge and skills. Like the end-of-project exam, about half of the end-of-course exam items should assess technical knowledge and skills, and half should assess literacy, mathematics, and science knowledge and skills. Some exam items may simultaneously address 21st century skills. Depending on the course and content area, this exam could be used as the basis for awarding an industry certification, academic credit, or dual credit for high school and college.

By the end of a CTE course built around powerful assignments, teachers will have a range of measures to provide evidence that students have made progress on the learning goals of the project. These include products developed for each project, engineering notebooks or journals, written reports and oral presentations, examples of math and science projects completed, as well as achievement on end-of-project and end-of-course exams.

Step 10: Support All CTE Teachers to Shift Instructional Practices to Inspire Deeper Learning Through Powerful Project-Based Assignments

CTE teachers need support and encouragement to transition to a teaching approach in which students take greater responsibility for completing complex assignments that require them to use a mix of skills. It is important that the powerful CTE assignment development team engages both career pathway and academic teachers as they consider what supports they will need to create a classroom culture in which teams of students take ownership of the learning process guided by a teacher who facilitates learning. This undertaking will require some big shifts in school and classroom expectations for both CTE *and* academic teachers, including the following:

- A shift from teacher-directed, guided, step-by-step assignments to open-ended project assignments requiring students to research and prepare their own plans for completing the work.

- A shift from a classroom culture in which only teachers hold students accountable to one in which student team members hold one another accountable for completing the assigned task and mastering the necessary standards, while also learning from and supporting one another.

- A shift from the CTE teacher being the sole source of knowledge and skills to the CTE teacher partnering with academic teachers, industry mentors, and others to ensure students acquire the knowledge and skills needed to complete the rigorous project.

- A shift from a teacher-driven schedule to a student-focused schedule that enables students to pace their efforts while holding themselves accountable for meeting the deadlines with quality work.

- A shift from academic teachers viewing CTE classrooms as a place to teach only technical skills to one where students learn and apply high school–level academic knowledge and skills. This shift can best be done when CTE teachers and academic teachers partner in planning connected assignments to support students in learning and applying academic knowledge and skills to complete a rigorous CTE project.

- A shift from a classroom culture that allows some students to meet a lower level of expectation to one in which all students are expected to achieve at high levels and produce quality work.

Powerful Assignments "Wall-to-Wall" in Five Years

Several years ago, as the new director of the Columbia Career and Technology Center in Columbia, Missouri, Randy Gooch launched a five-year journey to redesign CTE classes around rigorous, open-ended, project-based assignments. With the support of district and teacher leaders, the school set out to engage students in applying a mix of academic, technical, technology, cognitive, digital, and 21st century skills to complete challenging assignments.

Gooch made an agreement with teachers that, rather than having a different professional development focus each year, they would focus the next five years on designing and implementing what Gooch calls "the gold standard of project-based assignments–learning experiences that meet all the criteria of *powerful assignments*." Gooch tells the story of the Missouri technology center's transformation in his own words:

I promised teachers we would become a lighthouse school where CTE and academic teachers could come and witness students engaged in higher-level learning, and we would accomplish this by using the nonteaching days built into their existing contracts. For three consecutive years, we engaged a project-based trainer with a proven record of working with CTE teachers to design rigorous project-based assignments.

Several teachers quickly grasped the concept of designing powerful assignments in the first year, and they became our lead teachers who supported other teachers in developing quality project-based assignments. These lead teachers have now become trainers who work continuously with existing staff and new teachers.

We also had our share of teachers who were not enthusiastic about the effort in the beginning. However, they became motivated as business and industry leaders began endorsing the effort, telling us that these projects reflect the type of work they want their employees to be able to do. Teachers became more motivated as they witnessed greater student motivation, ownership of learning, and effort from students completing the project-based assignments.

In five years, we went wall-to-wall with project-based assignments in all classes. About 75 percent of our projects now meet the gold standard, but that's part of our continuous improvement journey.

We learned several lessons along the way. First, do not begin by asking teachers to design a new project-based assignment; rather, ask them to redesign an existing assignment to meet the gold standard.

Second, it is important to develop your own trainers over time to work with new teachers on designing project-based assignments, because this is a continuous process of revision and improvement.

Third, the director and other administrators must attend all professional development sessions with teachers so that school leaders understand the vision and can support teachers.

Fourth, you need to engage the business and postsecondary community so they can support your efforts and help resistant teachers understand that deeper learning experiences are essential in preparing students for an ever-changing world.

And lastly, showcase teachers' results and recognize the good work that they are doing. This motivates them to design more projects that meet the goal standard.

We have seen evidence of the success of project-based assignments. In 2018, more than 80 percent of our seniors agreed that their assignments are rigorous.[48] About 90 percent of students earn dual credit and are pursuing postsecondary studies. Enrollment at the center has continued to grow as more parents recognize the value of intellectually demanding projects in preparing students for both careers and postsecondary studies. And CTE and academic teachers from other schools now come to our center to observe project-based learning.

Our teachers take pride in becoming a true lighthouse center. We have shown that it is possible to go wall-to-wall with project-based learning using a carefully planned five-year process.

A Theory of Action for Implementing Powerful Assignments in CTE Courses

As Randy Gooch's story demonstrates, schools can successfully take on the challenge of creating and implementing CTE pathway courses organized around powerful assignments to engage students in deeper learning. Consider the outcomes that might arise from this model "theory of action"—presented as "if/then" scenarios:

If . . .

- The powerful CTE assignment development team provides at least eight days annually over three to five years for teams of CTE and academic teachers to design powerful assignments that advance students' readiness for both careers and postsecondary studies . . .
- Time is built into the schedule for career pathway and academic teachers to plan connected lessons for a common cohort of students . . .
- CTE teachers are given external coaching to help them shift from procedural-based instruction to instruction that engages students in higher-level learning . . .
- The powerful CTE assignment development team adopts or creates a classroom observation rubric that can be used to assess teachers' progress at regular intervals and provide feedback to career pathway and academic teachers regarding actionable items they can address . . .
- The preceding actions are taken with district and school support over a three- to five-year process to engage students in higher-level learning in CTE and career pathway classes . . .

then your school has the potential to become a lighthouse model for your region, state, and the nation.

The powerful CTE assignment development team will need to create its own "if/then" statements—actions that must occur to successfully make the shift to engaging students in higher-level learning in CTE classes.

Powerful Assignments: Practical Steps Schools Can Take Now

Schools that are not ready or able to make the full investment of time necessary to design and implement powerful assignments in all career path courses can take the following steps now to improve the rigor of CTE assignments—using a more limited initial strategy:

- Adopt already-developed CTE curricula (such as SREB's Advanced Career curricula) that engage students in rigorous, real-world assignments.
- Incorporate higher-level math into existing assignments using the Math-in-CTE model from the National Research Center for Career and Technical Education (NRCCTE).

- Discontinue assignments that provide students with step-by-step instructions on how to proceed; rather, ask them to do background research and develop their own work plan for completing an assignment.
- Use the 12 criteria for powerful assignments (Figure 4.3) to expand an existing assignment in one or more CTE courses into a powerful assignment, following the modified version of the 10 steps outlined in this chapter.
- Form a *pathfinder team* that includes one or more career pathway teachers partnering with English language arts, mathematics, and science teachers to design a project-based assignment.
- Invite industry partners who have employed recent graduates and postsecondary institutions who enrolled recent graduates to provide feedback on graduates' strengths and weaknesses in terms of academic, technical, and 21st century skills.
- Interview former graduates to discern what knowledge and skills *they wish had been emphasized more* in their high school CTE and academic classes.
- Use the template provided in Appendix C to write a project-based assignment that meets the 12 criteria for powerful assignments (Figure 4.3).
- Consider designing one fully developed project unit, including a pacing guide and an assessment plan. After implementing this one project, the pathfinder team can use the lessons learned to begin working on a second project, as team members share what they've learned with other CTE and academic teachers.

Summing Up and Looking Ahead

Powerful assignments like the ones described in this chapter can prepare students for uncertain and rapidly changing careers and for postsecondary readiness. A framework for developing and implementing such assignments across all CTE career pathway courses (including assignment criteria and detailed procedural steps) can guide schools in improving students' readiness for careers and postsecondary studies.

Chapter 5 will examine how powerful, multistep, abstract, and real-world assignments can advance students' ability to reason, understand, and use mathematics knowledge and skills, so that more leave high school prepared to succeed in careers and postsecondary studies.

5

Developing Powerful
Mathematics Assignments

Walk the crowded halls of most middle and high schools, mention "math class," and you'll quickly hear more than one student say, "I don't get it, "I don't like it," "I don't need it."

Little wonder that the United States faces a growing gap between the problem-solving mathematics skills high school graduates have and the skills required for 21st century careers and postsecondary studies. As technology takes over the production of goods and services, the demand for individuals with STEM-related skills—employees who can manage processes and work across departmental boundaries to solve problems—has grown since 2008 by nearly 20 percent.[49]

Yet the majority of the 2019 graduating class departed high school without the mathematics skills needed to succeed in high-skill, high-wage jobs, and many college professors report having to spend considerable instructional time reviewing math skills that students should have learned in high school. The challenge is even more pronounced for many students of color and for those from low-socioeconomic backgrounds. Nearly 2 million students who begin college each year drop out before earning a degree, with math being one significant barrier to degree attainment. A national survey of high school graduates in 2014 shows that only one in four graduates reported high school had high academic expectations for college and career, which was unchanged from a similar survey in 2004. Graduates agreed that high school students would work harder if high schools connected rigorous academic studies with career studies leading to middle-class earning opportunities.[50]

This disconnect between the math skills students need and the skills they are developing is not limited to the post–high school or high school level. In 2019, only 34 percent of 8th graders performed at or above the Proficient level on the mathematics portion of the National Assessment of Educational Progress. Although this number was 19 percentage points higher than in 1990, the data reveal that the increases have not occurred equitably across student groups. About 64 percent of Asian students achieved at the Proficient level and above, whereas 44 percent of white students, 20 percent of Hispanic students, and 14 percent of Black students reached an achievement level indicating they were well prepared to succeed in college preparatory mathematics courses upon entering high school.[51] It's clear that significant changes are needed in K–12 classrooms—and specifically, in math instruction—if we are to provide every student a path forward into the middle class.[52]

The Root Causes of the Math Achievement Gap

The math achievement gap in the United States is best explained by the disconnect between the assignments students are completing in middle school and high school and the expectations of colleges, universities, and employers. **High school math teachers are expected to cover a great deal of content; and to do so, many rely on step-by-step assignments and direct instruction that does not provide students with opportunities to explore, discuss, and make sense of what they are learning.** The focus is on helping students recall information long enough to pass multiple-choice tests—not on developing their understanding of essential concepts and building the critical problem-solving skills they will need to succeed in postsecondary studies and good jobs in the real world.

The math achievement gap is also explained by the variance in the quality of mathematical teaching. Due in part to social and parental pressure, the most effective teachers are often assigned to teach the best students, and the new and less experienced teachers and those who do not have a strong math background are assigned to teach the most challenging students. The problem is not that we need to flip the teachers; we need to prepare *all* teachers to meet a high standard.

In 2011, after looking at data from more than a third of U.S. states, the SREB Middle Grades Commission concluded that many math teachers in grades 6 through 8 lack the mathematics background necessary to prepare students for algebra. The commission recommended states require 7th and 8th grade math teachers to work toward full high school certification to better prepare students for the advanced courses in grades 9 through 12.[53]

What Schools Can Do to Close the Math Achievement Gap

To address the issues in math education, schools must become proactive and consider *what* math content is taught in their classrooms and *how* it is taught.[54] To strengthen math curriculum and instruction across the board, schools serving grades 6 through 12 should establish a powerful mathematics assignment (PMA) action team to develop and implement an action plan using the Plan, Do, Study, Act process described in Chapter 3. This plan should describe ways to engage students in mathematics assignments that advance their ability to understand, reason, and use mathematical knowledge to solve multistep abstract and real-world problems in math, science, and CTE classes. It also must include strategies for extensive support for reengaging every student who fails to demonstrate mastery of math concepts and skills at the college- and career-readiness level at key points along the learning continuum.

The PMA action team should draw its members from both the high school and the main feeder middle school and include at least two math teachers; a science teacher, an English language arts teacher, and a CTE/exploratory teacher; a school leader; and a parent. Representatives from postsecondary institutions and business who understand the mathematics needed for success in college and careers should also be involved.

The PMA action team should begin by developing a *statement of need* that reports the percentage of current 8th grade students who demonstrate mathematics knowledge and skills needed for college preparatory Algebra I and career pathway courses in 9th grade—and the percentage of 12th graders who are prepared to succeed in postsecondary mathematics and in careers—overall and by subgroups. The team can begin by analyzing data gathered by the school's data, accountability, and policy action team. With the data in hand, the team can identify possible primary root causes for gaps in readiness. (See Chapter 3 for more information on data analysis.)

As part of this process, the PMA action team will need to define the indicators of readiness for high school college preparatory Algebra I at the end of 8th grade and readiness for postsecondary studies and careers at the end of 12th grade.

What Are the Math-Readiness Indicators for High School, College, and Careers?

To better define *what needs to be taught*, schools, districts, and states must carefully define what incoming 9th graders and graduating 12th graders *should know and be able to do to succeed in their next step*. For example, SREB worked with a panel of teachers and math experts from southeastern states to develop five indicators that would suggest a student is ready for Algebra I and for the math demands of postsecondary studies and careers.[55] These five indicators represent essential skills found in all areas of mathematics:

1. **Real-world problem solving.** Before Algebra I, students can solve two-step problems with multiple solution paths, solve problems with insufficient information, and solve problems that require choosing correct strategies. By the end of high school, students can determine if and what information is missing from a problem and discriminate between necessary and unnecessary information that may be present in a problem.

2. **Reading and communicating.** By the end of 8th grade, students can read problems, effectively interpret what the problem is asking them to do, and explain their thinking and the concepts and strategies they used to solve the problem, both orally and in writing. By the end of high school, students can understand and use algebraic and geometric vocabulary confidently, identify number systems, recognize and interpret algebraic symbols, recognize and interpret geometric theorems, and convert between verbal and symbolic mathematical representations.

3. **Estimating and verifying answers and solutions.** By the end of 8th grade, students can recognize when answers can and cannot be negative, know when to use estimation strategies, and recognize shortcuts to make the problem-solving process easier. By the end of high school, students can use estimation to determine accuracy and reasonableness of answers, identify the inverse of a function, and find solutions from multiple representations (e.g., tables, graphs, and symbols).

4. **Logical reasoning.** By the end of 8th grade, students can make and evaluate their own arguments and critique the arguments of others. High school graduates can evaluate the reasonableness of multiple solution paths and understand and use deductive and inductive reasoning.

5. **Using technology.** By the end of 8th grade, students can use a scientific calculator and use graphing software to create bar, line, and circle graphs. High school graduates can interpret information from a graph, determine a regression equation using a scientific calculator, use a scientific calculator to solve systems of equations and graph functions, and describe transformations of functions.

Providing more students with this set of skills and knowledge will require teachers to change *how* they teach. Researchers believe greater emphasis on exploration and discourse is the gateway toward improvement,[56] and the National Council of Teachers of Mathematics (NCTM) advocates regular and ongoing opportunities for *productive struggle* through multistep, problem-solving assignments. Students need opportunities to explore a variety of possible solution paths, discuss solutions with their peers, and apply the essential math skills they are learning in real-world contexts. Such learning opportunities promote deeper understanding by *enabling students to develop their own solutions and address their own misconceptions.*[57]

The PMA action team will need to prepare a statement of proven practices that can benefit all students, and particularly students who are failing to meet college- and career-readiness mathematical standards. The powerful mathematics practices offer a successful framework to begin this exploration.

What Are the Powerful Mathematics Practices?

The following powerful mathematics practices (PMPs) are a set of instructional practices that help teachers shift away from a "sit-and-get" model and instead create *student-led learning environments that facilitate procedural fluency and mathematical reasoning*:

1. Plan for and ensure a balanced approach to mathematics.
2. Engage students in assignments that matter.
3. Use questioning and feedback for deeper student understanding.
4. Use formative assessment data to plan reengagement lessons for students.
5. Foster a classroom environment that supports student ownership of learning.
6. Reflect on teaching practices.

The PMPs challenge students with complex assignments that engage them in a productive struggle and use formative assessment lessons (FALs) to help teachers check students' understanding of math concepts and guide them in correcting their misunderstandings. Through these strategies, students also learn from one another how to clarify and share learning intentions, engage in effective discussions and questions, provide feedback to move forward, recognize connections among mathematical concepts when solving complex problems, and take ownership of their learning.

The six PMPs align well with the eight effective mathematics teaching practices identified by the NCTM and developed by seasoned math teachers from all levels to strengthen math teaching and learning:[58]

1. Establish goals.
2. Promote reasoning and problem solving.
3. Pose purposeful questions.
4. Make connections to other classes and to events outside the school.
5. Facilitate discourse.

6. Elicit student thinking.
7. Support productive struggle.
8. Build procedural fluency.

Both sets of practices share common goals: *to eliminate racial and socioeconomic achievement gaps in math* while raising all students to college and career readiness; and *to graduate more students college- and career-ready and prepared for STEM careers.*[59]

The Six PMPs: A Closer Look

Let's examine the six powerful mathematics practices more closely.

PMP 1: Plan for and Ensure a Balanced Approach to Mathematics

The first PMP encourages teachers to use nonroutine instruction tasks and assessments that represent both abstract and real-world scenarios to *promote a balance of factual, procedural, and conceptual knowledge.* A balanced approach allows students to explore and discuss multiple ways to solve a problem, reflect upon which method is most efficient, explain why certain procedures work, and critique one another's strategies.

Both the National Mathematics Advisory Panel and the National Research Council have emphasized the importance of a balanced approach to mathematics that builds both conceptual knowledge and procedural fluency.[60] When students have procedural fluency, they are able to choose from multiple strategies to solve problems based on appropriateness and fit.[61]

Fluency is built through deepening conceptual understanding and making connections between strategies.[62] When students make these connections, their problem-solving skills and understanding of math concepts improve[63]—and with a greater problem-solving skill set at their disposal, students are better able to understand the operations involved in a strategy and select the right solution path.[64]

Memorization, conversely, fails to build fluency and can lead to math anxiety as students' capacity to recall steps they don't fully understand fades over time.[65] The more effective approach to building students' fluency is to allow them to explore various strategies through application and discussion in the context of complex assignments.[66]

Reason making is key. A math teacher in North Carolina witnessed firsthand what student-centered, aligned, and rigorous math lessons look like. They've implemented the strategies alongside local trainers, and she continues to see an increase in quality instruction and mathematical discourse in these classrooms. Students are engaged in reason making instead of answer getting.[67]

PMP 2: Engage Students in Assignments That Matter

This second practice challenges students with meaningful, complex assignments that require problem solving, deductive reasoning, and mathematical modeling. Through this practice, teachers advance students' learning by prompting them with guiding questions rather than giving them step-by-step instructions for how to complete an assignment.

Assignments that matter are built around complex problem tasks that motivate students to think and learn while working through problems, as opposed to routine, formulaic work.[68] Complex assignments create *productive struggle*, pushing students to deepen their understanding of the problems they are solving and to see connections among the strategies being used to solve the problem.[69]

The benefits of productive struggle are illustrated by a math teacher in Mississippi. After receiving training on using PMPs, he found a way to engage students successfully with productive struggle. "Students' productive struggle became evident in my classroom, and the results were amazing," he says. "There was so much conversation and discussion around all the different approaches to solving problems." In the first year of implementing PMPs, students in the class showed improvement on the schoolwide benchmark assessments. The average number of correct responses increased by 14 in the first quarter, 16 in the second quarter, and 4 in the third quarter.[70]

Complex tasks work best when teachers construct balanced assignments that draw upon students' prior knowledge and connect that knowledge to another class, experiences students have outside class, and real-world workplace applications. Authentic assignments have proven effective in increasing students' motivation, extending their problem-solving skills, and encouraging perseverance.[71]

Despite their benefits, implementing these types of tasks can be challenging for many teachers because they often feel the need to intervene when students do not immediately produce the correct answers—a phenomenon researchers refer to as "rescuing."[72] *Teachers must embrace struggle* and allow it to happen as part of the learning process, so that their students also learn to embrace cognitively demanding tasks.

> **Hands-off teaching.** A math teacher in Georgia found that through using FALs (formative assessment lessons), students have an opportunity to explore and engage in the material without much teacher direction. She finds it difficult not to lead students in a certain direction, but she notices more learning occurs when she does not lead her students to the answer.

Good assignments engage students in productive discussions with peers, through which students help each other complete complex tasks, share ideas and solutions, get feedback, and build reasoning skills and a shared understanding of math concepts. Teachers use grouping strategies to facilitate such discussions among sets of students who have similar levels of mathematical knowledge and skills. (Students should be grouped with a comparative group of their peers. Grouping a low-performing student with a team of high-performing students, for example, may not provide the low-performing student with ample opportunity to participate and struggle through the process.) Turn-and-talks, a type of peer discussion, have also been shown to be effective in eliciting student thinking and can serve as a segue into small-group or whole-group discussions.

Strategically organized discussion groups allow students to observe how their classmates approached and solved a problem, and how their classmates' solution paths paralleled or differed from their own. Working in groups, students can address their misconceptions and generate a better understanding of how to apply learned skills, while teachers use good questioning to keep groups moving forward.

PMP 3: Use Questioning and Feedback for Deeper Student Understanding

Purposeful questioning is a key component of high-quality math classrooms. Without good questions, teachers cannot know what students understand and where their misconceptions lie. Moreover, good questions push students not only to recall critical facts, but also to apply their knowledge, explain their reasoning, predict outcomes, and connect ideas and concepts, which accelerates learning.[73] Well-crafted questions help students think more deeply about the content, particularly when they have time to formulate responses to questions and can share their ideas in groups, building on the questions asked by their teacher.

Strategic questioning is a skill that takes time to master. When done well, teachers use a variety of questions that hit at all levels of knowledge and understanding and enable them to assess student progress in real time.[74] Teachers must be prepared to respond to student ideas in ways that build fluency and reasoning.[75]

Cognitively demanding authentic tasks are designed to stretch student thinking, building higher-order thinking skills that are key to higher math achievement.[76] These learning tasks are enhanced when teachers ask good questions that reveal student thinking and pinpoint student progress toward achieving the desired learning goal.[77]

The impact of good questioning. As a participant in PMP training, a middle school math teacher from North Carolina became more cognizant of the questions she asked in class. She now poses questions that require students to brainstorm with their neighbors to develop solutions to assigned problems. After a full school year of training, her students outperformed their grade-level peers across the state on the North Carolina State Assessments. More than 90 percent scored at the Proficient level on the Math I assessment for 8th grade, compared with 50 percent statewide.[78]

PMP 4: Use Formative Assessment Data to Plan Reengagement Lessons for Students

Ongoing formative assessment is an essential part of effective math instruction because it generates evidence of what students know and their gaps in learning. Beyond helping teachers to reengage students in learning, formative assessment helps students reflect on the purpose of each lesson, assess their own understandings and misconceptions, and work with their teachers to create a plan to advance their learning. Without high-quality formative assessment, teachers have less information about learning gaps and cannot address all their students' learning needs.[79]

Formative assessment is an effective method because it moves beyond determining whether students have the right or wrong answer; it delves into the strategies they used to reach their answers, the mistakes made, and the misconceptions formed.[80] Teachers adept at using formative assessment can track student progress over time, so instruction can be personalized.[81] The end result is targeted learning objectives driven by student data.

Formative assessment can come in a variety of forms, including purposeful questioning, peer discussion, or examining snippets of student work. Formative assessment lessons are designed to inform teachers about what students understand and enable them to adjust instruction to reinforce key concepts as needed. (For open-source resources on more than 100 FALs, visit http://map.mathshell.org.) By focusing on students' understanding of mathematical concepts, FALs help teachers assess how students think using mathematics and determine what to change in content and instructional strategies so students can master the standards. This is not feasible when individual procedural skills are taught through worksheets.

To be effective, FALs must be aligned to what is being taught. Teachers select formative assessment lessons that match well with the relevant mathematical topics or concepts being studied and gauge how much information students have retained.

Transformational PD. When a high school math teacher from North Carolina was first told about the PMP professional development she was to attend, she was unsure the workshop would benefit her and her students. She refused to book the hotel room until she attended the first day to see if she thought it was something that would work for her students. By lunchtime, she knew she was staying. The first formative assessment lesson was a transformational experience, and she was hooked. She found that after she began implementing PMPs, the pass rate in her Math III class increased from 38 percent in 2014-15 to 61 percent in 2015-16. She presented PMP lessons multiple times during instructional rounds. When teachers visited her room, there was always conversation that included comments like 'They are all working!' 'They are trying!' or 'Wow, I can't believe you got them to work!'[82]

PMP 5: Foster a Classroom Environment That Supports Student Ownership of Learning

Teachers adopting this PMP strategy encourage students to have a voice in the classroom—to openly share ideas, confidently justify their problem-solving approaches using precise language, critique one another's reasoning, and provide one another with meaningful feedback. These opportunities help students establish connections between concepts and strategies, clarify misunderstandings, and build fluency.[83]

As students participate in robust discussions and respond to peer questioning (in pairs, small groups, and whole-group settings), they are forming a community of learners in math class. Teachers do not hand off all ownership of the teaching process; instead, they facilitate this community conversation by encouraging discourse, using purposeful questioning, and guiding discussions so students remain on-topic and move toward their learning goals.[84]

> **Increasing teachable moments.** A math teacher from Georgia found students more willing to share their answers after collaborating with a partner. Students showed more ownership, and the number of teachable moments increased when students were discussing problems.[85]

Achieving a balance between teacher-led instruction and increased student discourse can be difficult at first. Over time, teachers perfect their ways to honor students' ideas while maintaining focus on the learning target. Doing so requires thought and planning before beginning the actual lesson—strategically developing the activities and questions that will provoke meaningful discussion.[86] In working toward the right balance, teachers strive to practice research-based strategies for facilitating student talk, including anticipating responses, monitoring engagement, selecting certain students to present or share ideas, sequencing students' responses to create a natural progression, and connecting students' ideas to the overall goal of the lesson.

Like several of the PMPs, increased student discourse can help generate productive struggle, encouraging students to engage with content at deeper levels while learning to persevere and work toward a solution. When students engage in productive struggle with the support of their teachers and peers, they can view misconceptions as learning opportunities and develop a growth mindset. In short, productive struggle supports perseverance and deepens the conceptual understanding needed to solve complex, authentic, and abstract tasks.[87]

PMP 6: Reflect on Teaching Practices

Teacher reflection is critical to improving instructional practice and a vital component of setting goals and evaluating progress toward meeting those goals.[88]

Deep reflection does not come naturally. It is deliberate, structured, ongoing, and often collaborative.

Teachers who adopt this practice join with colleagues to reflect on evidence of student learning and discuss ways to adapt instruction to better meet students' needs. When teachers reflect on the goals they have set and the progress students have made, they can reengage students more effectively and differentiate their instruction to support both struggling and advanced learners. This reengagement process is essential to ensuring students comprehend key mathematical concepts.[89]

> **Adapting and adjusting.** A math teacher from Georgia found that using formative assessment data helped adapt and adjust instruction after administering a formative assessment lesson. It helped to reflect on the strategies used and how well the students understood the content.

Learning goals can help guide teachers' self-reflection, as well as their assessment of students' understanding. When written appropriately, learning goals address all concepts and ideas included in the lesson and the learning that should occur as a result. A lack of explicit learning goals inhibits a teacher's ability to determine whether reengagement and additional instruction are needed.[90]

The Impact of Powerful Mathematics Practices

Using the six PMPs, the PMA action team should develop a multiyear plan of action for supporting teachers to make the desired instructional shifts that will, over time, result in *95 percent of 9th grade students successfully completing Algebra I and 90 percent of 12th graders meeting college- and career-readiness math standards.*

Understanding and sharing the potential impact of the PMPs will be important as the PMA action team works to engage teachers in a long-term transformational process. Data collected from teachers and students who have experienced what math education is like in PMP-based classrooms will help.

Changes in Teachers' Perceptions

Surveys can help schools better understand teachers' perceptions about the impact of professional development and classroom coaching. Before implementing PMPs, surveying teachers to determine current practices will establish a baseline and provide data for talking points when the PMPs are introduced. As implementation rolls out, additional surveys should ask teachers to report on the PMPs they are using in their classrooms, the student behaviors they observe after implementation, and the coaching and support they are receiving to facilitate implementation and professional growth.

The Southern Regional Education Board administered a survey to more than 200 teachers across three states who received two years of professional development and on-site coaching to shift their mathematics instruction in ways that align with the six PMPs. The results indicated teachers believed professional development and coaching benefited them as practitioners and improved their ability to shift from a procedural focus to a greater emphasis on students' conceptual understanding. Furthermore, most teachers believed their new instructional practices were helping students learn more mathematical concepts. And teachers who reported using practices like the PMPs described in this chapter were more likely to have classroom environments that promoted student-centered learning and helped students understand how to take ownership of their learning.

The survey also found that schoolwide adoption of student-centered practices was more likely to be found in schools where principals encouraged use of such practices, attended trainings, and provided implementation support. According to teachers responding to the survey, principals are key in spreading PMPs to all math teachers. Principals who understood the practices, attended trainings with teachers, supported teachers by designating collaborative planning time, and conducted classroom observations with feedback were significantly more likely to see improved instruction and student achievement.

Changes in Students' Perceptions and Achievement

Students also perceive the difference that PMPs can make in their instruction and classroom experiences. A survey of more than 11,000 students—some of whom had teachers who had received intensive professional development and external coaching on implementing the PMPs, and some who were in classrooms where teachers had not received formal professional development—showed that *teachers who received PMP training were more effective in helping their students' build conceptual knowledge of math strategies and apply that knowledge to solve real-world problems.*

Teachers trained in PMPs were more likely to have student-centered classrooms, and their students were engaged in activities that promote student ownership more often than students in comparison classrooms. And the longer teachers were trained in using the PMPs, the more students perceived an impact in the classroom. Although data from the survey show that teachers who implemented the PMPs improved their instruction throughout the first and second years of training, it was not until year 3 that they made profound instructional shifts.

These data provide evidence that schools will see greater impacts if they invest in providing at least three years of training to help teachers master the PMPs. It is this type of investment—and not quick solutions or one-off professional development—that will result in the kind of instruction that increases college and career readiness.

The same survey also showed that the PMPs can be effective with math teachers of all course levels. Students in college preparatory, honors, and basic math courses who were exposed to the instructional practices rated their teachers significantly higher on all scales than did students in comparison classrooms.

Teachers of basic math courses received the highest ratings, signaling that the PMPs can be used to enhance learning experiences for struggling math learners. This finding is particularly noteworthy, as basic math courses are traditionally designed to focus on procedural repetition, with a heavy emphasis on worksheets that mimic common questions found on standardized assessments. The data suggest that when teachers receive sufficient professional training in the PMPs—and the freedom to put that learning to use—basic math classes can become much more engaging, student-driven, and effective.

The experience of a parish in Louisiana illustrates the need for ongoing professional development. Teachers in the parish participated in intensive professional development over three years, with strong support from the parish superintendent. They found that their students' mathematics achievement was improving at rates higher than the state average in both Algebra I and Geometry. Throughout their extended implementation of PMPs, the parish learned two big lessons: First, when a teacher retires or leaves a position, the new teacher must be provided with 60 to 70 hours of professional development and support over several months to implement PMPs. Second, ongoing support will help some teachers continue to sharpen their skills in implementing the powerful math practices. Districts must develop their own internal capacity to provide in-depth professional development to new teachers and administrators who do not understand the instructional shifts. Otherwise the progress made can be quickly undone.

Another example demonstrates that when districts provide the ongoing supports necessary to make the instructional shifts outlined in the PMPs, they can change not just students' perception of math but their achievement as well. Among 230 middle and high schools in North Carolina in which selected teachers received intensive professional development to use PMPs, 78 percent experienced schoolwide gains on end-of-grade assessments—and about one-half of those schools had gains greater than the average statewide gains on the same assessments.

A Theory of Action for Shifting Mathematics Instruction

When the PMA action team has analyzed gaps in mathematics achievement, determined the root causes for these gaps, identified best practices for closing the gaps, and outlined the instructional shifts needed to implement PMPs, it is ready to develop a theory of action.

The PMA action team uses the Plan, Do, Study, Act process outlined in Chapter 3 to identify actions needed ("if/then" statements) to ensure students exiting grades 8 and 12 are equipped with the mathematical knowledge and skills needed to succeed in challenging high school and postsecondary studies and in careers.

The PMA action team should come up with statements that are specific to their school and district setting, in addition to statements such as the following samples:

If . . .

- Schools support the development of a local math coach . . .
- Principals select two successful middle grade and two successful high school math teachers to become early adopters of the PMPs . . .
- Principals, early adopting teachers, and the local math coach participate in extended professional development, and each teacher is supported to design/select and use at least six formative assessment lessons in their first year of implementation . . .
- Principals receive special training on using a PMP classroom observation rubric . . .
- An external coach, the local math coach, the principal, and the PMA action team visit math classrooms four times each year during the learning and implementation period to provide feedback on adoption of PMPs, and use observations to design their next round of professional development . . .
- Principals schedule time for early-adopting math teachers to meet with other teachers and spread implementation of PMPs and lessons learned . . .

- Schools administer a PMP student survey to gauge the quality of implementation occurring in schools . . .

- All other math teachers ultimately participate in intensive professional development to implement the PMPs over three years; receive in-classroom observations and feedback every 45 days from early-adopting math teachers; lead math trainers and the principal use results to provide further professional development and other mentoring and collaborative support . . .

- Early adopting lead teachers receive further development to advance their skills and become coaches who can support other teachers in implementing the powerful math practices effectively . . .

- The PMA action team regularly collects data on improvements in classroom grades, exams, and student work, as well as data from assessments such as state exams, the SAT, the ACT, WorkKeys, and so on, to identify areas needing further improvement . . .

then over three years, the schools should expect to see the spread of powerful math practices in all math classes and should witness a significant increase in the percent of students meeting math-readiness standards.

Powerful Mathematics: Practical Steps Schools Can Take Now

Schools that are not ready to invest in the comprehensive, multiyear action plan to make schoolwide shifts across all mathematics courses can still work to begin improving mathematics learning and achievement. Here are steps to take:

- Require four years of mathematics for high school graduation.

- Discontinue different levels of math courses and teach all students to the same high standards with a focus on mathematical understanding, reasoning, and applying math knowledge and skills in a variety of situations.

- Have students keep a mathematics journal where they make daily or weekly entries on new mathematics insight gained and math applications they've made or observed in other classes, their home, and community.

- Group two or three students who have similar math knowledge and skills and allow them to work as a team to solve complex multistep problems.

- Give students short summative assessments at the end of each class and a longer assessment at the end of each major unit to identify misconceptions. Use the insights gathered to reengage them in additional learning tasks.

- Work with career pathway and science teachers in identifying math knowledge and skills their students are having difficulty applying and connect math assignments to their classes.

- Support all educators who are teaching a math course in grades 7 through 12 who do not hold a high school math certification to pursue advanced studies to acquire such certification.

Summing Up and Looking Ahead

The United States is facing a widening national gap between the math skills needed for STEM-related jobs and postsecondary studies and the skills students have acquired in high school. A balanced approach to middle school and high school mathematics instruction can help close this gap by shifting to *complex, multistep assignments* that advance mathematics understanding and reasoning and enable students to connect mathematics concepts to real-world scenarios. The six powerful mathematics practices outlined in this chapter provide a framework for making such shifts.

The next chapter will provide a framework for increasing students' literacy readiness through the use of powerful literacy-based assignments that advance both content achievement and literacy achievement in grades 6 through 12.

6

Developing Powerful Literacy-Based Assignments

by Gene Bottoms, Monique Whorton, & Jamie Lee Korns

To access the types of careers that will lead to satisfaction, fulfillment, and a middle-class lifestyle, students need more than just career-field knowledge. Business and industry leaders seek employees who can also apply literacy and mathematics skills to solve complex problems.[91] In the previous chapter, we discussed the importance of closing the mathematics readiness gap—but what about literacy?

The Need for Literacy-Based Assignments in Every Content Area

Adults entering the world of work in the 21st century will need advanced levels of literacy to perform their jobs, engage as active citizens, and conduct their personal lives—all while coping with the flood of information they will find everywhere they turn. They need to be able to absorb, synthesize, and process this information at home and on the job. They also need to be able to communicate clearly in speech *and* in writing. Describing the types of speaking and writing employers want from their employees, senior education consultant Cynthia Gewertz notes, "They want workers who can explain things concisely, support their requests with evidence, and understand the appropriate shifts in tone necessary for different audiences."[92]

To help more students master literacy skills at the level needed to succeed in their future, schools need to engage students in reading complex texts and communicating their understanding—not just in English language arts classes, but across all academic and career pathway courses. **Yet far too few teachers are prepared to create literacy-based assignments that engage students in mastering these types of skills while also gaining disciplinary skills and knowledge, resulting in significant gaps in students' literacy skills—particularly for students from traditionally underserved populations.[93]**

Literacy Readiness for High School, College, and Careers

In 2019, only about one-third of 8th grade students in the United States met literacy proficiency standards, indicating that they were achieving at grade level on the reading portion of the National Assessment of Educational Progress. A deeper dive into the data shows wide gaps between student groups, with 42 percent of white students, 22 percent of Hispanic students, and 15 percent of Black students reaching the Proficient level.[94]

These gaps persist as students advance through high school, affecting their readiness for college and careers. On the 2019 ACT exams—one standardized measurement of college readiness—45 percent of all students met the reading benchmark (54 percent of white students, 32 percent of Hispanic students, and 20 percent of Black students). On the English language arts test, 59 percent met the readiness benchmark (70 percent of white students, 40 percent of Hispanic students, and 32 percent of Black students). Students meeting these benchmarks and entering college are 50 percent more likely to earn a *B* or higher in a given subject.[95]

Alarmingly, the gap between the highest- and lowest-performing students is widening on assessments of college readiness, despite billions in federal funding designated specifically to help close it.[96] Numerous studies have linked reading proficiency to college completion, wherein 20 percent fewer Hispanic and Black students than white students completed in six years.[97]

The need for literacy skills is not limited to students who are planning to pursue postsecondary studies. The Armed Services Vocational Aptitude Battery, which is used to determine enlistment eligibility and assignments to military jobs, also measures literacy comprehension, among other skills, and screens out candidates who fail to meet armed services expectations. Furthermore, to land military jobs that translate to middle-class civilian jobs—administrative, intelligence, mechanical, medical, and computer roles—test-takers need high scores in word knowledge and paragraph comprehension.

Are schools responsible for these problems in literacy readiness? Educators, including those in secondary school, do have to accept some ownership of the literacy gap. Based on my work with middle and high schools over many decades, I can see one long-standing and overarching issue: the widespread failure among educators and education policymakers to understand or acknowledge the power of literacy-based assignments to advance students' content knowledge and literacy skills *across* the curriculum.

Improving Literacy Skills Across the Curriculum

Many policymakers believe there is no need to continue emphasizing literacy-based strategies in all coursework after 3rd or 4th grade. They fail to recognize that *literacy is a fundamental way students learn* throughout their educational journey—and never more so than in today's information-centered economy and the world of social media.[98]

As a result of this short-sightedness, most school districts fail to lobby for or earmark resources to prepare history, science, math, and CTE teachers to design literacy-based assignments for their classrooms. After decades of operating in this outdated paradigm, it's no surprise that many teachers and school leaders today do not fully understand the role that literacy plays in advancing all students to a level where they are prepared for college and careers.

State accountability systems can further exacerbate this problem by expecting English language arts teachers in middle and high schools to carry the entire burden of advancing students' ability to read and write effectively in all disciplines and CTE courses. It is unrealistic to ask English language arts teachers to cover all that needs to be taught about analyzing informational text and organizing writing in a clear, logical manner at the levels needed in science, social studies, and CTE courses.

We cannot eliminate the literacy gap by simply adding an extra reading teacher in middle or high school or by expecting English language arts teachers to develop students' discipline-specific literacy skills in other academic and CTE classes. *Both academic and CTE teachers must understand the need to engage students in reading grade-level documents in content areas and in expressing their understanding orally and in writing as a way to improve both literacy and content-area learning.* Until education funding and assessment systems are designed with the expectation that all subject matter and CTE teachers are accountable for advancing students' skills in these areas, the literacy achievement gap will persist—and the bold goal of having 90 percent of students graduate from high school with a high level of information literacy will remain elusive.

To address gaps in literacy skills, schools serving grades 6 through 12 should establish a powerful literacy-based assignment (PLBA) action team and charge this team to develop and implement an action plan for engaging students in all classes in literacy-based assignments that advance both their literacy and subject-matter knowledge and skills. (See Chapter 3 for steps the PLBA team will take in developing this plan.) The plan should define how each school will engage all students in literacy-based assignments to advance their abilities to read, comprehend, analyze, and express orally and in writing their understanding of grade-level information texts and discipline-specific materials, resulting in more students meeting academic- and career-readiness standards.

The PLBA action team should draw its members from both the high school and the main feeder middle school and should include two English language arts teachers, at least one teacher from each of the other academic areas, one CTE/exploratory teacher, and a school leader. The team should include a parent and representatives from postsecondary institutions and business/industry who understand the literacy level needed for success in college and careers.

The PLBA team's first step will be to identify gaps between their school's performance and the *bold goals*—with help from the data, accountability, and policy action team's findings—and then determine primary root causes of gaps in literacy achievement, especially for students from traditionally underserved backgrounds. They can begin with this question: *Are all of our students being engaged in comprehending and interacting with progressively more complex cross-curricular texts in grades 6 through 12 that would develop the literacy skills needed for good jobs and postsecondary studies?*

Literacy-Readiness Indicators for High School, College, and Careers

To engage teachers across all content areas, begin by adopting specific literacy standards for every discipline and incorporate them into the curriculum for grades 6 through 12 in both academic and CTE courses. These literacy standards define what students must be able to do as incoming 9th graders or graduating 12th graders, using indicators that suggest students are ready to make successful transitions to high school or to postsecondary studies and careers.[99] Literacy standards should include, at a minimum, these readiness indicators:

- **Reading Comprehension**

    o *Summarize, paraphrase, and categorize information.* This indicator provides ways that students can demonstrate comprehension of both nonfiction and fiction texts they have read. Ninth graders are expected to work with complex materials and extract key ideas, whether explicit or implied. Middle schoolers need opportunities to synthesize information from multiple sources and then formulate and express views based on that information. These skills extend beyond high school into postsecondary studies and careers. First-year college students are expected to convey the essential meaning of multiple complex materials and therefore need to have precollegiate experiences putting key ideas into their own words and classifying multiple ideas within and across texts in meaningful and efficient ways.

o *Connect what is read to personal experience and the world beyond the classroom.* High school students need to connect both nonfiction and fiction text they have read to something relevant in their own lives. In middle grades, students need practice using paired texts to make connections between varying perspectives and to connect what they read to previous learning experiences. This skill is also expected of college students. High school teachers must provide students with frequent opportunities to connect texts to their own lives through intentional questioning, open discussion, and writing assignments.

- **Writing**

  o *Compose writing that conveys a clear main point with logical support.* To prepare for high school expectations, middle school students need assignments that require them to state their point directly and to experiment with creative ways of making points. Similarly, high school students need multiple opportunities to organize their writing around main ideas and supporting details, as well as opportunities to construct their own arguments using a variety of strategies.

  o *Edit and revise writing for the strongest effect.* To learn to evaluate their own writing, middle school students need many opportunities to produce and revise their own writing to improve grammar, structure, and content. Likewise, for high school students to be prepared for postsecondary studies and careers, they need assignments requiring them to refine their message, ensuring it is clear, logical, and effective for their intended audience.

- **Speaking**

  o *Use appropriate organization, language, voice, delivery, style, and visual aids to match the audience and purpose of oral presentations.* By high school, students are expected to prepare and deliver presentations in front of an audience, in part because this increases their motivation to fully organize and present ideas. Expectations for quality oral communications increase as students' progress into postsecondary studies and a career. High school students need opportunities to research information, organize their thoughts, prepare oral presentations, share their work with others, and receive others' feedback.

- **Listening**

  o Use active-listening strategies to organize and respond to information presented in different formats for different purposes. High school success is contingent upon students using good listening and note-taking skills in the classroom and in small learning groups. The ability to accurately capture key ideas from teachers and other students and store them for later use can advance students' success in all classes. Middle and high school teachers must shift from writing notes on the board and having students copy them down to using strategies designed to engage students as active listeners—two-column note-taking activities, class interviews and discussions, and sharing with student learning groups. By the end of high school, students should be able to adjust their listening strategies to the purpose of the activity and be able to use a variety of note-taking strategies to organize and prioritize classroom lectures.

The PLBA action team should identify the literacy-readiness indicators that would signify students are ready for rigorous high school studies by the end of 8th grade or ready for success in postsecondary studies and careers by the end of 12th grade. The PLBA action team will need to determine the percentage of students currently meeting literacy-readiness indicators and specify the expected advancement of students' content knowledge and skills as a result of using literacy-based assignments.

Powerful Literacy Practices to Shift Instruction and Achievement

The powerful literacy practices (PLPs) described here offer a guiding framework to help schools make the instructional shifts necessary to provide more students with the skills needed to meet literacy-readiness standards for high school, college, and careers. Here are the six PLPs:

1. Include an authentic written product in literacy-based assignments that cites evidence from reading complex, grade-level texts that are aligned to the depth of knowledge of the standards.

2. Scaffold complex assignments using explicit comprehension strategies tied to literacy and content standards.

3. Establish clear and measurable learning targets that are communicated to students and assessed by the teacher.

4. Embed reading instruction and strategies into assignments to improve content retention and to advance literacy skills.

5. Use student discourse to promote students' ownership of learning and to facilitate the application of reading strategies and text comprehension.

6. Use formative and summative assessment in all aspects of the literacy learning process.

The following Powerful Literacy Practices offer a guiding framework to help schools make the instructional shifts necessary to provide more students with the skills needed to meet literacy-readiness standards for high school, college, and careers. Let's take a closer look at each of these.

PLP 1: Powerful Literacy Practices Will Shift Instruction and Achievement

Include an authentic written product in literacy-based assignments that cites evidence from reading complex, grade-level texts that are aligned to the depth of knowledge of the standards.

The teacher aligns content, texts, and written products to state content and literacy standards. Students complete extended written products that engage them in analyzing and synthesizing information from texts, using evidence from texts to make claims, and demonstrating critical thinking about essential content. Because students' engagement, literacy development, and knowledge acquisition are enhanced when they can exert some control over their learning,[100] assignments should offer students choices in the texts they read to complete the assignment.

The benefits of writing across the disciplines extend beyond the writing itself. Writing can improve reading comprehension and critical thinking and also deepen understanding and retention of disciplinary content.[101] Students who participate in disciplinary reading and writing activities across content areas outperform their peers on state assessments in both English language arts and in their content-specific domains.[102] Unfortunately, too few students are engaged in reading grade-level nonfiction texts and expressing their understanding in writing in science, social studies, and CTE courses, despite benefits reported in the literature.[103]

Literacy-based science assignments. A science teacher from Mississippi thought she did not have time to do literacy-based assignments because she had content to cover before the state biology exam. Her belief has changed drastically. Her first use of literacy-based assignments focused on a very hard concept. She was surprised at how well her students responded to the assignment. They asked deeper questions and scored better on the exam than any previous group she had taught.[104]

PLP 2: Scaffold with Explicit Strategies

Scaffold complex assignments using explicit comprehension strategies tied to literacy and content standards.

The teacher sets a purpose for student learning through sequenced, complex assignments, while introducing scaffolding supports to help students use explicit reading-comprehension strategies to make sense of texts.[105] Students move through the different stages of the learning process, with each lesson improving their ability to complete the culminating assignment.

A balanced sequence of lessons with built-in complexity can enable struggling readers to comprehend discipline-specific texts and vocabulary.[106] Teachers should provide students with ample opportunities to determine the meaning of words from the context of the text and to use new vocabulary through discussion, writing, and extended reading assignments.[107]

Scaffolding builds on learners' existing knowledge and skills by adding supports—such as modeling, questioning, and guided discussions—to build competency levels.[108] As teachers introduce texts that are more complex, they must prepare students to comprehend those texts by guiding them to use a variety of literacy strategies. Teachers can, for example, have students summarize the main ideas of what they have read through discussion or writing, periodically ask students reflective questions about what they have read, encourage students to draw inferences from texts, or have students develop graphic organizers.[109]

Many of these research-based strategies are well-known to reading and literacy specialists, but traditionally they have not been part of professional development programs in other disciplines. Yet it is clear that *content-specific* understanding and reading comprehension are the result of students' active participation in and application of these strategies.[110] Substantial gains in literacy skills and higher-order thinking come when students are supported to learn a variety of strategies for reading and writing that call for them to think independently, organize information read from a diverse range of informational texts, and construct written responses in a variety of mediums.

PLP 3: Establish, Communicate, and Assess Learning Targets

Establish clear and measurable learning targets that are communicated to students and assessed by the teacher.

The teacher posts, explains, and refers to the lesson's learning targets and links those targets to the overarching assignment. Learning goals communicate what students will learn, how they will learn, and how they will demonstrate their knowledge.[111] Student motivation and engagement are enhanced when teachers establish meaningful and engaging learning activities aligned to key ideas and standards.

Consider the following literacy-based assignment prompt from an agriculture teacher in Arkansas:

> *"Where's the beef?"* Should consumers purchase beef that has antibiotics, hormones, or additives? After reading primary and secondary texts, write an argumentative essay to address the question and argue your position concerning production practices of the beef industry. Support your position with evidence from documents and the text. Be sure to acknowledge competing views.

With a prompt like this, students can quickly identify what they will be asked to learn and how they will successfully demonstrate new learning.

Using this practice, the teacher assesses students' progress and provides feedback. Students in small groups discuss how the learning targets relate to the assignment and reflect on progress toward meeting the target. Frequent teacher feedback can help ensure students stay attentive to the learning process.[112] Positive feedback that praises student effort and provides valuable information (e.g., on writing, vocabulary) helps students view their mistakes as learning opportunities.[113] When giving feedback, teachers provide detailed explanations of how to use a reading strategy, and they help students set realistic goals for their learning.[114]

> **Rethinking assignment planning.** A principal from West Virginia found that teachers planning literacy-based assignments resulted in discipline-area teachers rethinking their assignments and instructional strategies. They now plan with the end in mind and with students becoming more engaged in reading grade-level text and documents. The biggest change is that students have taken ownership and want to give their best.

PLP 4: Embed Reading Instruction and Strategies

Embed reading instruction and strategies into assignments to improve content retention and advance literacy skills.

Across content areas, direct, explicit reading instruction is a powerful strategy for developing students' vocabulary and comprehension when working with informational text.[115] Direct reading instruction includes explanations, guided practice, feedback, and modeling.[116]

When first introducing a reading strategy (e.g., summarizing, predicting, making inferences), teachers should model the strategy with grade-appropriate texts.[117] Make sure students understand that *text comprehension is the goal* of the lesson. Too much focus on mastering strategies will cause students to lose sight of the true goal.[118] Demonstrating how the strategy works with multiple texts helps students apply the strategy independently and judge when the strategy is appropriate.[119]

To ease into a new strategy, students can use guided practice in small groups. This approach gives teachers an opportunity to check how well students are using the strategy and to provide feedback that encourages independent practice.[120] Building student confidence and understanding early on will prove beneficial to independent practice.

PLP 5: Use Student Discourse to Promote Ownership and Aid Comprehension

Use student discourse to promote students' ownership of learning and to facilitate the application of reading strategies and text comprehension.

The teacher organizes small groups in which students discuss the text and documents they've read. The groups engage with progressively higher-level questions; they ask questions of their peers and actively listen to make independent decisions about how to connect what they read to their writing products. The teacher's role is to ensure students explain their thinking, provide examples from the text to support their positions, and protect the productivity of the discussion by including all students and valuing all perspectives.

As students gain more ownership, they begin to ask questions to monitor their own learning (e.g., "Am I considering more than one point of view?"). They are also asking their peers questions in ways that increase one another's comprehension—and they are encouraged to ask teachers pivotal questions that can expand their foundational knowledge. The teacher should not steer students toward one point of view, but rather open the classroom up to different perspectives and interpretations[121] and expand student knowledge by creating deeper engagement.[122]

When teachers provide extended opportunities for students to discuss the meaning and interpretation of texts,[123] students achieve deeper comprehension and understanding of content knowledge and skills.[124] Student discussions allow opportunities for sharing and critiquing ideas.[125] They encourage students to dig deeper into texts to support their arguments with evidence, and they create a framework for students to gain valuable feedback and opposing viewpoints from classmates.[126]

> **Writing beyond the test.** A curriculum supervisor in a large district in Alabama said before they began literacy professional development, teachers never expected students to prepare a written product other than to take a test. It was about teaching to the test. Literacy-based assignments enable teachers to raise their expectations of what students can do. The result is that students are doing the work and learning more.

PLP 6: Employ Continuous Formative and Summative Assessments

Use formative and summative assessments in all aspects of the literacy learning process.

Formative assessment is assessment *for learning,* as opposed to assessments *of learning,* which are devised to determine whether students can produce the right answers to questions/tasks at a given moment in time.[127]

Content-area teachers develop *formative assessment* that allows students to demonstrate their knowledge and thinking.[128] They then analyze and apply the data they've gathered to adapt instruction, design interventions for struggling students, enhance assignments, and gauge whether students are using critical-thinking skills to analyze and comprehend texts.[129] Students, in turn, use descriptive feedback on daily lessons and culminating assignments to revise their work.

A good *summative assessment*—typically provided only at the end of a unit or grading period—asks a balanced set of questions based on Webb's Depth of Knowledge framework.[130] The questions should enable teachers to determine whether the student has mastered content knowledge and learning skills at the level necessary to meet college- and career-readiness standards for a given grade level. In the case of literacy-based instruction, summative exam items should require students to read grade-level texts in the discipline area and answer higher-level questions.[131]

The key to establishing an effective assessment program is to connect and align formative and summative assessments so that formative assessment prepares students for summative assessments. Reflecting on the teacher roles described in the powerful literacy practices, the PLBA action team researches and prepares a statement of proven effective practices that benefit all students, and particularly students who presently are failing to meet high school or college- and career-readiness literacy standards.

> **Active listening and questioning.** An English teacher from Mississippi explained that her students often engaged in an active discussion about what they were reading, but it was structured so students had to ask questions, listen, and take notes. They were eager to discuss what they read.[132] At the beginning of the implementation year, she estimated that 40 percent of her students would pass the state literacy test. At the end of the year, she had a 70 percent pass rate.

Designing Literacy-Based Assignments

Creating literacy-based assignments and adopting powerful literacy practices across the curriculum will require intensive preparation of teachers and school leaders. When students are guided by teachers who have engaged in thoughtful planning, they become active learners and take greater ownership in completing the assignment.

The following steps provide a starting place for teachers to work toward full implementation of literacy-based assignments:

- **Step 1:** Identify which focus standards will guide the work. (Focus standards to be embedded in assignments should be drawn from either the national Common Core State Standards for Literacy in History/Social Studies, Science, and Technical Subjects, or from related grade-level state reading and writing standards.) A triad of one content standard, one reading standard, and one writing standard lends relevance to the thinking work students are asked to complete.

- **Step 2:** Determine which informational texts and documents will be used to drive the work.

- **Step 3:** Determine the content knowledge that will guide the development of students' written assignment.

- **Step 4:** Determine which writing product best suits the learning expectations for this assignment.

- **Step 5:** Design a prompt that surpasses basic recall of information and instead engages students in higher-level thinking. Strong writing prompts, along with reading and writing standards to support content standards, can help create engaging literacy assignments in all academic discipline and career pathway classes.

Examples of Literacy-Based Assignment Prompts

The prompts presented here were developed by the Literacy Design Collaborative, which offers templates to guide teachers in writing stronger literacy-based assignments. (See Appendix H at www.ascd.org/CareerTechEdTools for additional prompts.) A full overview of the process can be found at this link: https://ldc-production-secure.s3.amazonaws.com/resource_files/files/000/000/045/original/LDCBrief1-FillinTask_Final_0.pdf.

Consider the following sets of high school prompts and identify those that explicitly define the task, explain what is sought by the teacher, and help students understand what elements their final product should include.

From an English language arts class:

- Example 1: Write an essay comparing and contrasting elements of *Animal Farm* with the Russian Revolution of 1917.
- Example 2: After reading George Orwell's *Animal Farm*, "Totalitarianism," and "Revolutions in Russia," write a literary analysis in which you analyze how Orwell uses allegory to depict key events from the Russian Revolution of 1917. Support your discussion with evidence from the text(s).

From a health services career class:

- Example 1: Write an essay explaining the stages of life and the aging process.
- Example 2: After researching informational texts on human growth from conception to death, write a brochure for a target audience in which you define life stages and explain key changes throughout the aging process. Support your discussion with evidence from the text(s). What conclusions or implications can you draw?

The PLBA action team should reflect on this question: *How will the teachers in our school learn to write higher-level assignment prompts that link content standards to writing and reading standards?* There are no quick fixes. Short, one-time professional development events will build neither principals' nor teachers' capacities to make the necessary instructional shifts in ways that will advance students' mastery of content and their literacy skills.

Spreading the use of literacy-based assignments across a school takes time and commitment. In middle and secondary schools, a core group of lead teachers from each content area—supported by a strong principal and guided by an external professional with a strong literacy background—can help build success. This investment has a return that schools cannot afford to pass up: designing literacy-based assignments within all discipline areas in middle and high school will provide the higher-level learning needed to prepare more students, especially those from traditionally marginalized backgrounds, for career and postsecondary success.

The Impact of PLPs on Classroom Experiences and Achievement

Can the powerful literacy practices *really* help more students succeed in science, math, social studies, and CTE courses? The Southern Regional Education Board surveyed nearly 700 teachers who had participated in two full years of professional development to implement powerful literacy-based practices, to determine their perceptions of the impact of literacy-based assignments. Here's what they found.

Teachers who believed literacy-based assignments were engaging students in deeper learning were more likely to implement such assignments with fidelity and experience student achievement gains. Use of literacy-based assignments was greatest among teachers who said they received strong support from their principals, and principal involvement was positively correlated with the spread of literacy-based assignments across a school. In fact, principal support was the only common *must-have* ingredient in efforts to spread the use of higher-level learning assignments in these schools—which speaks to the influence principals have over teacher behaviors.

A survey of students whose teachers had received varying levels of training in implementing literacy-based assignments found a clear correlation between teacher preparation, years of implementation, and student engagement. More specifically, the more preparation teachers received and the greater their familiarity with using literacy-based assignments to engage students in higher-level learning, the more students perceived that their own classroom experiences were linked to higher-level learning and to greater achievement.

It takes well-focused and sustained professional development to drive up achievement and spark transformation around literacy-based assignments. Short-term staff development efforts with weak follow-up consistently fail.

Supportive district and school leadership, and an assigned literacy coach, are key to successful, schoolwide implementation of literacy-based assignments. When principals recognize outstanding early adopters, attend professional development sessions, and support teachers with time to meet and plan literacy-based assignments, the level of student engagement and achievement increases.

The need for supportive leadership extends to teacher leaders as well. Success increases when early adopting teachers participate in three years of professional development and collaborate with other teachers in designing literacy-based assignments. **And fidelity of implementation improves when principals and teacher leaders use classroom observation information, examples of student work, classroom and external assessment data, and student survey information to adjust professional development and model success to other teachers.**

Evidence from the field demonstrates the impact of powerful literacy practices. Here are some examples:[133]

- After two years of professional development to assist teachers in preparing literacy-based assignments in English language arts and social studies, Eddy Middle School—a majority-minority school in Columbus, Georgia—saw significant jumps in their 6th, 7th, and 8th grade scores on criterion-referenced competency tests in reading, English language arts, and social studies.[134]

- Thanks to a USDOE Investing in Innovation (i3) grant, thousands of teachers from New York City and the Los Angeles Unified School District received training from the Literacy Design Collaborative (LDC). These teachers implemented literacy-based assignments across more than 100 schools serving predominantly disadvantaged students, with the following results:

  o In both districts, middle school students exposed to literacy-based instruction in English language arts, social studies/history, and science showed statistically significant learning gains and large positive effect sizes over a matched comparison pair of students, controlling for prior student, teacher, and school performance, and student demographics.

  o As reported by an independent evaluator, the quasi-experimental study showed that among Los Angeles students who received the ideal dosage of literacy-based instruction, the "effect sizes translated to a striking 9.4 months of additional learning compared to similar peers."[135] Even among the average middle school students who received any literacy-based instructional assignments, the effect was equivalent to 4.1 months of learning.

  o New York City students whose teachers were just in their first year of literacy-based training saw remarkable growth in English language arts test scores, translating to nearly 7 months of additional learning over matched-pair, control students.[136]

Gains of such magnitude are rare for an educational intervention. In both New York City and Los Angeles, these powerful results occurred when students' English language arts, science, and social studies/history teachers were supported by the Literacy Design Collaborative—meaning they followed LDC's optimal implementation model. When students received instruction from multiple teachers engaged in the LDC-supported professional learning, the results for students were multiplicative. For more information and news about the latest results, contact the LDC (ldc.org).

A Theory of Action for Implementing Literacy-Based Assignments

After the PLBA action team identifies gaps in literacy readiness, determines the root causes of these gaps, researches best practices for closing the gaps, and identifies the instructional shifts needed to implement literacy-based assignments across the curriculum, the team develops a theory of action ("if/then" statements) to achieve their goal.

The team will need to consider action statements that are specific to the desired goals and the school and district setting. Here are some examples:

If . . .

- Schools or districts support the development of a local literacy coach . . .
- Four successful middle school teachers and four high school teachers—English, social studies, science, and career pathway/exploratory—are engaged in becoming early adopters of literacy-based assignments . . .
- Early adopters, a local literacy coach, and the principal participate in extended professional development, and each teacher is supported to design and use at least six literacy-based assignments in their first year of implementation . . .
- Principals and literacy coaches receive special training on using a classroom observation rubric to evaluate implementation of literacy-based assignments . . .
- The principal and a member of the PLBA team visit classrooms four times each year to observe implementation of literacy-based assignments, provide feedback, and use observations to design the next round of professional development . . .
- Early adopting teachers are given time to meet with other teachers to spread implementation of literacy-based assignments and discuss lessons learned . . .
- Schools administer a student survey to gauge students' perceptions about the implementation of literacy-based assignments . . .
- All other core academic, CTE, and exploratory teachers participate in intensive professional development to implement literacy-based assignments over three years, and receive in-classroom observations and feedback . . .
- The PLBA team regularly collects data on improvements in classroom grades, exams, and student work, as well as assessment data (e.g., state exams, the SAT, the ACT, WorkKeys) to identify areas needing further improvement . . .

then over three years, the school should expect to see the spread of literacy-based assignments and strategies effectively in most classrooms and should witness significant increases in the percent of students meeting literacy-readiness and content standards for high school, postsecondary studies, and careers.

Powerful Literacy Assignments: Practical Steps Schools Can Take Now

Districts and school that are not ready to make a full commitment to high-quality literacy-based assignments across the curriculum can begin with a few key actions to improve literacy achievement:

- In each course, assign grade-level texts and documents for all students to read; assign each student responsibility for sharing with other team members and with the class information they gleaned from the reading; and have students write an analysis of the document, based on the teacher's specifications, and receive feedback from their team members.

- Ask each student to read at least one nonfiction book of their choosing each semester, related to the subject being studied, and prepare a written report or presentation meeting the specifications set by the teacher.

- Ask teachers to use the literacy design template for assignments presented in Appendix H to advance students' comprehension of grade-level texts and their ability to express their understanding orally and in writing.

Summing Up and Looking Ahead

Advanced literacy skills in reading, writing, speaking, and listening are essential for 21st century jobs, civic engagement, and everyday personal life. Yet few teachers outside English language arts are equipped to create literacy-based assignments. Training teachers across the curriculum to develop such assignments using the powerful literacy practices outlined in this chapter can lead to improvements in students' content knowledge as well as their literacy skills, thus advancing their readiness for their post–high school experience.

Chapter 7 presents an overview of how middle school and 9th grade teams can work together to have more students leave 8th grade ready to complete a true college-ready academic core and a rigorous career pathway or academic concentration in high school.

7

Building Successful Transitions into High School

Many students enter today's high schools unprepared to succeed in challenging courses, and many graduate unprepared for a career or postsecondary studies. To change this outcome, middle and high school leaders must work together to accelerate student learning in literacy and mathematics, especially in grades 6 to 9.

As transition teams determine the percentage of your students entering high school prepared for *true* college preparatory courses, consider this national context from the 2019 National Assessment of Educational Progress.[137] Assuming that scores in the midrange between Basic and Proficient translate to readiness for college prep courses in 9th grade, about half of the nation's students entering 9th grade were not prepared to become independent learners and read grade-level texts and documents in college prep science, social studies, English language arts, and rigorous career pathway courses. And half had not developed the mathematical reasoning and understanding necessary to succeed in college prep Algebra I or to perform the kinds of mathematical operations required in science and advanced career pathway classes. Despite much work by schools and educators to address racial achievement gaps, in 2019 there continued to be major differences in the percentages of white (55 percent), Hispanic (30 percent), and Black (25 percent) students demonstrating readiness for challenging college prep high school courses. Hispanic and Black students now make up a significant portion of the high school population in the United States, and middle schools must work even harder to ensure they are receiving the types of high-quality educational experiences that can eliminate these gaps.[138]

These astonishing NAEP percentages clearly show why many students who are behind academically never catch up in high school—leading to outcomes after high school that betray students' own hopes and dreams, affecting everything from the nation's economy to health care costs and social stability. This impact is why strengthening the transition from middle to high school matters more than we often realize. It truly affects students' lives and the overall outlook for communities and even the nation.

Major Causes for Gaps in High School Readiness

Students' own words can reveal a lot about why so many are entering high school ill-prepared for success. Through decades of school improvement work with SREB, I often interviewed groups of students during our in-depth reviews of middle and high schools. Here's a sampling of the insightful comments they offered when I asked them about the rigor of their courses and how they would improve their schools:

- "We're given worksheets—no comparison questions or anything like that."

- When most students in a group of 8th graders agreed that they were prepared for college preparatory high school English, one girl immediately challenged that statement: "Are you kidding?" she said. "Have you seen our numbers? If we're passing 'rigorous' English, it's because our teachers are making it too easy."

- "Being assigned to a low-level track course is like a black hole. You never get out."

- "In this class, we don't write essays. We're the dumb class. Students in other classes write them. I wonder why we don't. I wish our class was more challenging."

- "We don't need so many different levels of English and mathematics. Why not offer advanced English and math and expect all students to work hard? Have the ones who aren't doing well go to special sessions for extra help."

I would hear these kinds of comments over and over from students at many schools. The students could recognize when they were in classes with low expectations, with assignments that failed to engage them in the higher-level learning they needed to succeed in a college prep curriculum. In other words, students can see how they are sidelined by these school and classroom sorting practices. In many schools I visited, students got stuck in low-level tracks and eventually realized they had no hope of "learning" their way into higher-level courses. This situation is nothing less than tragic and discriminatory—and schools can and must change these practices.

The quality and rigor of students' classroom experiences matter. Middle school and 9th grade students want challenging learning experiences that engage them in a productive struggle and that allow them to use their social and emotional skills, talents, interests, and motivation to complete a meaningful learning task. Students deserve this opportunity. In fact, research clearly shows that most students—*once they are engaged*—respond well to accelerated learning opportunities. And they rarely have anything good to say about low-level, boring courses that lead nowhere.

Addressing these issues requires teachers, principals, and others to design assignments that engage students in higher-level cognitive learning experiences—lessons that students can relate to their own lives, in which they work in teams and learn from each other, and from which they learn to apply the habits of mind that characterize responsible learners.[139]

High schools, for their part, cannot continue to accept as a given the relatively low levels of achievement and skills many students bring to the 9th grade. Doing so perpetuates a system that widens rather than closes the gap between their performance and career- and college-readiness standards.

Without a joint effort by middle and high schools to ensure students arrive at high school prepared to succeed, many schools will never achieve the goals of graduating 95 percent of students entering the 9th grade and having 90 percent graduate from high school truly ready for postsecondary education, careers, or both. *The good news:* I know that the strategies outlined here can help solve this problem. They have worked successfully in many schools that admitted the problem and embraced them with fidelity.

What Schools Can Do to Improve the Transition from Middle School to 9th Grade

How can schools adopt approaches to make sure students are ready for rigorous high school courses, ultimately preparing them for any path they choose after high school? Two important steps in the process are forming a transition action team and developing a statement of need.

Form a Transition Action Team

District, school, teacher, and counselor leaders can form a middle to high transition (MHT) action team for the school district or for one high school and its feeder middle schools. The MHT action team's objective is to develop a plan that

- Provides accelerated literacy and mathematics instruction in grades 6, 7, 8, and 9, with extended time and support for students who need it.

- Identifies rising 9th graders who could succeed in challenging college-ready courses in 9th grade if they were assigned to the right teachers and received intensive, unconditional support.

- Identifies rising 9th graders who have major achievement deficits and will need extra time and extensive support to succeed in college preparatory English language arts, social studies, algebra, and science courses and a rigorous career pathway course.

Central to this plan will be *a redesigned schedule* to provide extended time and assistance to those needing extra support—and ensuring that students develop the habits of independent and responsible learners—so that at least 95 percent of students earn enough credits during their 9th grade year to successfully transition to 10th grade.

The MHT action team needs to establish a close partnership between 9th grade and middle school educators to reduce the percentages of students entering high school unprepared for challenging studies. I am not naïve about the long-standing blame game that can exist between middle and high school educators. The MHT action team will need to be straightforward in examining the attitudes of educators on both sides of the "wall" and finding a balanced approach to moving forward.

Members of the MHT action team should include the high school principal or assistant principal, a counselor, and lead English language arts, mathematics, science, and career pathway teachers. From the primary feeder middle school, the team should include a principal, a counselor, and English language arts, mathematics, science, and career exploratory teachers. The team may also include a concerned parent, a key leader from the district office, or an outside facilitator with expertise in middle to high school transition. Educators who have been successful teachers at both the middle and high school levels can bring important perspectives to the team.

Prepare a Statement of Need

To increase the percentages of students across all socioeconomic status (SES) and racial/ethnic groups who are on pace to graduate from high school and graduate college-ready, career-ready, or both, the MHT action team will need to determine a baseline and prepare a statement of need. In addition to data gathered by the data, accountability, and policy action team (as described in Chapter 3), this information should include the percentages of students who

- Are ready at the end of the 7th and 8th grades for challenging college preparatory courses.

- Need extended time and support to succeed in a college prep course of study in 9th grade.
- Need a proven teacher, intensive support, and extended time to complete college prep English language arts and Algebra I by the end of 9th grade.

Making these determinations involves studying 7th and 8th grade assessment data, as well as indicators such as student grades, attendance, and discipline issues. The MHT action team should also monitor annual increases in the percentages of students enrolled in and completing four truly college preparatory courses in 10th grade.

The MHT action team should also compile information around the following questions:

1. Which sequence of courses in 9th grade represents the true college preparatory curriculum? What are the indicators currently used to place students in the college prep courses (e.g., performance on state exams, performance in key 7th and 8th grade courses, teacher recommendations)?

2. Based on your high school's current indicators for enrolling students into college prep courses, how closely do the students chosen for these courses reflect the socioeconomic and racial demographics of the entire incoming 9th grade class? How might you modify your indicators to select an additional 25 percent (or more) to be mainstreamed into college prep courses in 9th grade? Would such an approach increase the percentage of low-SES or minority students who pursue this level of study?

3. Challenge yourself to look at this possibility differently and face your own potential biases: How do the learning experiences of students in grades 6 through 8 who fail to meet readiness indicators for college prep courses in grade 9 differ from students who meet your indicators with regard to types of assignments given, courses taken, and the experience and strengths of their teachers? (Additional questions that may be useful can be found in Chapter 3.)

After analyzing these and other data, the MHT action team must determine the root causes underlying gaps in students' readiness for a true college preparatory high school curriculum. The team must investigate and determine its blind spots by analyzing data and information collected around key questions such as these:

- How are the assignments and classroom assessments given to *prepared* students different from assignments and assessments given to *unprepared* students in grades 6 through 9?

- Are students in some classes more often engaged in meaningful higher-level learning than students in other classes? How and why?

- What are the differences in years of experience and education levels of the teachers assigned to classes with the best-prepared students compared with teachers whose classes are unprepared for high school?

- How do student-teacher ratios compare between teachers in classes with more students performing below grade level and teachers of advanced courses?

- Do teachers in the middle grades and grade 9 plan collaboratively by grade level and develop challenging and relevant assignments that all teachers can use to engage all students in learning experiences aligned to grade-level standards?

- If your school predominantly serves students of color or those from low-income families, and if many students' parents did not complete postsecondary studies, does your school receive more funding for extended-time support than schools that serve primarily middle- or higher-income families? Is extended-time funding used effectively, and is the resulting program effective in engaging students in grade-level relearning experiences?

The transition team also should determine the causes for the blind spots in school and classroom practices in grades 6 to 9 that perpetuate a continuing supply of students who did not have access to a challenging and meaningful curriculum that prepares them for college and careers.

The resulting analyses by the MHT action team can help schools recognize that the best instruction and assignments given to the best students must be given to *all* students—with extended time and support needed by some to achieve at a higher level. Otherwise, there is little hope that schools will significantly increase the percent of historically underserved students who can meet the bold goals and become successful in postsecondary studies and careers.

This I believe: If I were asked to underscore the most passionate personal belief I have shared in this book, I would paraphrase a statement by one of the 20th century's great educators, Arthur E. Wise: **"We must help our neighbors and elected officials understand that unless we provide more equitable educational opportunities [including in middle school and 9th grade], many of our children will be doomed to a jobless future, and our nation will suffer civic and economic losses."**[140] The MHT action team can strive to become the advocate for this cause.

The Major Shifts Needed to Achieve Bold Goals

After analyzing readiness gaps and possible root causes, the MHT action team then identifies best school and classroom practices in grades 6 to 9 for raising more students to college- and career-readiness standards in literacy and mathematics. These practices should be built around replacing low-level assignments with higher-level learning in which students find meaning and purpose. Here are some examples:

- **Place all students in courses aligned with college- and career-readiness standards,** and schedule time for extended support for students to meet grade-level expectations.

- **Expect all students to read grade-level text and documents**—and give them a reason to persist in understanding such texts. Prepare and expect teachers (academic, career exploratory, career pathway) to frequently use literacy-based assignments to engage students in researching, reading grade-level texts to accomplish a personal task, and expressing their understanding orally and in writing. (See Chapter 6 for strategies.)

- **Implement the powerful math instructional practices** outlined in Chapter 5 to engage students in real-world and abstract multistep math problems—problems that advance their reasoning powers and their ability to apply math concepts in a range of situations and contexts.

- **Provide students with higher-level, relevant assignments** related to their future goals and interests, and then provide them with the extra time and support needed to complete these assignments to high school readiness levels. Students become more motivated and persist in completing assigned tasks when learning matters to them—and when they know that their teachers believe they are capable of doing the work and that the school is prepared to provide any support they need.

- **Move from teacher isolation to collaborative team planning** in the middle grades and 9th grade. Connect grade-level math, English language arts, science, and social studies assignments to project-based assignments in STEM and career pathway courses.

- **Replace predominantly teacher-centered instruction with instructional practices that engage teams of students in a productive struggle** to complete their assignments. The teacher's role becomes one of facilitator, asking probing questions and enabling students to take ownership of assignments.

Actions That Help to Shift School and Classroom Practices

How can schools adopt approaches to make sure students are ready for truly rigorous high school courses, ultimately preparing them for any path they choose after high school? This section reviews several proven practices used by many high schools and middle schools participating in SREB's school improvement network. These practices help lower-performing students succeed in college prep courses. (See the Spotlight story about Polytech High in Chapter 3 for what these actions look like in 9th grade.)

Make Sure Students Take the Right Courses

Numerous SREB reports compared career/technical student achievement across high schools with similar demographic profiles. These reports revealed that schools making the greatest gains in achievement had significantly increased the percentage of students taking college prep English, four college prep math credits (including Algebra I and higher), and at least three college prep science and social studies credits.[141]

Provide Students with Rigorous, Project-Based Assignments

As Chapter 4 shows, there is ample evidence that providing rigorous project-based assignments in career pathway courses results in higher percentages of students meeting college-readiness standards. The middle school project-based exploratory courses organized around STEM and other emerging career fields described in Chapter 9 can similarly engage students in rigorous assignments that require them to apply literacy, math, and science concepts and skills to complete their projects.

Provide Teachers with Intensive, Classroom-Based Professional Development

Extended, classroom-based professional development can drastically affect school-wide adoption of proven practices. Chapters 5 and 6 provide evidence that such a professional learning model can enable teachers to implement powerful classroom practices and assignments that advance students' readiness for high school and post-secondary studies.

Adopt or Develop Transitional "Readiness Courses" Built Around Literacy-Based Assignments and Powerful Math Practices

Well-designed literacy-readiness courses for 8th or 9th grades can build students' capacity to read texts in college prep academic and rigorous career pathway courses and put more students on track to graduate from high school ready for college, careers, or both. The intent of such a course is to engage students in reading and analyzing informational texts about history, science, and technical subjects, as well as fictional texts. In an 8th grade literacy-readiness course, students learn to develop, organize, and defend their ideas and to increase their critical thinking and communication skills (both written and verbal). In short, such a course helps prepare students for the rigor of high school studies.

To improve mathematics readiness, schools should develop or adopt a mathematics course in 8th or 9th grade that uses the powerful math practices described in Chapter 5 to prepare more students for college prep Algebra I. The course must emphasize students' understanding of math concepts rather than just the memorization of formulas. Students should learn how to solve real-world, complex, multistep problems and apply critical-thinking skills to complete assignments. This course provides schools with an early-intervention strategy to reach unprepared students and get them back on track before or early in high school.

One example of such courses has proven successful in several Southern states: the high school literacy- and math-readiness courses developed by SREB in collaboration with state leaders, master teachers, and higher education literacy specialists as part of a long-term project supported by the Bill & Melinda Gates Foundation.[142] (For more on this and related courses, see www.sreb.org/publication/readiness-courses-preparing-students-college-and-careers.)

A curriculum director from one Southern state described the effects of the math-readiness course:

> Teachers like the high school math-readiness course because it is different from traditional math instruction. It engages students in a productive struggle to solve complex problems. It results in teachers using a more balanced approach to math instruction by having students use fewer worksheets and spend more time solving complex problems with the teacher serving as a facilitator.

A large school district in Mississippi began to teach the math-readiness course in all district high schools, as a stand-alone, 90-minute block scheduled course in the first semester of 9th grade. Students chosen for this course had low scores on 8th grade statewide math assessments and average grades below 70 percent in math.

Students who previously had not done well in math were more engaged in this class and persisted in solving difficult problems; they learned to "talk" mathematics with one another. Students enjoyed the math-readiness class because they were actively engaged in learning during the entire class period.

In the beginning (as we might expect), students preferred that the teacher give them the exact process for solving the problem. But in time, they took more ownership of their work and gained confidence in their ability to think through and solve problems and justify their answers. Students failing to demonstrate mastery of the course standards were provided extra time and intensive relearning experiences until they mastered the material.[143]

How did participating schools change their classroom practices after launching the course? Teachers in other math classes began to adopt some of the key strategies from the readiness courses, such as providing students with a pre-assessment before a math skill is introduced, assigning multistep word problems, and having students working in teams at times and independently at other times.[144]

Provide Time for Extended Support

Develop a school schedule with added time for students in 8th and 9th grades who need more time to complete grade-level assignments in 8th grade, and in college prep English language arts and Algebra I in 9th grade. **Quality relearning experiences are essential until students demonstrate at least B-level work on the expected knowledge and skills.** This observation from Robert Lynn Canady, professor emeritus at the University of Virginia, is worth noting: "When learning is the variable, time is the constant. When learning becomes a constant, then time must become the variable."[145]

Simply extending course time for students, however, does not necessarily lead to significant achievement gains. When some schools doubled the amount of time students spent in Algebra I, for example, achievement did not rise because instruction was dominated by the use of worksheets designed to help students only learn a procedure rather than understand how the procedure could be applied to solve problems in a number of different contexts. Additional time can produce positive results, but only when it is focused, assessment-based, and personal.[146]

Schools can consider a variety of options for extending learning time:

A pre-elective option for students whose assessments reveal large deficits in the skills necessary for success in college prep courses in English language arts, Algebra I, science, and social studies in 9th grade. Seventh and 8th grade students earning low *C*s and *D*s or failing grades in English or math most likely will not be prepared for college prep courses in 9th grade. Proven readiness courses in literacy and math can be offered as pre-elective options in either 8th or 9th grade. However, some students' skill levels may require such readiness courses to be offered in extended class periods so they can receive the support they need to succeed.

A parallel scheduling option that provides time for academic support in conjunction with students' regular courses. This is a good option for students who demonstrate on pre-assessments that they have mastered sufficient skills to benefit from college prep courses but need temporary, parallel support to address some of the specific skills they are still missing. For example, students with gaps in reading comprehension and analyzing grade-level texts in English, science, social studies, and career pathway classes could be enrolled in a parallel support class every other day, giving them additional time to complete literacy-based assignments and express their understanding both orally and in writing.

Students who need additional math skills when leaving 8th grade could be enrolled in a college prep Algebra I course and scheduled into a parallel class on alternate days, with relearning experiences based on their teachers' individual assessments. These strategies can extend beyond 9th grade, as well, as many students will continue to need additional support in 10th and 11th grades to reach the goal of 95 percent of students completing a full college preparatory curriculum.[147]

An intensive summer school for 8th graders with low grades and achievement levels on state exams in reading and mathematics. A four-week, six-hours-per-day, fast-paced mix of learning experiences can increase the percentage of students ready to succeed in college prep courses in 9th grade. The design for an intensive summer learning experience should engage students for about one hour each day to

- Read 9th grade–level informational texts in each core academic discipline and in technical fields and express written and oral understanding, as teachers provide guidance in key reading and writing strategies.

- Solve abstract and real-world math problems requiring the use of math concepts necessary for Algebra I.

- Work on a miniproject each week in a CTE lab, conducting research and designing a plan for completing the miniproject while successfully applying one or more essential math concepts.

In addition to these daily lessons, students participate in a 45-minute math and literacy lab that is coplanned and delivered by the English, math, and CTE teachers. In this lab, students

- Learn and apply the core habits of success in setting career and educational goals based on an assessment of student interest, aptitudes, and learning style, and from field trips and other experiences.

- Work in small groups to reduce gaps in literacy skills.

- Analyze and present data in a variety of formats.

- Use essential math concepts and skills to solve problems that they will encounter in different career pathway classes.

Each week, students update their portfolio summarizing in their own words what they learned, the study skills they used, new insights gained about themselves, and specific skill gaps they need to address and how they plan to do it. Students also should have a weekly field trip to a community college and a business or government organization to learn about the many careers in these settings and the education required for those fields.[148]

These strategies work. For instance, as a consequence of a summer program and extra help and extended time throughout the school year, Tri-County Regional Vocational Technical High School in Massachusetts in just one school year raised the percentages of students passing the Massachusetts Comprehensive Assessment System (MCAS) tests from 41 percent to 69 percent in English and from 40 percent to 65 percent in math.[149]

Provide Relearning Opportunities

Success options and *credit recovery* are two relearning experiences that can help students meet college- and career-readiness standards, as shown in Alan M. Blankstein's book *Failure Is Not an Option: Six Principles That Advance Student Achievement in Highly Effective Schools.*[150] In other words, if students are not succeeding, it is the school's responsibility to engage students in relearning experiences to help them master the skills they need to advance. Failure is literally not a choice students can make.

This "success option" for all students works in schools that commit themselves to it. SREB surveyed 342 high schools and 99 middle schools that had implemented the success option, and those schools reported numerous benefits from extended-time relearning sessions. Students earned higher grades and were more motivated in school than before. The schools also reported stronger communication with parents, higher rates of parent satisfaction, fewer course failures, and increased math and reading achievement and graduation rates.[151]

The schools most frequently applied the success option to three college prep courses—Algebra I, 9th grade English, and science—as alternatives to lower-level courses. Sixty percent of the schools that implemented the option for three years or longer reported "their primary means of extra help was teachers tutoring students in small-group sessions who had common deficits." The schools commonly used extended time—before, during, and after the school day, and sometimes on Saturdays—to support students in relearning experiences. Teachers were more open to the success option *if they believed their primary mission was to prepare each student for his or her next step in education.* This approach conveyed to students that their effort mattered, and that with continued support and persistent effort, they could master the material.[152]

In another approach, Henry W. Grady High School in Atlanta, Georgia, used *credit recovery* as its primary strategy, creating a series of credit-recovery courses called "Let's Do It Again" for subjects in which students were required to pass state exams to graduate. The credit-recovery courses provided 90-minute, standards-focused sessions for nine consecutive Saturdays. The result: more than 90 percent of participating students recovered the credits they needed for graduation.[153]

Another example is Springdale, Arkansas, where schools taught and retaught students until they learned at least 80 percent of the required content in Algebra I. When the program began, 42 percent of students scored below the 50th percentile in mathematics on the Stanford 9 exam given at the beginning of 10th grade. Five years later, only 27 percent scored below the 50th percentile. This gain occurred while this community experienced steady growth in the enrollment of students from families that spoke little English and who often struggled more than students had in the past.[154]

Establish a Culture of Connected Learning

Combining an interdisciplinary approach, the success option, and "looping" in 7th and 8th grades also can increase the percentage of students completing college prep courses in 9th grade. *Looping* is a strategy in which the same teachers stay with students for two or more consecutive years. Students might be chosen for looping when their grades or achievement on classroom or standardized assessments at the end of 6th grade suggest they will not succeed in 9th grade college prep courses without an accelerated curriculum and extra support.

Northwest Rankin Middle School in Jackson, Mississippi, used the "triple threat" (looping, the success option, and interdisciplinary teaching) beginning in 7th grade to prepare more students for high school. In the first year using this approach, the school raised 7th graders' math achievement from a grade level of 5.5 to 8.6 and reading from a grade level of 7.1 to 9.6. Similar results were achieved for 8th graders. After one semester, 58 of the program's 65 students earned grades of "incomplete," yet after the entire year, only two students were not promoted to the next grade. Expecting students to meet higher standards, along with the additional support from educators who believed the students could learn more, accounted for the significantly higher achievement during the second semester.[155]

Another example comes from Pasadena, Maryland, where an interdisciplinary curriculum at George Fox Middle School raised 8th grade achievement significantly and the state recognized the school for improved performance. Students selected for the new approach had below-average grades, low achievement on state tests, and a history of past course failures—and were considered at risk of failing again. Forty-four students took two academic classes every day for one hour and 45 minutes each. One class offered integrated mathematics and science, and the second integrated English language arts and social studies. Each pair of academic teachers met daily to plan connected lessons that reinforced each other and addressed students' gaps in knowledge and skills.[156]

The literacy- and math-readiness courses described earlier in this chapter represent another approach to building a connected learning environment. Teachers have planning time each day or week to create connected, project-based learning experiences in math and science in connection with STEM exploratory classes.

The same concept can be used in 9th grade: both math and science teachers, and English language arts and social studies teachers, can team up with career pathway teachers to develop major projects that require students to use their literacy and math skills successfully. These courses would target students needing considerable support to successfully complete college prep Algebra I, science, English language arts, and social studies. (See Chapter 4 for details on planning assignments that connect academics and CTE.)

Regardless of the options used, choosing the right teachers for this work is crucial. They need a record of successfully working with challenged students, and they need the time and collaborative skills to work with teachers from other discipline areas to develop connected learning experiences.

A Theory of Action for Building Successful Transitions to High School

After identifying gaps in high school readiness, determining the root causes of these gaps, researching best practices for closing the gaps, and identifying the instructional shifts needed, the MHT action team develops a theory of action for achieving the 9th grade transition goals described at the beginning of this chapter.

The evidence of success is out there in the real world. *Schools can have 95 percent of 9th graders complete a college prep core successfully.* That said, in every success story I have seen, middle and high schools made the commitment to provide additional support for each student who needs it, so that virtually all rising 10th graders are prepared to succeed in subsequent years of high school and beyond.

How can you know your school is heading for success? Consider this if/then exercise:

If . . .

- School and teacher leaders commit to enrolling all students in grades 6 through 8 in courses that lead them into college prep courses in 9th grade . . .

- The school provides intensive professional development for all academic, career pathway, and exploratory teachers in grades 6 through 10 to use literacy-based assignments (as described in Chapter 6) with defined levels of content and literacy standards required to earn at least a *B* . . .

- The school provides intensive professional development to mathematics teachers in grades 6 through 10 (as described in Chapter 5) to use a balanced approach in creating assignments with defined levels of expectations to earn at least a *B* . . .

- The school adopts proven readiness courses in literacy and mathematics for 8th or 9th grades, designed around literacy-based and powerful math practices, that require students to learn and apply literacy and math skills . . .

- Students who are not yet ready for college prep courses in 9th grade are enrolled in a rich, intensive summer learning experience . . .

- Schools adopt a schedule that provides time for extended, intensive support for students, with quality relearning experiences—and if the schedule provides teachers within and across disciplines with collaborative planning to design connected assignments and assessments . . .

- The teachers assigned to those classes in 8th and 9th grades with higher percentages of students of color or from low-income families have at least the same level of experience and student-teacher ratios as teachers in advanced-level courses in the upper grades . . .

then significant progress can be made each year toward having more students succeed in college prep courses in 9th grade.

The MHT action team should be responsible for creating the plan *and* for monitoring progress every 45 days and identifying the adjustments and actions that might be necessary. The MHT action team must develop the specific strategies that will ultimately lead to 95 percent of students exiting 9th grade having successfully completed college prep core academic courses.

Middle to High School Transition: Practical Steps Schools Can Take Now

Schools that may not be ready to adopt a comprehensive set of interventions could consider the following steps to help build momentum:

- Increase the percentage of incoming 9th graders enrolled in true college preparatory courses each year by 15 to 20 percentage points, until you reach at least 95 percent. Provide a parallel-scheduled class for students who need intensive support to meet specified standards and earn a *B*.

- Enroll 8th or 9th grade students with major skills gaps in literacy- and math-readiness courses for an 80- to 90-minute semester block. Provide 45-minute, alternate-day, extended-time courses for those students achieving below a *B* level. Then, in the second semester, enroll students in college prep Algebra I and English language arts, each with an 80- to 90-minute semester block and a 45-minute class for additional support. Enroll students failing to earn a *B* in either English or algebra or both in a summer program to address skills gaps and to achieve a higher grade.

- Enroll all students in a special career and educational development course for the first semester (as described in Chapter 9 at Fort Mill High School). For the second semester, enroll all students in a career pathway class organized around rigorous projects that require literacy and math skills to complete successfully.

Summing Up and Looking Ahead

Proven strategies can help middle and high schools free themselves from outdated practices and modes of thinking that assume many students—too often, students of color or those from low-income families—simply cannot learn at high levels. The strategies rely on extra support and deal with engaging all students in deeper learning that has meaning and purpose. **They call for teachers to collaborate across the disciplines so that students in middle and high school can see how learning is connected to their future aspirations.**

Chapter 8 focuses on strategies for achieving a successful transition from high school by designing the senior year to prepare students for postsecondary studies, a quality career path, or both.

8

Rethinking Senior Year:
A Launching Pad, Not a Rest Stop

The senior year of high school should be a launching pad for students, not a rest stop on their journey toward adulthood. Rather than offering only light schedules or easy courses, the senior year should offer demanding course options that build a seamless transition for every student into postsecondary studies, the workplace, or both. State, district, and school leaders need to develop the fortitude to reshape the senior year, because for too many students, it's not just a party—it's a dead end.

Despite what many educators, parents, and even students might believe, most high school seniors are *not* prepared to succeed in college or the workplace. Fifty-two percent of the U.S. high school graduating class of 2019 took the ACT test, and only 37 percent of those students met at least three of the four ACT benchmarks for college readiness in English language arts, reading, mathematics, and science.[157] Those achievement benchmarks indicate that students have a 50 percent chance of earning a *B* or higher in corresponding courses in their first year of college. The percentages of students meeting three or more of the benchmarks ranged widely across demographic groups: 62 percent of Asian students, 47 percent of white students, 23 of Hispanic students (the nation's fastest-growing group), and 11 percent of Black students.

This breakdown of data doesn't even include the 48 percent of high school seniors who did not take the ACT exam; most are likely to have been even less prepared for life after high school. The upshot: the actual percentage of students ready for careers and postsecondary studies was even lower in 2019 than the 37 percent indicated by the ACT data. Every school *must* do better.

The situation was marginally better for high school students headed straight for the workforce and job training: 41 percent of 2019 ACT test takers scored at the Gold and Platinum levels of the ACT WorkKeys National Career Readiness Certificate—meeting the academic career-readiness benchmarks that the ACT JobPro database shows are required for more than 9 out of 10 jobs today.[158] Another 31 percent would likely earn a Silver-level certificate, preparing them for about 69 percent of jobs profiled on the WorkKeys system, according to ACT.[159]

To summarize, out of all 2019 ACT test takers, a little more than one-third met most of the academic college-readiness benchmarks, and roughly three-fourths met the academic career-readiness benchmarks. Considering that two-thirds of the country's jobs soon will require an advanced career credential or an associate or bachelor's degree,[160] U.S. schools face a major challenge: closing students' academic-readiness gap for careers and postsecondary studies.

The readiness challenge is greatest among marginalized and minoritized learners. Just 9 percent of students in historically underserved minority groups, students from low-income families, and those whose parents did not attend college met three or more of the ACT college-readiness benchmarks.[161] These numbers quite simply are an affront to their future and a call to action for the American education system.

Consider what this situation means for the future of the U.S. workforce. With the demographic changes in society, the majority of students enrolled in many public secondary schools are members of at least one of these historically marginalized groups. Unless we transform high school, the nation faces an even greater gulf between the requirements to qualify for a good-paying job and the foundational and technical skills high school graduates have to meet those requirements.

Root Causes Behind Students' Lack of Readiness

Let's face it: many of us educators and policymakers haven't taken seriously the research showing that public school families overwhelmingly want their children prepared for both jobs and academic paths going forward. Most often we've just made the choice for them.[162]

One major weakness in U.S. schools is students' lack of preparation in math. Only 48 percent of white, 25 percent of Hispanic, and 12 percent of Black students who took the ACT met the math benchmark for postsecondary study and careers. Yet most states and school districts don't require high school students to take a fourth year of math. This omission doesn't make sense. Why can't all students who fail to meet math-readiness standards for college and careers at the end of 11th grade have a special 12th grade math course that engages them in learning a mix of math knowledge and skills essential for both careers and postsecondary studies?

We see the same trends in reading achievement, with less than half of ACT test takers demonstrating the ability to comprehend and analyze complex texts in different academic disciplines considered essential for postsecondary success, and wide gaps between racial groups. In an information-centered economy, the abilities to read, comprehend, analyze materials, and express one's understanding orally and in writing are key factors in postsecondary studies and in eventually earning a middle-class income. Why shouldn't students who fail to demonstrate the ability to read postsecondary-level texts by the end of 11th grade take a specially designed advanced literacy course in the senior year to strengthen their reading comprehension and communication skills?

And even students who seem to be on track for college readiness and are working toward college credit in high school may not be getting the true preparation they need. Although enrollment in dual-credit courses has soared in recent years, these classes don't always help reduce the number of credits still required to earn an advanced credential or degree—and this situation needs to change.[163] As the costs of postsecondary studies continue to rise, why can't high schools and postsecondary institutions blur the lines between grades 12 and 13 to enable students who meet college-readiness benchmarks to earn a full year of college credit toward an advanced career credential, an associate's degree, or a bachelor's degree—at a reduced cost?

As described in Chapter 2, a 2013 study of high school graduates found that nearly half (47 percent) completed neither a true college-ready academic core nor a career focus before graduation. This situation is a policy issue. State and local graduation policies must require demanding options that combine rigorous CTE studies with a college-ready academic core aimed at preparing students for both careers and postsecondary studies. (As described earlier in this book, Camden County Schools, Simpson County Schools, and Polytech High have seen the huge positive impact of moving beyond state requirements for high school graduation.)

The fact that many graduates are simply not prepared academically for postsecondary studies—or trained academically or technically for a job or advanced career studies—is simply unacceptable. **Yet, for many schools, it's been easier to allow students to state an aspirational goal for college and then look the other way, knowing that many students aren't taking the right courses to be prepared. It's easier to allow students to make random course choices, rather than ensuring they are enrolled in a focused, rigorous series of career courses connected to postsecondary studies and good jobs.** This current laissez-faire system amounts to "tracking" by default, creating a culture of inequality (which disproportionately disadvantages students of color and students from lower socioeconomic backgrounds) and leading to lower-level learning experiences for many students within and across schools.[164]

Rethinking the last year of high school to fully prepare every student for their next step in life will send shockwaves through this system. That would be a *bold goal* indeed.

Redesigning the senior year alone cannot completely close these readiness gaps, but it can make a significant difference. How do we know? Because some schools across the nation are doing it. As explained in a report from the Southern Regional Education Board, transforming the senior year "can be a first step in establishing a functional mission policy that schools are to prepare *all* students for postsecondary studies, a career, or both by designing demanding learning experiences in the senior year as the last opportunity to prepare students for postsecondary education and a career *at public expense.*"[165]

In spring 2018, SREB surveyed students from comprehensive high schools and career and technology centers in its school improvement networks about their senior year. On average, a significantly higher percentage of students at career and technology centers than at comprehensive high schools reported that their senior year was preparing them for their next step in education and life.[166] Let's think about what that means.

What Schools Can Do to Improve the Transition to College and Careers

There's a clear path for schools and educators to prepare far more students for college, the workplace, or both. We already know which research-based strategies work. In Chapter 7, we considered the actions required during the transition *into* high school. Now let's look more closely at high school itself.

High schools must take action to get more students ready for their next steps by the end of their junior year. High schools also must rethink the senior year to focus on students who plan to pursue various types of postsecondary studies but don't yet meet the benchmarks in reading and mathematics.

Schools can provide multiple options for students. "Ready" students can opt to complete their first year of postsecondary studies before they graduate from high school. For all other students, the focus of the senior year should be preparation for postsecondary studies and work. The goal should be for at least 90 percent of students to graduate from high school knowing they're college-ready, career-ready, or both. Accomplishing this goal can only be done if all students—especially those who traditionally have been relegated to low-level tracks—have more rigorous academic and career pathway options and support in their senior year.

Establish an Action Team

Begin the effort by establishing a senior-year transition (SYT) action team, and charge the team with creating an action plan to address three objectives:

1. Offer students who meet readiness standards opportunities to earn up to 30 hours of college credit during the senior year.

2. Use 12th grade readiness courses in math and literacy to prepare students not yet meeting readiness standards for postsecondary studies.

3. Provide career pathways in high-demand, high-wage fields and work-based learning experiences—internships and job shadowing—for students not interested in more formal postsecondary studies.

The point is that *every* student should be on a path to success after high school. Many students still don't have the chance to pursue different types of postsecondary education—even though the economy now clearly demands that virtually every student have some level of education or training beyond 12th grade. These students likely will be stuck in low-wage jobs forever. On a broader level, the United States' democracy and economic system are at risk unless every student has the academic, technical, advanced technology, and problem-solving skills now required for most jobs. If you doubt the economic impact of this goal, consider that during the COVID-19 pandemic, 60 percent of American workers with a bachelor's degree could work from home, but only 20 percent of workers with a high school degree or less had that flexibility.[167]

Remember, the senior year can no longer be a rest stop. It must be a launching pad to prepare students for success in postsecondary education and the increasingly complex workplace requirements of the 21st century.

Who should be on the SYT action team? The team will require a mix of both internal and external stakeholders to blur the lines between grades 12 and 13 and to achieve cooperation between public schools, higher education, and employers with different governing boards, policies, and operating norms. Along with educators, it's important that key employers and key postsecondary leaders be a part of the SYT action team, and all members should be committed to building a more meaningful senior year for all students.

Include strong advocates who see an accelerated senior year as the opportunity to do what's best for students, such as key policy and industry leaders, a local college president, and your local school superintendent. These leaders can drive policy changes that benefit your students, securing additional funding for your efforts or ensuring that dual-enrollment college courses count toward your state's high school graduation requirements. It's equally important to have a business and industry leader or workforce advocate involved who knows which high-wage, high-demand fields face shortages of qualified workers and which dual-enrollment courses can help give your students a jumpstart toward an advanced degree or credential.

The team's first task is to determine the percentage of the school's or district's graduates who meet postsecondary and career-readiness (both academic and technical) standards and to analyze the data by demographic and socioeconomic group to focus on the students who need the most support.[168] The report from the school's data, accountability, and policy action team is a good starting point for this analysis. (Also see Chapter 9 for additional data on national high school graduation rates by subgroups.)

The SYT action team can then begin building a stronger transition from high school into postsecondary education and the workforce by asking themselves and others (e.g., policymakers, school and district leaders, teachers, counselors) several important questions:

- Why do so many high school students who aspire to go to college never make it?

- Why do so many high school graduates attend college for one year or less, then fail to return?

- Why do so few students consider community and technical college as viable options for postsecondary study or advanced workplace credentials?

- Why do so few high school students complete a demanding career pathway linked directly to postsecondary studies and middle-class jobs?

The SYT action team must identify the primary root causes preventing their school from redesigning the senior year to give students who are ready a jumpstart on pursuing a college degree or advanced credentials and to prepare other students for a "ready" start toward postsecondary studies, a job, or both.

Determine the Readiness of Rising Seniors for Careers, Postsecondary Studies, or Both

You can't prepare more high school students for success in college and careers unless you know their readiness levels toward the end of their junior year. The SYT action team can help determine students' readiness.

Designate someone on the team to compile baseline data, answering some of the same questions outlined in Chapter 3 (e.g., What percentage of students plan to pursue some type of postsecondary education? What percentage of students then actually enroll? Why do so many students say they're headed to college but haven't taken the right courses?). National data sets on students' readiness for college and careers described in Chapter 9 also can help you.

The SYT action team also should determine the percentage of rising seniors who

- Meet college- and career-readiness standards that qualify them to earn up to 30 hours of college credit during their senior year.

- Plan to pursue postsecondary studies and are *approaching* the readiness benchmarks for reading and math set by the state or postsecondary institutions. Students who plan to pursue postsecondary studies but aren't close to meeting the standards have different needs. (See Chapter 1 for other indicators for being accepted into credit-bearing courses at four-year colleges and two-year community and technical colleges.)

- Don't plan to pursue postsecondary studies but meet academic career-readiness standards as defined in Chapter 1 or other indicators that employers accept.

- Fail to meet the college- and career-readiness benchmarks.

Once the SYT action team compiles and analyzes the data, its primary charge is to develop a three-part action plan to transform the school's senior year:

1. **For "postsecondary-ready" students (those meeting college- and career-readiness benchmarks), start an accelerated learning experience** in which they can earn up to 30 semester hours of college credit. Or ready students can choose to pursue advanced technical or workplace training at a vocational and technical education center, in an organized program of study with an employer, or with a postsecondary institution leading to shortened time to a degree or an advanced credential.

2. **For students *approaching* postsecondary-readiness levels, consider semester-long literacy- and math-readiness courses** that can help them attain specific foundational literacy and mathematics skills necessary for an advanced credential or a degree. If students reach the readiness standards in the first semester of their senior year, they can enroll in credit-bearing postsecondary courses. Students who still don't meet the standards could enroll in readiness courses offered by postsecondary institutions.

3. **For students performing well below college- and career-readiness benchmarks, provide a personalized plan** that includes intensive literacy- and math-readiness courses that lead to their next step

beyond high school. These students include those who say they're going to college but aren't prepared, students who don't plan to pursue postsecondary studies and aren't enrolled in a career pathway, *and* students who are in a career pathway but who lack the academic readiness to advance in a career earning a middle-class income.

The goal is to use the senior year to prepare every high school graduate for the next step—a career, postsecondary studies, or both. The rest of this chapter will help you design these options for students.

Option 1: An Accelerated Senior Year, Leading to a Degree or an Advanced Credential

The SYT action team, along with postsecondary and industry leaders and advocates, can craft a guided-pathway program of study that directly connects the last year of high school to postsecondary studies and a career. Rather than stressing dual enrollment for many students—often without a specific end goal in mind—a guided pathway requires well-thought-out agreement among the high school, the college, and even employers. It also can address the problem of additional time, cost, and credit hours that many students face in pursuing a degree or an industry credential.

At SREB, we learned that states and education systems should set a goal of requiring students to complete around 60 college credit hours to earn an associate's degree and about 120 hours for a bachelor's degree. Without setting such a goal, students' pathways can become filled with duplications and unnecessary steps that cost additional time and money—and do little to solve shortages of well-qualified workers in many high-wage fields.

In one state, for example, leaders and educators successfully reduced students' time-to-degree by about one-third by building a series of "stackable" credentials in nursing. The move was in response to the health industry's complaints that nurses' education journey lacked alignment with the industry's needs and many students were forced to waste time and money as they sought to upgrade their skills and earn degrees. A working committee involving higher education redesigned the courses, enabling students to earn a practical nursing certification, an associate's degree, and then a bachelor's degree in nursing in 136 hours rather than the original 180 hours. Setting 120 credit hours as the initial goal was critical in focusing all parties on the best ways to redesign courses and meet the state nursing board's qualifications for practical nursing certification, the college associate's degree, and a bachelor's degree in nursing.

As they work toward creating such a guided-pathway program of study—leading to an advanced credential or an associate or bachelor's degree—the SYT action team will need to ask and answer the following logistical questions:

- Who will teach the courses that lead to postsecondary credit—qualified high school faculty, postsecondary faculty, or a combination?

- Where will the courses be taught?

- Can structured work-based learning experience count as college credit?

- What criteria will be used to ensure courses are taught for the same number of hours and at the same pace and level of expectations set for college students taking the same courses?

- Will high school teachers use the very same syllabi, instructional materials, and classroom exams as college faculty?

- Who will pay for each course, and how much money can students save by earning up to one year of college credit while in high school?

- What assurances can be offered to students that successfully completing these courses will shorten the time toward a valuable credential or college degree?

- How will advocates ensure that dual-enrollment courses approved for postsecondary credit will also count toward high school graduation?

- Who will design and initiate a communication plan to inform parents, students, and high school and postsecondary faculty and counselors about the pathway?

- Who will create a road map describing the guided-pathway program of study leading to authentic, usable college credits? The road map would show

  o Key high school courses and performance levels that are required in *both* academic and career pathway courses and that students must meet to enroll in the accelerated senior-year program.

  o A sequence and description of each course, leading to 30 semester hours of college credit earned during the senior year.

  o A list of the additional courses (with their descriptions) required to complete an advanced industry credential or an associate or bachelor's degree.

The SYT action team must establish a set of indicators for measuring successful implementation of an accelerated senior-year program. Then it must conduct an annual review of how the plan is working and make modifications as needed.[169]

How a District and a Technical College Built an Advanced Manufacturing Career Pathway

A school district and a technical college in one southern state designed a "stackable" guided-career pathway in Advanced Manufacturing that leads to a NOCTI workforce competency credential by the end of high school. (NOCTI, the National Occupational Competency Testing Institute, provides services and resources for improving workforce preparedness.) The partnership used the SREB Advanced Career Integrated Production Technology curriculum as the high school pathway curriculum, connected to a college-ready core. Students who meet the readiness standards by the end of their junior year can earn at least 19 semester hours of college credit in their senior year toward an electrical engineering technology specialization at the technical college, with the option to continue toward a bachelor's degree in engineering technology.

The school district is located in a major manufacturing center. A manager of a manufacturing plant and the chair of the local workforce board said at the initial planning meeting for the pathway, "We could recruit more qualified workers for the manufacturing sector if we can show students and their parents a pathway to an associate and bachelor's degree."

Employers support the Advanced Manufacturing pathway, and their involvement proved to be a big motivator for student effort and retention. After two years of planning, the college and high school launched four sections of 24 students each in the Advanced Manufacturing pathway. In the second year, two sections of 24 students each registered for the second course, and 96 students registered for four sections of the first course.

Students in the pathway learn how to work together in groups to complete their assigned tasks. With the completion of each project-based assignment, they work toward applying the seven key steps of engineering in their work: (1) identify the need, (2) research the problem, (3) brainstorm possible solutions, (4) select a promising solution using engineering analysis, (5) create a prototype, (6) test the protype, (7) improve and redesign/manufacture a product.

District, high school, and college leaders involved in this project described two of the biggest challenges in their work to help more students earn an advanced credential and a college degree: (1) drawing enough students—having a large enough cohort for a schedule that allows high school advanced manufacturing instructors and English language arts, mathematics, and science teachers to share students and plan connected lessons; and (2) convincing businesses—increasing the number of employers who see the program as valuable and are willing to provide students with a range of workplace learning experiences in high school and beyond and then offer jobs to credentialed students.

Here is the Advanced Manufacturing guided pathway program of study developed by the high school and technical college, in engineering technology:[170]

High School Experience, Option 1:

- College preparatory curriculum, and
- CTE curriculum of Advanced Career Integrated Production Technology (AC-IPT)
  - o Advanced Technology for Design and Production
  - o Systems of Advanced Technology
  - o Mechatronic Systems for Advanced Production
  - o Design for Production of Advanced Products
- NOCTI workforce competency credential/digital badge
- Work-based learning with industry partners
- Graduate from high school meeting state college- and career-readiness standards

High School Experience, Option 2 (for students who are college-ready by the end of the junior year):

- College preparatory curriculum, and
- AC-IPT curriculum
- Dual college-high school enrollment during the senior year (total of 19 credit hours earned):
  - English Composition (Fall, 3 credits)
  - Intro to Engineering Tech (Fall, 3 credits)
  - Algebra (Fall, 3 credits)
  - Engineering Graphics (Spring, 4 credits)
  - Workplace and Technical Communications (Spring, 3 credits)
  - Public Speaking (Spring, 3 credits)

Degree Requirements: Post-High School (48 credit hours)

- General Education Core (9 credit hours)
  - Pre-Calculus (3 credits)
  - Social/Behavioral Science: U.S. or World History (3 credits)
  - Humanities: Art Appreciation (3 credits)
- Program-Specific Core (19 credit hours)
  - Chemistry I and Lab (4 credits)
  - English Literature and Composition (3 credits)
  - Calculus (4 credits)
  - Introduction to Physics I and Lab (4 credits)
  - Introduction to Physics II and Lab (4 credits)
- Electrical Engineering Technology Specialization (20 credit hours)
  - Circuit Analysis I (4 credits)
  - Circuit Analysis II (4 credits)
  - Digital Systems I (4 credits)
  - Calculus II (4 credits)
  - Electronic Circuits I (4 credits)

Sixty-seven total hours (high school and post-high school) for AAS electrical engineering technology specialization. Students may then pursue a bachelor's degree in engineering technology at a college offering an Engineering and Engineering Technology degree.

A Theory of Action for an Accelerated Senior Year for "Ready" Students

The SYT action team should develop a theory of action ("if/then" statements) to achieve a successful launch and continuation of accelerated learning opportunities that reach more students each year. For example,

If . . .

- The higher education governing boards, the state K–12 board of education, the local school board, the participating higher education institution, leading employers, and high school leaders and teachers agree to support the effort . . .

- High school leaders and counselors work collaboratively with postsecondary institutions in orienting faculty, parents, students, and employers to the program's benefits . . .

- Enough students show interest in the guided-pathway program of study to justify a cohort of students for college preparatory academic and career pathway teachers to plan connected learning to help more students meet college-readiness indicators by the end of 11th grade . . .

- The postsecondary institution arranges a senior-year cohort of students taught by the same general education and career pathway teachers, who can help students make connections in their learning . . .

- The SYT action team develops a system of indicators for measuring implementation, uses them to review progress at the end of the first and second semesters each year, and refines the program as necessary . . .

then it will be possible to provide most students who are postsecondary-ready at the end of 11th grade with an accelerated senior year that leads to advanced career credentials and college degrees.

Option 2: Senior-Year Strategies for Students Who Are Approaching Readiness Standards

Next, the SYT action team should develop a plan for students who are *approaching* math and literacy readiness levels for postsecondary and advanced career studies and for students who need more intensive support in learning the foundational skills that are crucial for advanced training and postsecondary studies.

The team can begin by identifying how many students are approaching the ACT's standards or locally set benchmarks, as well as how many are planning to pursue postsecondary studies but need more intensive preparation to meet the readiness standards. (Chapter 1 can help you select indicators to indicate students' readiness for postsecondary studies.) The academic career-readiness indicators may differ for students pursuing a degree versus a specialized credential or certificate.

This is where 12th grade readiness courses come in. The SYT action team can develop its own senior-year readiness courses, or it can adopt existing options such as the senior-year readiness courses developed by SREB in collaboration with higher education, state departments of education, and master teachers. (For more information on these courses, visit www.sreb.org/readiness-courses-literacy-math.)[171] Any readiness course should consistently include assignments aligned with college- and career-readiness standards that postsecondary institutions have agreed are essential for students' success after high school.

The chosen senior-year math-readiness course should emphasize the *understanding* of math concepts, not simply the memorization of formulas. By engaging students in real-world application, the course develops the critical-thinking skills they will use in college and careers. Jennifer L. Curtis, state math supervisor at the North Carolina Department of Public Instruction, offers this observation:

> Teachers and students in North Carolina are finding success with the ready-for-college-transition math courses as they transition from high school to college. The hands-on, conceptual approach to understanding mathematical concepts has benefited students.

The senior-year literacy-readiness course uses a discipline-based literacy approach, emphasizing college-level texts in English and literature, history, and science to improve students' reading skills and understanding of such texts. Students engage in reading comprehension, analysis, and oral and written expression to show their understanding of college-level material. Students learn to organize, develop, and present their ideas orally and in writing on a variety of topics. The course helps high school seniors master the literacy skills they'll need to avoid remedial courses in college and for continued success in postsecondary education and the workplace. The SYT action team can examine the effectiveness of these courses by reviewing three years of data and evidence of increasing levels of student readiness for careers and postsecondary studies.[172]

Mississippi and Oklahoma are among the states that have adopted senior-year literacy- and math-readiness courses. The Mississippi math-readiness course is required of students with ACT math benchmark scores between 15 and 18. The state also has implemented a math-ready "essentials" course for all seniors scoring below 15 on the ACT; it's the same course, but with increased time and support for students to help them meet readiness standards. Oklahoma enrolls students who have taken the ACT and scored between 14 and 18 in math in the state's math-readiness course.

In both states, students who perform well on the math-readiness course are not required to take remedial college math courses. The state higher education commission in Mississippi set a policy that students earning a score of at least 80 in the math-readiness course aren't required to take a college remedial math course, and eight colleges in Oklahoma agreed that students who earned a grade of B or higher in the math-readiness course will enroll directly in credit-bearing math courses.

State mathematics leaders in Mississippi and Oklahoma reported what they liked most about the math-readiness course.[173] Here are representative comments:

- "The average gains on the ACT exam were between two and three points for students who had taken the course, while students who did not take a math course in senior year had a decline in ACT score."
- "The depth and rigor of the curriculum . . . engages students in learning experiences beyond the traditional drill approach to instruction."
- "Students are engaged in problem-based learning in collaboration with other students."
- "Professors have noted that students taking the senior readiness math course have a deeper understanding of mathematics and a good approach to solving math problems."
- "Math teachers have begun to realize you do not need a lower-level math course for students. Rather, you need a rigorous course organized around real problems, and [an] instructional strategy that allows students to take ownership in solving the problem."

State leaders offer the following tips for successfully implementing readiness courses:[174]

- Select highly effective teachers to attend three days of training led by certified master teachers who have taught the course successfully and can engage colleagues in the pedagogical shifts required for unprepared students to become ready for postsecondary studies and careers.
- Have the principal or assistant principal attend the first day of training to understand his or her role in supporting the teachers implementing the course.
- Inform students and parents of the courses' benefits in moving students toward high school graduation, college, and careers.

A Theory of Action for Moving Students from "Approaching" to "Ready"

Similar to the process used to create a new option for "ready" students, the SYT action team should develop a series of "if/then" statements that, if implemented, can result in more unprepared students meeting literacy and mathematics readiness standards by the end of their senior year. The following statements are a good starting point, but the team should develop its own set of statements that are specific to the school and district context.

If . . .

- Unprepared students are enrolled in postsecondary/career-readiness literacy and mathematics courses that engage them in rigorous assignments, using a student-centered pedagogy in which the teacher serves as a facilitator and students are empowered to take ownership of their progress . . .
- School leaders communicate to faculty, counselors, parents, and students about the impact these courses can have on students' preparation for career and postsecondary studies . . .
- School leaders choose energetic teachers open to a new approach to teaching, who have a passion for working with more challenging students . . .
- School leaders support teachers in attending intensive professional development led by a qualified teacher, and also attend the training to support the SYT action team and teachers in implementation of the courses . . .
- Teachers frequently review student work and provide students who are failing to complete work at a satisfactory level with relearning experiences to bring their performance to at least a *B* level through an extended time schedule . . .
- Readiness-course teachers share with other teachers in 9th, 10th, and 11th grades the lessons learned for engaging more students in higher-level learning, resulting in fewer future 11th graders failing to meet readiness standards . . .
- The SYT action team develops a set of indicators for implementing the literacy- and math-readiness courses with fidelity and uses the indicators to observe instruction, review student work, and provide feedback to the teacher every 45 days to improve the course . . .

then it will be possible to significantly increase the percent of high school graduates who graduate ready for postsecondary options.

Option 3: Preparing Other Students for Their Next Steps

Finally, the SYT action team must develop senior-year plans for students who perform well below academic-readiness benchmarks for college and careers. These are students who have not completed four or more courses in a planned, career-focused program of study leading to high-demand, high-wage career fields; met literacy and math career-readiness levels; or made a plan for their next step after high school.

These students *can* become ready for postsecondary studies or career pursuits, with the right support. The SYT action team may propose a customized suite of services based on each student's goals and needs. Here are some examples:

- Enroll students in extended-time math- and literacy-readiness courses (for students planning to pursue postsecondary studies but failing to demonstrate readiness).

- Enroll students with a tentative career goal in a yearlong, three-hour, career pathway class that engages them in rigorous, real-world projects (as described in Chapter 4).

- Provide students with access to career pathway classes of their choice at their high school, career and technology center, or community college or through organized work-based study.

- Provide opportunities for students with no firm career goals to spend one day a week with a different employer during the first semester of senior year as part of a one-semester exploratory class. In this class, students take an interest and aptitude test, study the attributes of successful employees and citizens, learn time management and study skills, and visit local community or technical colleges to discover the available career opportunities. In the second semester, students would have the option to participate in a well-planned, on-site work-based training program while taking related CTE classes. Assign a professional to work with this group of students and local employers to engage them in quality work-based learning experiences that can lead to a good job.

This last strategy especially can be a game changer for many students who have not yet found their direction. Students need *high-quality* job experiences to understand what career options are available to them.

In 2010, the Southern Regional Education Board commissioned Stephen F. Hamilton and Rachel Sumner of Cornell University to examine the work-based learning of 12th grade students in schools that were part of the High Schools That Work network. In their unpublished study, the researchers concluded that high school staff were able to assist in finding job opportunities for students to gain work experience, especially students who were much less likely to find jobs on their own or with the help of their family.

This is an important finding, in view of the power of appropriate work experience to boost the development of employability skills among disadvantaged students. However, the challenge clearly identified by the study is for educators who are responsible for work-based learning programs to ensure that students most in need have *high-quality* work experiences. This effort requires schools and employers to exercise great care in selecting, planning, and monitoring school-related jobs, and it requires someone within the school system to build relationships with employers. This is time-consuming work, and too few school systems provide ample time and resources for these tasks.

While incorporating these readiness options, the SYT action team's plan must also ensure that all students will meet high school graduation requirements. The literacy-readiness course could meet the requirement for senior English, the math-readiness course could meet a requirement for a fourth math course, and other planned learning experiences can meet additional graduation requirements.

The objective is for each student to have a clear next step after high school and to use the senior year to prepare for that step. By the end of the senior year, students should be prepared to continue with an employer they worked with during the senior year, continue in a training program at the community college in their chosen career field, or pursue military service or other employment.

The Senior-Year Transition: Practical Steps Schools Can Take Now

For schools that are not ready to completely redesign the senior year, here are some practical actions to strengthen the senior year and help more students graduate career-ready, college-ready, or both:

- Assign a counselor to meet with each student and a parent or guardian during the last half of the junior year to develop a senior-year plan of study that prepares students for their next step after high school.

- Maximize the use of dual-credit courses for students meeting postsecondary readiness standards.

- Implement math- and literacy-readiness courses for students *approaching* postsecondary readiness and enroll students with more significant skill deficits in extended-time, yearlong literacy- and math-readiness courses to help those students meet at least the academic career-readiness indicators.

- Enroll students who aren't planning postsecondary studies in at least three career pathway courses in a career field of their choice at the high school, at a career and technology center, at a community technical college, or in an organized yearlong, work-based learning program.

Summing Up and Looking Ahead

Most public school parents and guardians expect students to be prepared for both career and college, and the senior year is the last chance for schools to launch students toward those goals. Using a three-fold plan, schools can strengthen and customize the senior year to meet the needs of a range of students: those ready for postsecondary studies and those who need varying degrees of time and support to reach academic and technical-career readiness for postsecondary studies or the workplace.

Chapter 9 guides schools in creating a counseling, exploring, and advising system that ensures each student has a plan, starting with a carefully defined course of study in middle and high school and leading to each student graduating career-ready, post-secondary-ready, or both.

Empowering Counselors and Teachers to Help Students Find Their Path to Success

As gaps widen between high-skill, high-paying job opportunities and the number of new employees ready to fill those openings, schools and districts need to consider what steps they are taking to actively connect their students to fulfilling careers that can lead to a middle-class lifestyle. **Although schools and parents often focus on grades, test scores, and the vague goal of students "going to college," what many students need most are caring adults who will help them find a meaningful path that will inspire their ongoing learning and achievement.**

Each school's counseling, exploring, and advising program should be organized to do just that: *counsel* students on potential paths that can lead to their desired career and educational outcomes, enable students to *explore* those paths, and *advise* students and parents about available opportunities and how to access them. Simply telling students they "need to go to college" is pointless and wasteful of human potential and educational resources.

When students lack information about growing career opportunities and about their unique talents and interests, they may struggle to see a connection between their daily learning and future careers and lifestyles. Students need opportunities to explore multiple career and educational options and to understand how challenging learning experiences during middle and high school will prepare them for their path to success—a path they must ultimately choose for themselves.

For these reasons, middle and high schools should establish a counseling, exploring, and advising (CEA) action team to help all students find a purpose or calling that will motivate them to advance their learning—and help students and parents understand how the right choices in middle and high school connect to future success and to students' aspirations. This team should consist of at least a counselor, an academic teacher, a CTE and career exploratory teacher, a principal or assistant principal, and parent representatives from the largest feeder middle school and the high school. In addition, the team should have persons who represent a postsecondary school that enrolls graduates from the high school, and a person who understands local and state-wide employment opportunities.

Charge the CEA team to create a system that enables counselors and advisors to meet the bold goals by

- Empowering counselors to lead a curriculum-based counseling, exploring, and advising system for middle grades through grade 12 to assist each student in building a path to success and understanding how school studies connect to that path.

- Providing each student, beginning in 6th grade and continuing throughout middle and high school, with learning experiences to explore potential career paths, to develop skills and habits to become independent and motivated learners, and to understand how characteristics such as honesty, fairness, and integrity are important to individual success.

- Providing all students and their parents/guardians with timely advising and counseling throughout middle and high school to assist them in planning, reviewing, and revising a guided program of studies linked to each student's goal.

Students have high aspirations; however, many students in middle and high school are not on a path to acquire the foundational academic, technical, technology, and personal skills to access fulfilling jobs and middle-class earning opportunities. Students from traditionally underserved groups often face gatekeeping barriers that prevent them from accessing the learning opportunities needed to prepare for emerging career opportunities. By working with school leaders, teachers, parents, and students, the CEA action team can help remove barriers that disproportionally affect low-income and minority students, so that they can access higher-level learning activities needed to prepare for emerging careers and postsecondary studies.

Identifying Gaps Between Students' Aspirations and Achievement

Before considering what structures are needed to provide each student with more effective counseling, schools need to identify whether the current system is working and where gaps may exist. The CEA team should use the bold goals outlined in Chapter 1, the questions provided in Chapter 3, and the report from the school's data, accountability, and policy team as starting points for this work.

Establishing benchmarks that show where the school stands can help the CEA action team create a sense of urgency for taking the steps necessary to close the gaps between the school's current success rate and the bold goals. The CEA action team might consider these benchmarking guidelines:

- *Bold goal:* **At least 95 percent of students who enter 9th grade graduate from high school.** Based on the adjusted cohort graduation rate (ACGR), *what is your school's true graduation rate, overall and by subpopulation?* The ACGR is calculated by identifying the cohort of first-time 9th graders in a particular school and determining how many in that cohort graduate four years later, adjusting for any students who transfer into the cohort after 9th grade and any students who transfer out, emigrate to another country, or die during high school. For the 2016–17 school year, for example, the national ACGR for public high schools was 85 percent overall (91 percent for Asian students, 89 percent for white students, 80 percent for Hispanic students, and 78 percent for Black students).[175]

- *Bold goal:* **At least 90 percent of students graduate college-ready, career-ready, or both, having mastered the power standards in literacy and mathematics critical to future success.** *What percentage of your most recent graduation class graduated college-ready, career-ready, or both, overall and by subgroups?* (See Chapter 8 for data related to graduation and college and career readiness, as well as the suggested indicators for measuring college and career readiness in Chapter 1.)

- *Bold goal:* **At least 70 percent of students enter 9th grade ready to succeed in true college preparatory academic courses (English language arts, social studies, science, and mathematics) and in challenging career pathway courses that require the academic skills to read, analyze, and comprehend a range of grade-level texts and materials in all subject areas.** *What percentage of your most recent entering 9th grade students (overall and by subgroup) were enrolled in a true college preparatory curriculum that engages students in higher-level learning?* (See Chapters 1, 2, and 7 for information on determining which academic courses truly prepare students for advanced studies.)

- *Bold goal:* **At least 80 percent of students go on to earn a credential or degree of value by age 25.** To determine progress toward this goal, the team should consider several indicators of post–high school achievement. Districts that have joined the National Student Clearinghouse can obtain information on the percentage of graduates who have earned a bachelor's degree, an associate's degree, or a certificate within six years of graduation (https://www.studentclearinghouse.org/high-schools/). More specifically, o *What percentage of graduates enroll in a two- or four-year college or university immediately after high school graduation (overall and by subgroups)?* In 2017, two-thirds of high school graduates enrolled in college, but a closer look at the data reveals disparities: 87 percent of Asian students, 69 percent of white students, 67 percent of Hispanic students, and 58 percent of Black students enrolled in college. More students from low-poverty schools enrolled than from high-poverty schools—69 percent versus 55 percent. (Low-poverty schools are defined as those in which less than half the students are eligible for free or reduced-price lunches.) And whereas 76 percent of ACT test takers in 2018 reported aspiring to some form of postsecondary education, only 65 percent enrolled in the fall following their high school graduation, meaning more than 200,000 graduates interested in attending college did not enroll at that time.[176]

o *What percentage of your recent graduates who entered postsecondary studies returned for the second year (overall and by subgroup)?* Once enrolled, 89 percent of students from low-poverty high schools return for the second year to college, compared with 79 percent from high-poverty high schools.[177]

o *What percentage graduate within 150 percent of normal time for degree completions from the first institution attended (overall and by subgroups)?* In 2013, 30 percent of students in two-year colleges graduated within three years of enrollment. And for four-year institutions in 2010, 60 percent of students graduated within six years of enrollment. Students from low-poverty high schools were twice as likely to earn a degree within six years of high school graduation (52 percent) compared with students from high-poverty schools (21 percent).[178]

o *What percentage of graduates, by age 25, obtain a bachelor's degree or higher, an associate's degree, or a certificate from a community college; complete an apprenticeship program; or earn through employer training an advanced credential?*

Possible Root Causes for Gaps

Why don't more students from historically underserved populations receive strong counseling and advising that encourages them to take the necessary academic and career pathway courses?

Gaps between students' achievement and their aspirations, and gaps in students' abilities to recognize their aspirations, arise when schools fail to help each student find a path to success. Noted child and adolescent development researcher William Damon argues that "anyone can find a purpose and pursue it with rich benefits to themselves and others." Optimism grounded in realism, ambition, and humility is something we should nurture in every student, Damon says, not just high achievers.[179]

When we focus on "college for all" as the goal, we lose sight of the need for *each* student to find and pursue his or her *own* goals and *own* paths to achieving those goals. The result is that many students have a stated aspiration to attend college but never enroll; many enroll but do not return for the second year; and many find themselves at age 25 without a credible credential because they never developed a clear sense of purpose for their life.

The singular focus on the traditional college prep pathway through high school ignores the value of two-year degrees and other advanced credentials that can lead students to successful careers. In part, the idea of "college for all" grew out of equity concerns that many students were being tracked into weak career programs. But what if those programs are strengthened and become challenging career pathways? Nearly 90 percent of parents reported in a 2017 survey that they want their students to become aware of educational paths leading to a variety of career opportunities.[180] Counselors, faculty, and school leaders need to reorient their thinking and become the leaders of a transformational plan to offer multiple rigorous career pathways that recognize the many different roads to post–high school success, and students need a rich selection of preparation options.

Once students and parents understand the full range of available career and education options and can set their goals, they need consistent counseling and advisement to form and follow their path to success. Too many students and parents fail to see that decisions made in middle and early high school will greatly affect readiness for careers and postsecondary studies. Clear aspirations are important, but students also need to be supported by the *right courses* and motivated to put forth the *effort required* to earn an advanced credential or degree.

In a 2018 survey of thousands of high school seniors, the majority reported that they planned to pursue further studies. Yet only 25 percent said they were encouraged by a teacher or counselor to take challenging mathematics, English language arts, and science courses—and the details of their school and classroom experiences reveal that most were not receiving support to connect their learning to a future career or further education. Between 50 and 80 percent of those surveyed reported they had never participated in an internship organized by the school, completed a project assignment that connected what they are learning in school to career opportunities, participated in job-shadowing experiences, or visited workplaces. Only 35 percent reported participating annually in a parent-teacher conference to plan and review their high school program of study.[181]

In many schools, the current structure of the counseling and advising system itself contributes to these gaps by limiting the process to professional counselors without the involvement of faculty and without the use of classroom curricula to provide learning experiences that help students discover their path to success. Most schools do not have enough counselors to work with every student individually and consistently. Instead, students are sorted into different tracks that too often disproportionately place low-income and minority students into lower-level classes. Unless this sorting system is replaced, many underserved students will not achieve their own goals—and schools will not achieve the bold goals.

A new approach is needed in which counselors and teachers join together through a comprehensive counseling, exploring, and advising system to remove the barriers preventing many students from having higher-level learning experiences and to empower them to succeed in achieving their goals.

Every school is different. The task of the CEA action team is to determine the root causes preventing *their* school from having 80 percent of graduates earning a credible credential or degree by the age of 25—and then to design and implement a plan of action for addressing those causes and closing the gaps through a comprehensive counseling, exploring, and advising system.

CEA Design Features: Helping Each Student Find a Path to Success

A counseling, exploring, and advising system can lift students up by enabling them to find their path to success. This type of comprehensive system educates students and parents, beginning in the middle grades, about emerging careers and connects them to multiple educational pathways leading to their goals. It provides *all students* with access to a qualified counselor in collaboration with a system of advisors who proactively support students to achieve their goals. Although the system can vary according to each school's needs and resources, it should have, at a minimum, these design features:

1. **Curriculum-based experiences for students to explore career and educational options in middle and high schools.** Embed authentic, real-world assignments within academic, CTE, and special courses. Such assignments allow students to discover their talents, interests,

aspirations, and values and to understand how each of these relates to future paths to success. Begin such experiences in middle and early high school, *before* students become stuck in lower-level courses.

2. **A counselor-led, diffused advising system in which all school staff members become advisors.** Counselors support advisors to help students and parents understand how learning in middle and high school is related to students' career and educational paths for success after high school.[182]

3. **Programs of study that are based on paths to success for all students.** Discontinue sorting students into fast, medium, and slow tracks. Place all students in a higher-level track connected to their aspirations and path to success, because tomorrow's opportunities require all students to experience higher-level learning in academic and career pathway classes.

4. **Parents as full partners in assisting students to choose a success path.** Counselors, advisors, and parents provide strong encouragement to students, assisting them to select the right courses in middle and high school and to analyze the pros and cons of different educational and career options—advanced training, an associate's degree, a bachelor's degree, or employment.

5. **New ways of thinking about college-bound and career-oriented student paths.** Both groups need advanced courses in English language arts, mathematics, and science. Counselors and advisors must advocate for designing multiple pathways through high school that blend college prep and CTE courses in ways that provide *each* student with rigorous, engaging, and relevant education experience.

6. **Counselors, advisors, and media center specialists who can provide information about future good jobs.** Informed support will assist students and parents in planning a program of study that prepares students for multiple post–high school options, including the recognition that many good jobs do not require a four-year college degree but still require the advanced academic knowledge and skills to progress to middle-class earnings.[183]

7. **The same counselor and teacher advisor for each student throughout middle and high school.** Ensure students are supported continuously by an advisor who knows them and their interests and can guide them in finding their path to success. This feature must become embedded in the cultures of middle and high schools, with a system of handoff between counselors and advisors as students transition from middle to high school. (See Polytech High School's story on pp. 63–67.)

These design principles can become the equalizer for success, because students are motivated to learn when they believe what they are being asked to learn is relevant to their lives and when they see adults willing to walk the extra mile to support them to achieve success.

What Works: Implementing Design Features in Middle and High Schools

This section details counseling, exploring, and advising practices that work in lifting up students in middle and high schools. In my experience, design systems that encompass these key features meet that ambitious goal.

Introduce Middle School and Early High School Students to Emerging Careers

Middle school and early high school students are a constantly changing mix of adolescents who differ in physical, social, emotional, and intellectual maturity and who are searching for their own identity in the context of their present and future environments. These young people do not passively develop into adults; they develop into the person they want to become through their experiences—and for many students, their experiences are limited.

Students in this age range benefit from curriculum-based experiences that blend hands-on and minds-on learning approaches with opportunities to explore broad career fields—to expand their images of who they might become—while discovering the connection between academic and career pathway studies.

Early learning is key to introducing students to rewarding career fields. In a Microsoft-commissioned survey of students and parents, four out of five college students studying science, technology, engineering, and math fields (STEM) said they decided to study STEM in high school. One in five decided in the middle grades.[184]

Middle schools can raise students' career awareness through exploratory courses organized around rigorous, real-world projects (see Appendix A) that actively engage students in

- Assuming responsibility for a variety of roles that mirror types of career fields.
- Working as a member of a team to take ownership of completing an authentic project.

- Participating in real-world projects that allow them to move around physically, to explore, to take a chance—as a break from traditional instruction.

- Encountering and interviewing positive adult role models and hearing stories of the journey that prepared them for their current job.

- Completing challenging assignment tasks involving researching, analyzing, problem solving, and interpreting information while discovering a relationship to their interests, aptitudes, school, and careers.

The Impact of Real-World Projects

Sarah Bailey, a science teacher at Buffalo Middle School in West Virginia, saw firsthand the impact that rigorous, real-world projects can have on middle school students' learning and career development. Her insights have been edited for clarity and length.[185]

When I implemented the project "Design, Construct, and Test a Wind Turbine," I was surprised by how quickly middle-grade students would take ownership for completing a difficult assignment. They were motivated by the opportunity to work with local engineers and to receive feedback from them. That was evident in the level of questions students asked the engineers and the students' ability to organize information into a written design plan for completing the project.

Students become highly motivated when they are engaged in a real-world project assignment in which they have an interest. Sometimes, as teachers, we are satisfied with just covering the content. This experience taught me that content coverage alone does not engage students in the deeper learning that a well-developed authentic project inspires.

Parents noticed the difference, too. Numerous parents told me they had never seen their child as excited about school as they were while doing the wind turbine project.

Several students discovered they like solving problems and are considering careers where the engineering process can be applied. Such project assignments enable students to reflect on their interest and aptitudes in different career fields.

Two Approaches to Curriculum-Based Career Exploration

Students need clear aspirations. They also need to understand the connection between school experiences and their aspirations. Once they do, they're motivated to apply themselves to their coursework. Two schools—Polytech High School in Delaware and Fort Mill High School in South Carolina—have developed purpose-driven programs that foster motivation in students by helping them find a purpose for their learning.

As detailed in the Spotlight on pages 63-67, Polytech helps each student set an informed career and educational goal, beginning with a career exploration course in the 9th grade. By the end of the school year, students have chosen a final career pathway—and 95 percent are placed in their pathway of first choice.

An Introduction to High School course (IHSC) at Fort Mill High School helps each student develop a focused program of study linked to career and postsecondary goals. This course, which launched in 2000 at Fort Mill, has now been adopted by all high schools in the county and is required for high school graduation. The primary goals of the IHSC are to have 9th graders see a connection between high school studies and a path to success and to awaken students to the many opportunities for success in their high school, community, and state.

The Introduction to High School course was created to help address high failure rates in 9th grade, high rates of absenteeism, and high rates of deficiency in literacy and mathematics. The school determined these problems were connected to a failure to help students develop personal habits for success early in high school and to connect their interests and aspirations to a personalized program of study.

The course addresses topics such as orientation to high school, learning styles, study skills, goal setting, and academic and career planning. Students take field trips, interview adults, maintain a self-reflection journal, improve reading and writing skills, and broaden their views of themselves to become fully engaged in meaningful and rigorous learning experiences.

At the end of each six-week period, IHSC teachers identify failing 9th graders and provide them with support based on a customized education plan. Teachers work with students to help them become aware of the importance of making efforts to succeed. One long-term benefit has been the positive relationships that develop between students and IHSC teachers; students continue to seek them out for special advice throughout high school.

Each year, IHSC teachers identify what worked and what did not and use that information to adjust the course content and how it is taught. A 101+ curriculum was developed for students transferring into Fort Mill High during the junior or senior year to make them fully aware of issues they must address to be ready for their next step after high school.

Fort Mill Principal Gales Scroggs believes a successful IHSC is based on clearly defined needs and the selection of passionate and energetic teachers who teach the course. Scroggs credits IHSC with dramatically reducing the 9th grade failure rate, and he believes the IHSC has contributed to the school's 95 percent graduation rate and to being ranked as the seventh best high school in South Carolina.

Implement a Counselor-Led Advisory System

Effective counselor-led advisory systems can lead students to complete academic and career pathway courses that are more advanced, resulting in students being better prepared for further education and jobs.[186] In such a system, all school professionals across grades 6 through 12—teachers, school leaders, counselors, media specialists, and others—serve as advisors, led by the counseling team. In an ideal setting, advisors are part of a team that includes a grade-level administrator and a counselor who works with the same cohort of students throughout their time at the school. By providing frequent, consistent contact, advisors in middle school and the early years of high school can rescue students from disengagement before they lose hope in themselves and in school. They call parents and guardians when students are absent and connect failing students with extra help. When necessary, the advisors work with the counselor to provide students with additional support that advisors are not able to provide alone.

The counselors and advisors work as a cohesive unit to ensure better outcomes for students. These teams can advocate for alternatives to traditional sorting of students, which too often results in students being grouped along racial and socioeconomic lines. This team should lead the school in enrolling *all* students into higher-level courses aligned with an academic or career focus and supporting students as they adjust to more demanding middle and high school curricula. They can also establish criteria through which students could earn honors credits in college prep and career pathway courses, based on completing higher-level assignments.

With guidance from the counseling team—and input from school leaders, faculty, parents, and key postsecondary and industry leaders—advisors organize advisory sessions each year around broad topics with planned lessons. The topics addressed are those most important at each grade level in supporting students to achieve their path to success and to make the right decisions for completing a program of studies linked to their career and educational goals.[187] Here are examples of such topics:

- Grade 8: Preparing students for high school success and for choosing the right courses needed for both college and careers.

- Grade 9: Assisting each student to design a customized five-year pathway program of studies that connects high school to postsecondary studies and careers.

- Grade 10: Reviewing progress toward students' stated goals and graduation requirements and making needed changes.

- Grade 11: Assisting students to plan a senior-year experience through which they can earn postsecondary credit; complete specialized curricula to meet college- and career-readiness standards; or graduate from high school with the literacy, math, and technical skills needed for immediate employment.

- Grade 12: Assisting each student to make a successful transition to his or her next step.

Advisors meet weekly or biweekly for 30-minute mini-advisory lessons with their group of advisees (preferably 15 to 18 students per advisor) to address broad topics such as those outlined above. The counseling team can ask two-person advisor teams to develop four lesson plans on a topic that interests them. At least two teachers then review lessons developed for each topic and provide feedback for preparing the final draft. After completing a unit, advisors provide feedback for revising the unit lessons for the following year. A sample template for developing an advisement lesson is provided in Appendix I at www.ascd.org/CareerTechEdTools.

Conduct Annual Counseling and Advising Sessions with Students and Parents/Guardians

Counseling and advising all students to take higher-level academic courses aligned to their career and educational path improves students' outcomes. Students who have been encouraged by counselors, teachers, and parents to take true college preparatory courses consistently meet literacy- and math-readiness goals at higher rates than students who do not receive such encouragement.[188]

Making an annual advisory session with each student a part of school culture—and involving not only the counselors/advisors but also parents/guardians—can result in stronger support for students to take and succeed in higher-level courses. This step is especially beneficial to historically underserved groups, including students of color, students experiencing poverty, students learning English as a second language, and students whose parents did not complete coursework beyond high school and who may be less familiar with postsecondary opportunities.

All students need help in setting career and educational goals, in developing a plan of studies connected to their goals, and in obtaining continued support to stay on track and achieve their goals. Annual advisory sessions with students and guardians can provide this help by

- Involving parents in supporting the student to develop a path to success and in annually reviewing the status of the student's preparation for college, career, or both.

- Establishing a plan of study through high school and beyond that can be reviewed and revised annually.

- Making each student, along with the parents/guardians and the advisor, aware of the student's interests and aptitudes, how these link to different career fields, and how the right academic and career pathway courses can prepare the student for both college and career.

- Informing parents/guardians why it is best for students to take college preparatory academic courses in 9th grade and beyond and how the school will support each student to complete higher-level assignments.

It takes planning and time to have an effective annual advisory session that makes parents true partners in their child's education—and achieves the goal of having more students meet college- and career-readiness standards. The counseling team works with school leaders to plan the logistics for getting parents to attend these annual sessions and helps each advisor/counselor to set the agenda and prepare for the sessions (including securing translators for parents who do not speak English).

Some schools schedule evening sessions, but others schedule sessions during workdays. To get parents to attend, one high school in southeast Georgia used local radio and newspaper advertisements to inform parents about the importance of their attendance. Other schools have used a range of incentives, from meals to rewards, to increase parents' participation.

When planning advising sessions, it's important to recognize that some parents did not have a pleasant high school experience. The moment they walk into the school, their old insecurities and unpleasant memories may return. The school must make a concerted effort to ensure that all parents feel welcome and realize they have an important role to play in the advisory process.

Use Interest and Aptitude Assessments

Interest and aptitude assessments are a valuable tool in helping students expand their understanding of the many career and educational opportunities available to them. Such assessments can become part of an Introduction to High School course or an advisory lesson activity, or the basis for discussion during annual advising sessions with students and their parents/guardians in grades 9 and 10.

Many young people do not pursue expanding career fields simply because they do not know about them or do not believe they would be good at those particular careers. At the same time, the U.S. labor market continues to have major gaps between the skills employers need and the number of job seekers who possess those skills.[189] Women and minorities continue to be underrepresented in some sectors of the labor market with growing opportunities, such as STEM fields,[190] and many students may not be able to see themselves in specific career fields because they don't fit the demographics of people who have historically occupied those roles.

Based on their current knowledge and experiences, students may have low interest in a career field, *but they may have a high aptitude for it.* In a pilot study in Georgia, 52 percent of male students expressed high interest in the field of computer technology, a high-demand career field in that state, and 57 percent had high aptitude. Only 30 percent of female students expressed high interest, but 58 percent had high aptitude for the field. Similarly, 39 percent of male students had high interest in healthcare, but 61 percent had high aptitude for this career field. Almost five times more female students had high aptitude for six engineering fields than had expressed high interest. Understanding they have high aptitude in a field could lead more students to further investigate their opportunities and learn more about the nature of the work.

To help overcome this disconnect between the types of careers students can succeed in and the types they know about or think are available to them, schools should implement assessments that measure not only students' interests but also their aptitudes. *Advisement tools based only on interests may perpetuate gender-biased skills gaps.* Linking measures of aptitudes and interests to high-demand, high-wage career fields can help more students consider a broader set of career recommendations.[191]

New tools exist that can support the work of counselors and teacher advisors, such as the Buyer Beware tool from the Georgetown University Center on Education and the Workforce.[192] The tool shows students and parents the potential earnings related to different majors at different institutions. **It is important to pay attention not only to the choice of institution but also to the major students choose to ensure they are selecting options that have a track record of producing graduates who can obtain a good job.**[193]

Rome City High School in Georgia implemented the *YouScience* interest and aptitude assessment connected to six high-demand and high-wage STEM careers to help inform students about their interest and aptitudes and to engage them in investigating the six career fields. As a result, the percentage of students choosing the computer programming pathway doubled, and participation in career pathways linked to the other expanding career fields also increased.[194]

A Theory of Action to Empower Counselors and Teachers to Help Students Find a Path to Success

Once the CEA action team has identified gaps between the school's current status and its bold goals, agreed on major causes for the gaps, and established its own design principles for a program to help each student find a path to success, the team is ready to consider specific actions to achieve full implementation of a comprehensive counseling, exploring, and advising system. Use the Plan, Do, Study, Act process outlined in Chapter 3 to identify actions that are needed.

In middle schools, the team can develop a series of "if/then" statements such as these:

If . . .

- School leaders and faculty agree to align all courses in grades 6 through 8 to college- and career-readiness standards . . .
- The school offers a two- or three-year exploratory course to introduce students to STEM and other career fields and provide them with a foundation for planning a success path in high school . . .
- The CEA action team implements a system that connects each student to one counselor/advisor who remains with the student from grades 6 through 8 . . .
- Counselors and advisors meet regularly throughout the year with their advisee group for planned sessions . . .
- Counselors and advisors meet annually with each student and the students' parents/guardians to review progress in an accelerated curriculum and explore additional actions needed by the school, the student, and the parents/guardians . . .
- Counselors and advisors meet with each 7th grader (and parents/guardians) who needs to be enrolled in special literacy- and math-readiness courses in 8th grade to become ready for college preparatory courses in 9th grade . . .
- The middle school CEA action team reviews actions every 45 days to determine whether they are being implemented with fidelity and to make needed adjustments . . .

then more parents will support their student to succeed in the accelerated curriculum, and more students will be motivated to make greater effort. In time, at least 70 percent of entering 9th graders will meet the bold goal for high school readiness.

In high schools, the team can develop a series of "if/then" statements such as these:

If . . .

- The CEA action team works collaboratively with the middle school(s) to improve the transition into high school by orienting middle school faculty, parents, and students to expectations for successfully completing high school career-ready, college-ready, or both . . .

- Counselors and advisors, with the support of faculty and school leaders, enroll all incoming 9th grade students into college preparatory academic courses with extended time and intensive support for some students . . .

- Counselors and advisors schedule a meeting with students and parents/ guardians early in high school to review the results of each student's interest and aptitude assessment as one basis for choosing either an academic or a career focus in high school . . .

- The high school provides an exploratory experience to help each student acquire the habits of successful learners and in planning a personalized program of study to graduate career- and college-ready . . .

- Counselors and advisors conduct an annual meeting with each student and the student's parents/guardians to review the range of careers and postsecondary education options available, discuss the pros and cons of each, and review progress (or lack thereof) toward a stated goal with next-step actions . . .

- The high school establishes an advisory system involving every faculty member in working with a group of students throughout high school and leading students through planned lessons around critical and timely topics . . .

- Scheduled sessions are provided during the last half of students' junior year to help each develop an individualized plan for using the senior year to prepare for the next step . . .

- The CEA action team collects and analyzes data every 45 days on the extent to which actions are being implemented and makes revisions as needed . . .

then the high school should make continuous progress toward graduating 95 percent of the students, with at least 90 percent of students postsecondary-ready, career-ready, or both, and 80 percent having earned by age 25 an advanced degree or a credential aligned to middle-class earning opportunities.

Counseling, Exploring, and Advising: Practical Steps Schools Can Take Now

Middle and high schools that are not ready to implement a comprehensive counseling, exploring, and advising system can still take an incremental approach to helping more students find their success path and graduate career- and college-ready. The ideas in this list may require the middle and high school to work together.

An appointed counselor and faculty counseling, exploring, and advising team should

- Work with all faculty and leadership to increase annually by at least 15 percent the number of students enrolled in true college preparatory classes—along with either an advanced academic focus or a four-course career pathway leading to middle-class earnings.

- Plan annual meetings with each student and the student's parents/guardians, beginning in 6th grade, to educate them about how the right courses can affect future educational and career options.

- Establish checkpoint systems at the end of grades 6, 7, 8, 9, and 10 to identify students failing to meet career- and college-readiness standards and implement an extended summer program or special support during the next school year to have more students meeting the standards.

- Advocate for high school faculty—academic, CTE, special education, fine arts, physical arts, media center, and others—to develop learning assignments that enable students to see a connection between courses taken and future success.

- Engage the entire faculty in encouraging each student to develop his or her path to success and to reflect on how school studies provide preparation for a path to success.

Summing Up and Looking Ahead

Schools can use several strategies to provide learning experiences and to empower counselors and teachers to lift students up by unlocking the school from traditional practices that prevent too many students from accessing higher-level learning experiences and support. The changes proposed in this and previous chapters will require major shifts in school culture.

The final chapter of this book addresses the shifts in attitudes and beliefs about school and classroom practices that must occur if each student is to graduate career-ready, college-ready, or both.

10

Acting on Our Beliefs to Achieve Bold Goals and Transform Our Schools

In a recent essay on the Brookings Institution blog, senior fellow Jon Valant offered his ideas about the most pressing issue facing our public schools: "While we were preoccupied with preparing students for the 21st century economy," he wrote, "we failed to prepare them for our 21st century democracy."[195] Valant cited the profound impact of the internet and social media tools on the way we interact and "how we learn about the world and one another"—and the negative effects of a sensation-hungry, technology-driven media that isolates many citizens from a broad range of views or opportunities for wide public conversations. Offering evidence of the breakdown of civil discourse and shared American values—marked by events such as the storming of the U.S. Capitol in January 2021—Valant argued that the most important work schools can do today is to help students acquire "a discrete set of skills and dispositions that don't come naturally" to navigate this new terrain and help rebuild civil society.

Valant's list of areas where schools should place more emphasis included media literacy, digital citizenship and empathy, and intellectual humility. "These aren't issues that will be resolved with yet more attention to math and English language arts," he wrote. "They reflect shortcomings that are different and deeper."

How do I, the author of a book that argues we need to put *even more emphasis* on the teaching of math, literacy, and career preparation, respond to the criticism by Valant and others? First, I share Valant's concerns about the need to help students develop skills and dispositions to sustain American democracy in the face of the threats he describes. I agree with Valant's conclusion that "we need to remember that schools serve democratic purposes as well as economic purposes."

My argument throughout this book has been that public education in the United States has *not* been successful in preparing many of its students for economic success in the 21st century—that we have, for the most part, created a two-track system that has relegated half of our students to low-end jobs that are now quickly vanishing. Inside our secondary schools, we've created a culture of low expectations for these young people by accepting the myth that "those" students cannot do challenging work in school.

I contend that unless we transform our schools in the ways described in this book, we will not cure our societal ills. Instead, we will produce a growing percentage of Americans who do not have a stake in America's economic *or* democratic future. In effect, we will feed the discontent and sense of disenfranchisement that is already dividing the United States in dramatic ways. The bold goal for secondary schools in the United States has to be this: *We will fully prepare and graduate every student so that he or she is ready for postsecondary studies and career opportunities leading to an economically, socially, and civically rewarding life.*

Full-scale achievement of this goal will require a seismic shift in attitudes and beliefs. Convincing educators and the public that just about every student in our schools is capable of mastering college prep academic subjects and advanced career studies at a high level will be a hard sell. It pushes back on the entrenched thinking of many Americans—including many educators—who are comfortable with the traditional view of education as a sorting process with fairly predictable outcomes based on economic status, race, family background, and so on.

"School has always been like this," the thinking goes. It may be the educator's job to "bring out the best" in each student, but underlying that easy profession of faith, many educators, political leaders, and folks on the street are certain that some students simply don't have what it takes to gain all the skills and knowledge they need to really be successful. *"They won't make it, and it won't be our fault."*

"Ability is fixed." That belief is the number one barrier to school transformation. Over the last 30 years, an avalanche of research and modeling by expert teachers has established that every student *does* have the potential to grow. When we do our job, students see themselves as capable learners, and they begin to soar. But *we* have to soar first.

If school board members, district leaders, teachers, counselors, and school leaders continue to believe that some students will underperform—particularly students of color, students experiencing poverty, students learning English, and students whose parents did not attend college—then their high schools will never graduate at least 95 percent of students, with 90 percent being college-ready, career-ready, or both.

Educational experts promote the importance of helping students adopt a growth mindset, but many school leaders and teachers haven't fully bought into the idea of growth mindset themselves. How do we change that?

Seeing Is Believing

School-turnaround expert Stephanie Johnson has an answer to the puzzle of changing hearts and minds—an answer she discovered through her own work with schools where students were being tracked into low-level courses and denied the opportunity to achieve more. Johnson says that when educators and policymakers are given the chance to see lower-achieving students excel as the result of good teaching and extra support—"when they actually see it happening before their eyes"—most will come to recognize that effort and attitude lead to self-efficacy, and that students' belief in their ability to learn makes a difference in motivating students to prepare themselves to become productive adults and prepared citizens.

Johnson, a passionate educator, is Georgia's Deputy State Superintendent for School Improvement, School and District Effectiveness, and Professional Development. Before joining the Georgia State Department of Education, she led the transformation of three low-performing schools in Georgia—two high schools and a middle school—using many of the principles developed in the SREB High Schools That Work initiative.

During her five years as principal of inner-city Atlanta's Maynard H. Jackson High School, once among the 5 percent lowest-performing schools in the state, Johnson and her staff worked in distributed leadership teams to redesign curriculum and reimagine instruction, creating academic and career pathways powered by student-centered learning strategies. These efforts earned MJHS recognition as a "Beating the Odds School" in the state's accountability system.

I can think of no better way to change attitudes and beliefs than to share some of my conversation with Johnson about what she learned in the process of leading three successful school turnarounds and now applying that knowledge to the creation of a statewide school-improvement framework. You will find excerpts from our conversation embedded in the nine beliefs that follow.

Nine Beliefs to Help Educators Make a Difference

Public schools educate more than 90 percent of American students, nearly half of whom belong to historically marginalized groups, with most of that half coming from low-income families with parents who likely did not pursue education beyond high school.[196] And the proportion continues to shift: the percentage of students qualifying for free or reduced-priced lunches, for example, grew from 38 percent in the 2000–01 academic year to 52 percent in 2015–16.[197]

Historically, education has been a bridge to a better future; but presently, almost 50 percent of high school graduates are not prepared for either college or careers, let alone both. Add in the number of students who do not graduate from high school, and that number grows to more than 60 percent. Too many graduates and high school dropouts are on a bridge to nowhere, and that bridge is coming up faster and faster as technology advances and traditional subsistence jobs disappear.

Today in the United States it is more difficult than in other industrialized countries to achieve upward mobility from a position of lower socioeconomic status.[198] From 1979 to 2018, real income in the United States increased by 4 percent for the bottom 10 percent of earners, by 14 percent for the median earner, and by 56 percent for the top 10 percent of earners.[199] Multiple studies have found that between 50 and 60 percent of students' achievement is explained by family circumstances—most significantly, by income.[200] And some argue that the most thoughtful and well-intended school reform program cannot improve educational outcome if it ignores the single greatest predictor of student achievement: household income.[201]

I do not accept this fatalistic view that schools cannot make a greater difference in the lives of more underserved students. At the same time, to accept things as they are and ignore that the current playing field is tilted against such students specifically in middle and high school only validates this fatalistic view.

In this book, we have identified many of the blind spots that still exist in our school and classroom practices. And we have acknowledged—and acknowledge again here—that there are many dedicated school and teacher leaders who are not satisfied with current practices and who want to leave a legacy of fully serving the historically underserved students who now make up so much of the public school population. But unless we systemically address the beliefs and attitudes on which current practices are based, education cannot become a bridge that leads more students toward upward mobility and self-fulfillment. Successful school transformation—reform that lifts all students—occurs when 90 percent of students (and that means 90 percent of students from historically underserved groups, as well) graduate from high school, pursue postsecondary studies, obtain a credible credential or degree, and get a good job.

What can middle and high schools do to change this trajectory? Schooling accounts for only 40 to 50 percent of the factors that drive student achievement, with quality teaching being a major factor. So what beliefs must we adopt and act upon to maximize the impact of schooling on advancing the opportunity for all students? I've identified nine beliefs that I contend are the most essential. Let's examine each belief in detail.

Belief 1: High Expectations

We—district, school, and teacher leaders—have to set high expectations for all students and support them to succeed in relevant and challenging learning opportunities.

To buy into the effectiveness of the actions outlined in previous chapters, educators need to buy into the idea that all students can meet high expectations. Setting high expectations for all means abandoning a deeply rooted tracking system in high schools—and increasingly in middle schools—that preselects different objectives and experiences for different groups of students.

How can students ever "catch up" when we consistently enroll them in lower-level courses, under the false pretense that lower expectations will close the achievement gap? Stephanie Johnson has this to say about changing hearts and minds:

> You first engage the faculty in looking at their own data and asking the question: *Why are our students failing to meet the higher performance standards?* Then you pose the question: *How do you think the norms and expectations of classroom instruction might be different in schools similar to ours but where students perform at much higher levels?*
>
> Then you engage teachers and school leaders in looking at instructional plans of teachers who are engaging their students in higher-level learning experiences aligned to grade-level college- and career-readiness standards, and ask: *How are these plans different from what is occurring in our school? Why are those students able to do more than our students?*
>
> At the same time, district and school leaders need to be saying that our current strategies aren't working and we're going to shift away from tracking students into lower-level classes and provide the additional time and support for students to meet the higher standards.

Many comprehensive high schools have failed to move beyond the concept of American high schools presented in 1959—the high school as a place in which the differences presented by students couldn't be altered in any significant way[202]—because district and school leaders haven't confronted the faulty assumptions that some students are not capable of engaging successfully in higher-level learning opportunities.[203] In one study of high schools, Keeping Track: How Schools Structure Inequality, educational theorist and researcher Jeannie Oakes found that tracking students into different levels of academic courses is done routinely in schools as the best thing to do for all groups of students. It is so accepted that few question the evidence and beliefs on which it is based.[204]

Oakes's study, published in 1985, describes to a large degree the situation in many high schools today. Tracking is based on the beliefs that students learn better and develop more positive attitudes about themselves when tracked by ability, that the process used to separate students into groups accurately and fairly reflects past achievement and native ability, and that it is easier for teachers to accommodate individual differences in a homogeneous group.[205] Although this last belief may hold some truth, is providing the easiest route for the few teachers who teach only the top students reason enough to sacrifice the success of other students and teachers?

Research has clearly demonstrated that tracking

> results in capable students being denied opportunities to advance their abilities and achievement through higher-level learning opportunities. Instead, they receive a steady diet of low-level assignments that fail to engage them in deeper learning experiences resulting in widening the achievement gap.[206]

Three decades after her first book on tracking, Oakes suggested combining rigorous academic courses with rigorous career studies as a strategy to move beyond tracking:

> On the academic side, such an approach is likely to increase the challenge and relevance of high school curriculum and, as a consequence, boost academic achievement and motivate students to stay in school. On the career preparation side, such an approach fits the analyst claims that jobs of the future require higher-level cognitive skills as well as specific technical competencies.[207]

Other research suggests that such an approach—when designed with choice, interests, and engagement in mind—can motivate students' learning and increase the retention of academic concepts at a deeper level by allowing students to apply what they have learned in academic courses in a career context.[208]

There is one proven way to overcome the lack of access to higher-level learning opportunities for underserved students: enroll them in demanding middle and high school courses with the extended time and support needed to succeed. Across more than 30 years of student survey and achievement data, the Southern Regional Education Board consistently found that the most powerful factor for increasing the percentage of career-oriented students who met college- and career-readiness standards was *enrollment in higher-track courses, with special support for those needing it.*[209] Success rates were highest when those courses engaged students in complex assignments that emphasize problem-solving and inquiry.[210] To help shift attitudes and beliefs across the school and district about the truth of this statement, schools can consider a gradual process for enrolling more students into the higher-level classes, enabling doubters to see that most students can meet expectations *when assigned highly qualified teachers* who have been prepared to create and engage them *in meaningful and rigorous assignments.*

Belief 2: Family Engagement

It is up to us—schools, teachers, and counselors—to engage all families in helping make choices about the best learning opportunities for their students.

Because families have the greatest influence on the educational outcomes of their students, they must be engaged by and with the school to make sure their students use their time wisely in middle and high school to prepare for future opportunities. The challenge for school leaders, counselors, and teachers is to find ways to engage parents and guardians of underserved students in assisting their students to make informed choices.

According to *Phi Delta Kappan*'s annual poll of the public's attitudes toward public schools, 75 percent of all parents say schools should prepare students academically for college *and* for employment. Nearly half of parents with incomes of less than $50,000 want their students to pursue full-time enrollment in postsecondary studies, and almost 90 percent of public school parents want their children to know about careers.[211]

Families from historically marginalized groups have similar goals for their children as do more privileged families, but they may not have the experiences or access to know the best ways to help their student achieve those goals. Aggressively developing and implementing strategies to engage (not simply "involve") more families in the education of their students throughout middle and high school can help close this opportunity gap and increase the percentages of disenfranchised students achieving upward mobility.

A 2020 review of research concluded that purposeful parent/guardian engagement improves student academic and social progress.[212] Effectively engaging parents/guardians, regardless of their SES background, can result in more students

- Becoming motivated by formulating career and educational goals as a path forward for themselves.

- Passing classes, earning higher grades, having higher test scores, and enrolling in higher-level courses in middle and high school.

- Attending school regularly, graduating from high school, and going on to postsecondary education to earn a credible credential or degree.

- Having better social skills, better study skills, and fewer behavioral problems.

Engaging parents of all backgrounds will require adaptation to a local context. Garden City High School, for example, is located in a community in western Kansas where many parents speak little English. To increase family engagement, school leaders established flexible time for advisory sessions with pre-arranged interpreters. This resulted in a trusting relationship between the school and parents.

Again, Stephanie Johnson shares her experience, this time on the topic of connecting faculty and community:

> One of the lessons I learned was to engage my faculty with a cross-section of parents— single, traditional family, grandmother-guardian—along with business, community, and faith-based leaders, who all want the same quality of education experiences for disenfranchised students that the school is providing to high-performing students.
>
> As teachers listen to these voices, they begin to see the need to revise the curriculum and implement more challenging learning experiences for all groups of students. This outside support for change becomes their rationale for creating a higher-performing learning culture.

Belief 3: Student Vision

It is our job—school leaders, teachers, and counselors—to help each student develop a clear vision for the future—because a student with a vision is a motivated student.

Students can never aspire to middle-class earning opportunities without knowing what those opportunities are and what is required to get to the point where they are realistic options. To improve outcomes for traditionally underserved groups of students, middle and high school counselors and teachers must make it possible for them to see themselves in higher-paying jobs with growing opportunities. Counselors and teachers must help each student develop a vision for who that student can become and understand the effort needed to achieve that end.

School leaders and teachers must adopt the belief that one role of schools is to engage all students in a journey to firm up a purpose for their life—beginning in middle school and continuing in high school. Students who have defined a purpose and path forward for themselves are more motivated and will make a greater effort to succeed.

The focus should not be limited to just four-year colleges. Employees with bachelor's degrees tend to perform better in the long run, compared with individuals who earn career certificates; however, as a *Wall Street Journal* report noted in 2020, "There are a lot of certificates where bachelor's degree salaries will never catch up."[213] In this era of rising student debt, schools must consider how to ensure students understand affordable postsecondary options leading to high-wage career fields. Among other steps, this will require schools to identify majors within two- and four-year colleges with a strong history of preparing students for good jobs.

Once schools have helped students set career and educational goals, they must provide the support and learning opportunities that will motivate students to make the effort to succeed in completing higher-level assignments *connected to a goal that students hold for themselves.* Here are Stephanie Johnson's observations on this point:

> If students have a career goal for which they have some passion, they are more moti-vated to learn in both academic and CTE courses. Parents see this, and they become passionate too.
>
> In the case of poor and disenfranchised students, the increase in parent engage-ment helps change teacher and counselor views about what we might expect from these students. As counselors, teachers, and school leaders accept responsibility to assist every student to find a career path, they realize the need to provide them with a full range of opportunities—including job shadowing and access to postsecondary and career days—to expand their vision of what they might become.

The belief of individual students in their ability to accomplish career-related tasks is a critical predictor of career choice. Higher-level assignments in areas connected to their career interest can help students become engaged in deeper cognitive processes and allow them to imagine themselves in a given career role.[214]

Authentic tasks in academic or CTE pathway classes that involve collaboration with other students, experimentation, simulation, debate, role playing, and presen-tation of work to outside mentors can expand students' vision for themselves and motivate them to pursue deeper learning. The most effective career-exploring assign-ments for students require homework and interpretation of information about the world of work, social support, and—a truly potent motivator—exposure to role mod-els in different career fields of interest who know how to connect well with young people.[215] Such engagement is essential if we are to lift historically underserved groups into middle-class opportunities.[216]

Belief 4: Different Paths

We—every leader and educator in our system—must respect and value different paths to success, including rigorous CTE pathways of study connected to a college-ready academic core and postsecondary studies.

Too many high schools send a message to students and parents that an academic, college preparatory path is the only way to win. Motivation and effort are enhanced when students have more than one path to success. (Polytech High School, spotlighted in Chapter 3, offers an example of how to provide multiple pathways for preparing stu-dents for both college and careers.)

The authors of a review of CTE in secondary schools found that although CTE has largely remained on the margins of secondary education, "the continuing technology evolution . . . requires the integration of career preparation into the fabric of secondary education as one means for preparing our nation's youth for the society and economy they will inherit and the economy that they will direct."[217] They conclude that full attention to CTE programs will be required to fulfill the broader agenda of education reform.

Yet some educational leaders believe that the role of CTE programs is limited to preparing students for local jobs, many of which do not provide a middle-class income, or to provide a holding place for students who cannot handle higher-level academic and cognitive learning but are not yet old enough to leave school. If such beliefs continue to prevail, we lose the potential to help students benefit from a new brand of high-quality CTE—the advanced pathway of study.

A national multidiscipline panel appointed by the National Research Council and the Institute of Medicine (now the National Academy of Medicine) presented a view of CTE pathways as another way for students and parents to win. This distinguished panel viewed intellectually demanding CTE pathways—connected to college-ready academic curricula, postsecondary studies, and worksite learning opportunities—as the catalyst for high school reform that would motivate and engage more students in higher-level learning and lift them into middle-class-opportunities.[218] The panel recommended organizing high schools around small learning communities (SLCs) in which adult and student *relationships* are maximized and higher-level academics are connected to rigorous assignments in career pathway classes.

Such SLCs can replace the traditional placement of students into higher- or lower-level academic tracks and help both teachers and students shift their beliefs about students' abilities to perform higher-level work. They create an atmosphere in which teachers—academic and CTE—press students to achieve higher-level learning and students quickly receive the support needed to complete challenging, authentic tasks. Giving students autonomy in selecting methods for completing assignments can result in an active learning climate as opposed to the more passive learning climate found in teacher-centered classrooms.[219] Students see the usefulness of what they are learning when they see how it affects others and connects to employment and continuing educational opportunities.[220]

Successful implementation of optional career pathways through SLCs requires school leaders who believe strongly that such pathways can lead to a good job and postsecondary studies. Otherwise the SLC strategy risks becoming another low-level attempt to warehouse students who are perceived to be low-achievers. When implemented under the conditions presented in this book, the strategy becomes another way for more students to win—provided the small learning communities are staffed by career pathway and academic teachers who believe that "ability" is a variable that can be expanded through the principles of a growth mindset.

Belief 5: Growth Mindset

It is imperative that we—school, teacher, and counselor leaders—approach each student with a belief in a growth mindset and the certainty that their ability is not fixed.

Research conducted in Japan and the United States suggests that in Japan, effort is viewed as a primary determinant of achievement, whereas in the United States, educators and parents place more emphasis on innate student ability.[221] Changing results for underserved groups of students in the United States requires school leaders and teachers themselves to adopt a growth mindset—a belief that ability is not fixed and that students' ability can grow through engagement in higher-level learning experiences.

Stephanie Johnson stresses the importance of voicing bold goals in no uncertain terms:

> At the beginning of the school improvement process, district and school leaders need to make clear, bold statements about goals. We are going to discontinue teaching students in remedial classes. We are going to teach all students in the middle grades and high school to grade-level college- and career-readiness standards. And we are going to provide the additional time and support they need to meet the higher standards. Leadership needs to make the commitment and send the message.

Teachers' beliefs about students' ability shapes the level of learning and instruction they provide to students. A teacher of history who believes ability is fixed will be more likely to assign students believed to be lower-achievers tasks requiring only memorization of a series of facts, dates, and anecdotal information. Teachers who believe in a growth mindset will see such students capable of understanding the nature of historical events and appreciating the meaning history has for their everyday lives.[222]

Growth Mindset in Action

In her book *Mindset: The New Psychology of Success*, psychologist and educational researcher Carol Dweck offers several strategies school leaders and teachers can use to change both students' and their own perceptions about whether traditionally marginalized students can do higher-level work:[223]

- If you praise an outcome, make sure to talk to students about the process that led to the outcome. When a student fails, help them figure out why by asking questions such as: What strategies did you use? Why did they not work? What did you learn and what would you do different next time?

- Link effort and outcome by giving students a pretest before a unit of study. As students progress through the learning process, give the test again. This allows students to track their growth.

- Do not just tell students to try harder to complete an incomplete task. Rather, identify what the student does not understand and help the student figure out what to try next. Simply telling students to try harder can lead to discouragement if that increased effort does not lead to success.

- When students fail to complete an assignment correctly, work with them to figure out what they did incorrectly and what they could do.

- Do not give students an easy task and praise them for their success; that will not advance their abilities. Instead, give students meaningful and challenging assignments that require productive struggle, and shift the teacher's role to one of a facilitator, enabling students to take ownership of and confidence in their ability to complete higher-level work.

- Continually stress with students the value of effort, strategies, and appropriate help-seeking—and the belief that sustained, smart effort over time is key to higher achievement, not some special ability that they do or do not possess.

Belief 6: Teacher Expertise

We—school board, district, and school leaders—cannot underestimate the power of teacher expertise to transform student outcomes.

Teacher qualification has an enormous effect on student learning. Research finds that student learning gains are directly related to teachers having a strong academic background, quality preparation before teaching, certification in the field taught, and three or more years of experience as a teacher. Taken together, these factors account for most of student learning gains associated with schooling.[224] Conversely, students taught by underqualified teachers have significantly lower achievement in reading and mathematics.[225] In a 2020 poll of public school parents, 85 percent said they would like the administration in Washington, DC, to focus more on attracting and retaining good teachers.[226]

Stephanie Johnson has this to say on the topic of rethinking teacher assignments:

> I learned early on that low-performing students are often assigned to the most inexperienced teachers and the best teachers are assigned to high-performing students. To create a rationale for changing this pattern, we engage school and teacher leaders to do classroom observations to understand the differences in the quality of instruction received by the high-performing students versus the poor and disenfranchised students. We then ask them to consider whether if the low performers were given the same high-quality teaching and learning experiences, with extended support, they would perform at higher levels. Most agree they would.

It is essential that students who come from the most underserved population are assigned highly qualified teachers, so more can leave middle and high school ready to pursue advanced credentials or college degrees. Yet these are precisely the students who are often assigned to the newest and most inexperienced teachers—teachers who frequently are juggling large course loads and extracurricular duties with little support from school leaders or senior colleagues.[227] Qualified teachers can go beyond expected norms—not just covering materials, testing isolated sets of skills and knowledge, and teaching in isolation from other teachers, but engaging students (often in collaboration with colleagues) in relevant and demanding assignments that improve their achievement.

Middle and high school teachers need to work together to improve student readiness, as Stephanie Johnson observes:

> Early on [in the work of transformation], school and teacher leaders will recognize students entering grade 9 must be better prepared if they are going to meet higher expectations in high school. High school leaders work with district leaders to engage school and teacher leaders from the middle grades. They look at the data and see the percentage of students entering high school who are performing below grade level. Seeing is believing. This leads to some deep conversation and to exploring how to align middle school courses to college- and career-readiness standards and how to teach all middle school students an accelerated curriculum with extended support to do grade-level work.

Belief 7: Teacher Growth

We—school board, district, school, and teacher leaders—cannot underestimate the power of all teachers to grow with our full support.

To ensure highly qualified teachers are placed in all classrooms—and particularly in classrooms with students who have been considered the most challenging to teach—districts and school leaders must have a vision for high-quality professional development and must take responsibility for upgrading both the content knowledge and the skill capacity among existing staff to engage all students in higher-level learning.

This undertaking will require intensive, job-embedded professional learning experiences that extend over time and include in-class observation, follow-up, and feedback from other teachers and school leaders. And the professional development cannot be limited to only the teachers. Principals, too, must participate in a level of professional learning that ensures they will understand the shifts in classroom instruction that are expected.

Stephanie Johnson explains the key role of classroom observations in enabling teachers to learn from each other:

Once teachers, principals, and counselors participate in classroom observations, they quickly begin to see differences in the quality of teaching and assignments experienced by disenfranchised students. In time they recognize the need for a collaborative planning process in which all teachers participate within and across disciplines. This planning produces meaningful multiday, standards-based assignments with a sequence of planned daily lessons to engage and motivate students in higher-level learning.

It is really important to get teachers outside their own classrooms observing other teachers within their own school and other schools. This is a powerful change activity, and it rarely happens unless we make it happen.

We've used Skype and other mediums to let teachers and principals observe classrooms of similar-aged students and learn firsthand that highly qualified teachers know how to engage and get greater effort out of students very similar to their own. This process gradually builds an understanding that students are not the problem—it's the system that prevents them from performing at a higher level.

Proven professional development practices change how teachers teach, how they engage students in deeper learning, and how they work with their colleagues to improve teaching and learning.[228] A review of selected research studies revealed a positive link between in-depth, school-embedded professional development and both teaching practices and student outcomes. However, growth in teachers' effectiveness is influenced greatly by the quality of support they receive from district and school leaders. Lasting effects from professional development efforts will require a strong belief among district and school leaders that one-day, one-shot efforts and jumping from one popular topic to another will not result in the instructional shifts that engage all students successfully in higher-level learning.

Professional development focused on learner-driven teaching is most needed in mathematics and science classes to ensure that all students are taught these subjects at the level at which we currently teach the best students. Student-centered learning is important in every subject, of course. But in my experience, the problem of teacher-centric instruction is greatest in mathematics and science, where teachers are more likely to be tracked as low-level or high-level instructors with marked differences in teaching strategies.[229]

Research-Based Professional Development Practices

1. Conduct curriculum and instructional review in affected schools before professional development, followed by an initial one-day workshop with key district, school, and teacher leaders to analyze problems of practices.

2. Provide sufficient hours of professional development for middle and high school mathematics and science teachers who lack a major in their teaching field to obtain the equivalent. This effort may involve online courses to advance teachers' content knowledge.

3. Provide at least 10 to 12 days of professional development spread over three years to address common problems of practice, such as
   - Creating and implementing discipline-specific, literacy-based assignments and strategies in core academic and CTE courses.
   - Creating and adapting formative assessment lessons and powerful math practices to engage students in multistep abstract and real-world mathematical problems.
   - Engaging and supporting CTE teachers in formulating and implementing rigorous, real-world, project-based assignments.
   - Engaging cross-discipline teams of academic and career pathway teachers in planning assignments that connect academic content to challenging assignments in career-exploratory classes and CTE courses.

4. Develop full-time lead teachers in each core academic discipline and CTE to deliver professional development, coaching, and modeling of best practices to new and developing teachers.

5. Provide training for school leaders on the instructional shift teachers are being prepared to make and on the leader's role in supporting the creation and sustainment of professional learning communities. If principals do not understand and support the changes teachers are expected to make, it is unlikely that investment in professional development will have a lasting impact.

6. Assist schools in establishing professional learning communities, led by teachers who are proven leaders, through which teachers within and across disciplines plan rigorous assignments linked to college- and career-readiness standards.

7. Conduct frequent classroom observations using a valid and reliable rubric to determine whether the desired instructional shifts, including engaging students in higher-level learning experiences, are occurring. Classroom observations should be led by the principal, lead teachers, and external coaches, who then provide feedback to teachers, professional development providers, and leaders of professional learning communities.

8. Conduct an annual survey of students' and teachers' perceptions to measure the extent to which the desired shifts from covering materials through low-level assignments to engaging students in higher-level learning experiences are occurring.

The real measure of professional development's effect on teachers' beliefs about traditionally underserved groups will come from hard evidence drawn from classroom and external assessments of higher-level learning. In rural Rutherford County School District in North Carolina, for example, teachers implemented powerful math practices and literacy-based assignments. After two full years of implementation, students' growth increased across all seven of the district's schools, with 96 percent of participating teachers meeting or exceeding growth expectations, as measured by the Educational Value-Added Assessment System. For comparison, on average, 74 percent of teachers in all North Carolina public schools met or exceeded growth expectations.[230]

Belief 8: Boards and Leaders as Allies

It is critical that school and teacher leaders see school boards and district leaders as allies in providing underserved students with access to the same learning opportunities provided to the students we have traditionally served well.

When the Elementary and Secondary Education Act was signed into law in 1965,[231] a former college professor of mine informed me that it would not work—that providing students from low-income families with remedial, low-learning opportunities would not work. The professor explained that the best way to raise their achievement was to teach them as if they were the best students. That statement has remained in my memory for almost six decades. And almost six decades later, *we still have not accepted the fact* that we cannot bring students up to grade-level standards by providing them with below-grade-level instructional experiences.

Looking at the situation from a monetary perspective, Stephanie Johnson urges districts to "make the money matter" by involving teachers and school administrators in devising improvement strategies:

> One of the big mistakes district and school leaders make is to use money the way it's always been used rather than aligning the money strategically. In our experience, school districts get better results when they allow school leaders to engage teams of teachers with outside experts to figure out the primary causes for student deficits, what the school can do differently, and how they will use their resources to implement proven practices.
> When teachers and school leaders have some say over how money is invested and have gone through a thoughtful process to come up with sound solutions, they will be more committed to make it work than when answers are handed down from the district office with the dollars attached.

To break away from the failed practice of sorting students by perceived ability—to implement new practices based on the belief that most students can learn at high levels—*districts must provide assertive and enlightened leadership and support to schools.* The district can engage middle and high schools in creating a vision of what learning opportunities look like that will prepare *all* students for careers, college, or both. Districts should choose leaders who embrace this vision and who accept the mission to provide students with access to extraordinary learning opportunities that advance their innate abilities and talents to a higher level.

A principal's sense of collective efficacy—a belief that the school's staff can have a positive impact on student achievement despite other influences in students' lives that challenge their success—is key to the principal's influence on teaching and learning.[232] This finding is consistent with an analysis of survey and achievement data that yielded small but statistically significant effects of principal efficacy on student results.

How can districts grow the sense of collective efficacy in their school leaders? More than half of the principals in the study identified seven district behaviors as possible influences on their sense of efficacy, and these are generally consistent with behaviors identified by the Southern Regional Education Board:[233]

1. **Establish a clear focus and a strategic framework of core beliefs, effective practices, and goals to guide improving student achievement.** This can be a mission statement, such as "striving for excellence—no exceptions, no excuses." Or it can be a living framework collectively adopted and developed by the community over a period of time and continuously monitored and revised by an active school board.

2. **Organize and engage the school board and district office in support of each school.** The school board continuously focuses on improving student achievement, and central office personnel spend the majority of their time in the schools, working with principals and teachers to create cultures of success. Principals are given the authority to make hiring and firing decisions for their schools and are expected to be (and supported as) instructional leaders.

3. **Provide instructional coherence and support.** District leaders understand the challenging work principals must do and support the principals' focus on instruction and model that priority by publicly focusing on curriculum and instruction in school board and superintendent's meetings with staff and school leaders.

4. **Invest heavily in instruction-related professional learning for principals, teacher leaders, and district staff.** District leaders give principals tools to be effective instructional leaders and continuous learners by setting aside time for collective learning and instruction focused professional development, and provide beginning principals with induction and mentoring to increase their chances of success as effective instructional leaders.

5. **Provide highly qualified data that link student achievement to school and classroom practices and assist schools to use data effectively.** Supportive districts have adopted strategies to help principals disaggregate, analyze, and interpret their student achievement data quickly to discern student deficits and identify weaknesses in school and classroom practices.

6. **Optimize the use of resources to improve student learning.** District leaders provide principals with resources—human and financial—and

the flexibility to use those resources to address unique school needs while remaining consistent with school and district improvement vision. Schools with the greater needs receive greater resources and assistance in assessing what schools and classroom practices are working and in eliminating ineffective practices. They support outside coaches and facilitators who are skilled in assisting the school and teacher leaders to address how low-income and minority students are being taught and how instruction must change if achievement gaps are to be closed.

7. **Use open, credible processes to involve key school and community leaders in shaping a vision for improving schools.** Such districts engage the whole community in setting a common vision for student learning. They seek principals' and teacher leaders' ideas on major decisions about district policies, changes in curriculum and instructional improvements, use of professional development resources, and the district's budget. They encourage principals to use leadership teams to lead their schools and to engage the school community and in setting a vision and creating a school improvement plan.

District Strategies for Supporting School Leaders to Achieve Higher Levels of Learning for All Students[234]

- Set bold goals for preparing all students to graduate college-ready, career-ready, or both and for creating opportunities for all rising 9th graders to succeed in a college preparatory program of study and rigorous career pathway courses.

- Organize the central office—including human resources, finance, curriculum and instruction, data analysis, and technical assistance—to support principals and school leadership teams in implementing their own strategic improvement plan within a district framework of mission, goals, proven practices, and values.

- Encourage schools to engage teacher leaders, parents, and key community leaders in preparing all students for careers, postsecondary studies, or both.

- Provide principals with autonomy in selecting and assigning qualified staff, establishing a schedule, and using discretionary resources.

- Provide necessary resources for

  o Intensive professional development linked to the school-approved improvement plan;

  o Extended time for reteaching students who need assistance to meet higher expectations;

  o Attracting and retaining highly qualified teachers; and

  o Building cross-discipline professional learning communities for teacher collaboration and the sharing of professional norms for high-quality teaching and instruction.

- Establish a vision of what a college- and career-ready curriculum would look like in middle and high schools, including having all students complete a true college preparatory academic core and either an academic or a career focus.
- Provide an accelerated curriculum path that prepares some students for postsecondary studies and a career by the end of 11th grade and that uses the senior year to prepare the remaining students for postsecondary studies and careers.
- Establish indicators for assessing
  o District staff effectiveness in establishing a collaborative and supportive process for empowering principals and school leadership teams to take ownership of problems and implement proven solutions; and
  o Improvement in school practices, classroom practices, and student learning, using the school's annual improvement plan as a basis for auditing progress and providing feedback and added support to principals and distributed-leadership teams.
- Provide high-quality data analysis that links students' perceptions of the school and their classroom experiences to student achievement on both internal and external assessments and assist the school in using data effectively.

Belief 9: Principal Leadership

We—school boards, district leaders, teachers, and parents—can never forget that the principal's leadership is absolutely critical as we set out to take big actions and achieve big goals.

A 2010 study commissioned by the Wallace Foundation found that "principal leadership is second only to classroom instruction among all school-related factors that contribute to what students learn at school."[235] If teachers are the most important determinant of student success, the principal is the most important determinant of whether teaching and learning in every classroom across the school is as good as it can be. Whereas a single teacher affects 120 or more students each year, the principal's leadership affects all students in a middle school or high school. Selecting and investing in school leaders who understand effective instructional strategies and who can work with faculty to engage all students in higher-level learning is a cost-effective way to raise achievement among all students.

Based on my experience of working with more than 3,000 middle schools and high schools over 30 years, too many secondary school leaders and teachers base instruction for underserved groups of students on the assumption that those students lack the ability to do higher-level work. Schools won't break free of this educator culture of low expectations without administrators who understand this assumption is false—who are prepared and committed to create a new narrative about what historically underserved students can do.

What is an effective principal? Effective principals are those leaders who "strike a balance between stability and change by emphasizing two priorities: developing and supporting faculty to do their best, and designing school organizations to improve effectiveness."[236] They understand the change process and have the leadership and facilitation skills to manage effectively by keeping score on critical indicators, sharing results with the faculty, supporting teachers to search out new ideas, encouraging faculty teams to accept leadership roles and address critical problems, and staying focused on a long-term improvement agenda around quality instruction.

What Are Transformative Principals Able to Do?

In my conversation with Stephanie Johnson, I asked her to share the key principles that her department has developed for successful leadership in low-performing schools. Here is her response:

We support principals and teacher leaders to develop certain skill sets that we know make a difference for all groups of students, and particularly for minorities and disenfranchised students. These are some of the things great principals do to turn around and transform schools:

- Have technical knowledge about what good teaching and learning looks like, engage teachers in doing frequent classroom observations to learn from each other, and engage teachers in reflecting on what they've learned from observing others.

- Engage the faculty through distributed leadership teams in determining the schoolwide and classroom practices that are resulting in disenfranchised students having major learning gaps; assessing and selecting possible remedies for these gaps; and developing plans for implementing them with fidelity.

- Work with teacher leaders in setting expectations for classroom planning, assignments, and daily lesson plans to engage students in mastering and completing major assignments; establishing a system through which these expectations are achieved, assessed, refined and improved; and providing classroom walks each week for leaders and teachers to observe and determine if these practices are being implemented.

- Establish strong distributed-leadership teams within and across disciplines to implement major improvements such as literacy-based assignments in all academic and career pathway classes and planning connected mathematics lessons involving math, science, and career pathway teachers.

- Use their resources to draw upon expertise within and outside the school to grow existing faculty and to recruit, grow, and sustain new faculty as needed.

- With district support, use financial resources and external providers to create enriched learning experiences for every student that result in having a larger percentage of students each year meet college- and career-readiness standards.

- Insist on a transparent process that assesses the fidelity of implementation of new school and classroom strategies and ensures needed adjustments are made as part of a continuous school improvement culture.

- To ensure continuity, get support from the district to select the most promising members of the faculty who express a desire to become school leaders and initiate a mentoring/internship process that will prepare them to continue the work at the current school or to lead a continuous improvement effort at another school.

When all is said and done, Stephanie Johnson believes, district leaders and school board members who want great schools for all students need to keep one question in the forefront at all times: *Does every school in our system have a principal with the adaptive capacity to sustain the progress we are making and engage the faculty in a continuous improvement process, no matter what ongoing and emerging challenges we may face?* As she explains,

> In education we are good at trying new things, but we often do not plan how we are going to support teachers to implement them successfully, nor do we take time to check to see if they are being implemented as envisioned. If we are achieving expected student outcomes, and if we are making all the corrections and adjustments needed to keep our improvement efforts on track, effective principals make sure all these things happen. We won't have great schools without them.

Effective principals are less likely to achieve meaningful and lasting school transformation in top-down systems where major reform initiatives are owned and micromanaged at the district level. To realize the maximum impact of effective leadership on school culture, classroom practices, and student achievement, districts must provide the framework for school transformation based on goals and proven practices—and then develop, empower, engage, and support school and teacher leaders as key players in doing the challenging day-to-day work of reform.[237]

Summing Up

The nine beliefs described in this chapter provide the basis for designing school and classroom practices that provide all students—including those from historically underserved backgrounds—with learning opportunities to achieve upward mobility. Basing school and classroom practices on the nine beliefs requires the involvement of district, school, teacher, and other leaders in finding successful solutions that will ensure greater access to higher-level learning experiences and will enable tomorrow's high schools to achieve their *bold goals*.

Acknowledgments

I am forever grateful to SREB presidents Winfred Godwin, Mark Musick, and David Spence for their encouragement and support, spanning more than 30 years, and for giving me the opportunity to pursue a continuous improvement learning journey that made writing this book possible.

I'd like to offer a special thanks to the many staff at the Southern Regional Education Board who worked with me in leading the nation's largest network of high schools, middle schools, and career and technology centers implementing comprehensive school reform. Working alongside these educators and learning from them made it possible to present a vision of *Tomorrow's High Schools: Creating Pathways for Preparing Students for College and Careers.*

I am fortunate to have two coauthors who worked with me in writing Chapter 6. Monique Whorton served as an English teacher for 27 years at a majority-minority high school in Georgia. After retiring, she worked in multiple districts across the nation, helping academic and CTE teachers design and implement literacy-based assignments in their discipline area. For almost two decades, Jamie Lee Korns worked as an English teacher and a teacher trainer in both K–12 and higher education. She is passionate about using literacy-based assignments to bridge achievement gaps in support of a mission of social justice.

Thank you to Emily Kagey, whose transformation of my wordy dictated drafts led to a coherent and more concise set of chapters; John Norton, whose tireless effort to comb through the entire book added clarity, sharpness, and consistency to my ideas; and staff at ASCD, whose constant guidance helped make this book a presentable product in which I take great satisfaction.

This book would not have been possible without the lessons learned from school and teacher leaders who were part of the network of schools we worked with over the past 31 years. Their willingness to have students complete biannual surveys enabled the Educational Testing Service to connect students' school experiences reported in the surveys to their performance on National Assessment of Educational Progress exams in reading, math, and science. This provided a database that validates that schools that were willing to implement the vision set forth in this book witness significant improvements in student achievement, especially for disenfranchised students.

Thank you to the many school and teacher leaders who have taken ideas in this book as a framework for comprehensive school improvement and have shown that when you teach all students as if they were our best students, many become high-performers.

I want to thank states, foundations, and national governmental agencies for financially supporting our comprehensive school reform work for more than three decades, without which this book would not be possible.

I owe a debt of gratitude to those professionals who have been willing for me to interview them and include their statements in this book to provide validity that achieving bold goals is possible for all students.

Thank you to Beth Andrews, my administrative assistant for more than 25 years. During the writing of this book, she has constantly answered the phone to instruct me on some computer functions I had not mastered, and she typed up my heavily edited drafts of each chapter.

Finally, and most important, I'm eternally grateful to Helen, my wife of more than 60 years, who has supported me every step of this long journey in pursuit of a higher quality of education for every student in our high schools.

Downloadable Appendixes

The following appendixes are available online at www.ascd.org/CareerTechEdTools.

Appendix A: Designing Project-Based Exploratory Courses Around Six Personality Types

Appendix B: Example of an Assignment That Connects Academic and CTE Classes

Appendix C: Template for Planning a Powerful Project-Based Assignment

Appendix D: The Engineering Notebook

Appendix E: Example of a Model Pacing Calendar

Appendix F: Assessing an Engineering Notebook

Appendix G: Assessing 21st Century Skills

Appendix H: Prompts for Secondary-Level Activities Addressing Various Cognitive Demands

Appendix I: Developing an Advisement Lesson

Notes

1. Carnevale, A. P., Smith, N., & Strohl, J. (2013). *Recovery: Job growth and education requirements through 2020*. Georgetown Public Policy Institute, Georgetown University. cew.georgetown.edu/recovery2020

2. Ross, M., & Prchal Svajlenka, N. (2016, May 24). *Employment and disconnection among teens and young adults: The role of place, race, and education*. Brookings Institution. https://www.brookings.edu/research/employment-and-disconnection-among-teens-and-young-adults-the-role-of-place-race-and-education/

3. SREB. (2020, November). *The pandemic's dual threat for vulnerable workers: Accelerated automation and post-pandemic impacts could displace millions*. https://www.sreb.org/publication/pandemics-dual-threat-vulnerable-workers

4. Carnevale, A. P., Smith, N., & Strohl, J. (2013). *Recovery: Job growth and education requirements through 2020*. Georgetown Public Policy Institute, Georgetown University. cew.georgetown.edu/recovery2020

5. This story has been adapted, in part, from SREB's blog post, "Small-Town School, a Pacesetter" (April 19, 2018). For more details, see https://www.sreb.org/blog-post/small-town-school-pacesetter.

6. Bound, J., Lovenheim, M. F., & Turner, S. (2010). Why have college completion rates declined? An analysis of changing student preparation and collegiate resources. *American Economic Journal: Applied Economics, 2*(3): 129–157. https://www.ncbi.nlm.nih.gov/pmc/articles/PMC3140225

7. U.S. Census Bureau American Community Survey. https://www.census.gov/programs-surveys/acs

8. Georgetown Center on Education and Workforce. 2018. *Three educational pathways to good jobs, 2018*. https://cew.georgetown.edu/cew-reports/3pathways/

9. ACT. (2019). The condition of college and career readiness *2019* [Annual report]. http://www.act.org/content/act/en/research/reports/act-publications/condition-of-college-and-career-readiness-2019.html

10. SREB. (2011). *A new mission for the middle grades: Preparing students for a changing world*. https://www.sreb.org/publication/new-mission-middle-grades

11. Ibid.

12. Carnevale, A., Jayasundera, T., & Gulish, A. (2015). *Good jobs are back: College graduates are first in line*. Georgetown University Center on Education and the Workforce, p. 9. https://cew.georgetown.edu/cew-reports/goodjobsareback/

13. Ibid.

14. Bottoms, G., & Sundell, K. E. (2017). *Valuing both Cs in college- and career-readiness accountability systems: How states can use career pathways to close credential attainment and skills gaps*. SREB. https://www.sreb.org/ValuingBothCs

15. Carnevale, A., Jayasundera, T., & Gulish, A. (2015). *Good jobs are back: College graduates are first in line*. Georgetown University Center on Education and the Workforce, p. 9. https://cew.georgetown.edu/cew-reports/goodjobsareback/

16. Personal conversation with James Flynn, May 22, 2019.

17. SREB. (2017). *Connecting classrooms, careers and college: SREB's Making Schools Work school improvement process.* https://www.sreb.org/publication/connecting-classrooms-careers-and-college

18. SREB. (2011). *A new mission for the middle grades: Preparing students for a changing world.* https://www.sreb.org/publication/new-mission-middle-grades

19. Ibid.

20. Grovenstein, E. (2015). Transforming developmental education in North Carolina's community colleges. *Concepts.* The Hunt Institute. https://hunt-institute.org/resources/2015/04/transforming-developmental-education-in-north-carolinas-community-colleges-2/

21. Bottoms, G., & Sundell, K. E. (2017). *Valuing both Cs in college- and career-readiness accountability systems: How states can use career pathways to close credential attainment and skills gaps.* SREB. https://www.sreb.org/ValuingBothCs

22. Ibid.

23. Ibid.

24. Bromberg, M., & Theokas, C. (2016). *Meandering toward graduation: Transcript outcomes of high school graduates.* The Education Trust. https://edtrust.org/resource/meandering-toward-graduation/

25. Doughtery, S. M. (2016, April). *Career and technical education in high school: Does it improve student outcomes?* Thomas B. Fordham Institute. https://fordhaminstitute.org/national/research/career-and-technical-education-high-school-does-it-improve-student-outcomes

26. SREB Commission on Computer Science and Information Technology. (2016, November). *Bridging the computer science education gap.* SREB. https://www.sreb.org/publication/bridging-computer-science-education-gap

27. Carnevale, A. P., Fasules, M. L., Quinn, M. C., & Campbell, K. P. (2019). *Born to win, schooled to lose: Why equally talented students don't get equal chances to be all they can be.* Georgetown University Center on Education and the Workplace. https://1gyhoq479ufd3yna29x7ubjn-wpengine.netdna-ssl.com/wp-content/uploads/FR-Born_to_win-schooled_to_lose.pdf

28. Ibid.

29. Carnevale, A. P., Smith, N., & Strohl, J. (2013). *Recovery: Job growth and education requirements through 2020.* Georgetown Public Policy Institute, Georgetown University. cew.georgetown.edu/recovery2020

30. Career Key. (n.d.). *Holland's six personality types.* https://www.careerkey.org/fit/personality/holland-personality-types

31. Kemple, J. J., & Scott-Clayton, J. (2004, March). *Career academies: Impacts on labor market outcomes and education attainment.* MDRC. https://files.eric.ed.gov/fulltext/ED484616.pdf

32. National Research Council & Institute of Medicine. (2004). *Engaging schools: Fostering high school students' motivation to learn.* National Academies Press, p. 83.

33. Ibid., pp. 80–81.

34. Ibid., pp. 68–69.

35. Oakes, J., & Saunders, M. (2008). *Beyond tracking: Multiple pathways to college, career, and civic participation.* Harvard Education Press, p. 204.

36. Allred, S. G., & Foster, K. A. (2018). *Without trumpets: Continuous educational improvement, journey to sustainability.* Rowman & Littlefield, p. 68.

37. Herlihy, C. M., & Quint, J. (2006). *Emerging evidence on improving high school student achievement and graduation rates: The effects of four popular improvement programs.* National High School Center, American Institutes for Research. https://www.mdrc.org/sites/default/files/Emerging%20Evidence%20full.pdf

38. Dewey, J. (1916). Thinking in education. In J. Dewey, *Democracy and education: An introduction to the philosophy of education* (pp. 179–192). Free Press, p. 191.

39. Gray, K., & Koncz, A. (2017). The key attributes employers seek on students' résumés. National Association of Colleges and Employers (NACE).

40. Bottoms, G. (2014a). *High Schools That Work 2014 assessment and survey report.* SREB; Bottoms, G. (2014b). *The Advanced Career spring 2014 assessment and survey report.* SREB; Bottoms, G. (2020, March). The voice of CTE success. *Techniques,* 20–22.

41. SREB. *Analysis of 2012 and 2014 High Schools That Work assessment and student survey data;* Bottoms, G. (2020, March). The voice of CTE success. *Techniques,* 20–22.

42. Trends across more than 30 years of data from the Southern Regional Education Board's *High Schools That Work* assessment and student survey. Bottoms, G., & Winkler, D. (2019, February). Powerful assignments matter in CTE classes. *Techniques,* 23.

43. SREB. (2014). *Kentucky report: From two systems to one world-class system of technical centers.* https://education.ky.gov/CTE/Documents/ky_report_with_appendices_rev_5-22-14.pdf

44. Bottoms, G., & Sundell, K. (2016). *Career pathways: Accelerating access to the middle class.* SREB. https://www.sreb.org/publication/career-pathways

45. SREB. (2009). *The next generation of school accountability: A blueprint for raising high school achievement and graduation rates in SREB states.* https://www.sreb.org/publication/next-generation-school-accountability

46. **Disclaimer:** All AC curriculum and assessment materials are the property of SREB as established under U.S. Copyright Laws. SREB grants access to these materials for review. Only teachers who successfully complete training may use these materials in their classrooms. These materials cannot be duplicated, shared, or distributed without the express written permission of SREB. For more information about the SREB Advanced Career (AC) Curriculum, visit www.sreb.org/publication/clone-college-or-career-O.

47. For more information on formative and summative assessments, see Chapter 7 in G. Bottoms, D. Pucel, & I. Phillips, *Designing challenging vocational courses* (1997), SREB.

48. Results from the Southern Regional Education Board's 2018 *Technology Centers That Work* student survey.

49. Langdon, D., McKittrick, G., Beede, D., Khan, B., & Doms, M. (2011). STEM: Good jobs now and for the future. U.S. Department of Commerce.

50. ACT. (2019). *The condition of college and career readiness 2019* [Annual report]. http://www.act.org/content/act/en/research/reports/act-publications/condition-of-college-and-career-readiness-2019.html

51. National Assessment of Educational Progress. (2019). *NAEP report card: Mathematics.* National Center for Education Statistics. https://www.nationsreportcard.gov/mathematics/?grade=8

52. Hess, F. (2018, June 6). The college dropout problem. *Forbes.* https://www.forbes.com/sites/frederickhess/2018/06/06/the-college-dropout-problem/?sh=25f7735b5fd2

53. Bottoms, G. (2011). *A new mission for the middle grades: Preparing students for a changing world.* SREB.

54. Gonser, S. (2017, October 31). *Without changes in education, the future of work will leave more people behind* [Hechinger report]. https://hechingerreport.org/without-changes-education-future-work-will-leave-people-behind/

55. Bottoms, G. (2010) *Getting students ready for college and careers: Transitional senior mathematics.* SREB.

56. Kramarski, B., Mevarech, Z. R., & Arami, M. (2002). The effects of metacognitive instruction on solving mathematical authentic tasks. *Educational Studies in Mathematics, 49,* 225–250.

57. National Council of Teachers of Mathematics (NCTM). (2014). *Principles to actions: Ensuring mathematical success for all.*

58. Ibid.

59. Fuson, K. C., Kalchman, M., & Bransford, J. D. (2005). Mathematical understanding: An introduction. In M. S. Donovan & J. D. Bransford (Eds.), *How students learn: History, mathematics, and science in the classroom* (pp. 217–256). National Research Council, National Academies Press; Jitendra, A. K., Peterson-Brown, S., Lein, A. E., Zaslofsky, A. F., Kunkel, A. K., Jung, P.-G., et al. (2015). Teaching mathematical word problem solving: The quality of evidence for strategy instruction priming the problem structure.

Journal of Learning Disabilities, 48(1), 51–72; Lesh, R., Post, T. R., & Behr, M. (1987). Representations and translations among representations in mathematics learning and problem solving. In C. Janvier (Ed.), *Problems of representation in the teaching and learning of mathematics* (pp. 33–40). Erlbaum.

60. National Mathematics Advisory Panel (NMAP). (2008). *Foundations for success: The final report of the National Mathematics Advisory Panel.* U.S. Department of Education. https://files.eric.ed.gov/fulltext/ ED500486.pdf; National Research Council. (2001). *Adding it up: Helping children learn mathematics.* National Academies Press.

61. National Council of Teachers of Mathematics (NCTM). (2014). *Principles to actions: Ensuring mathematical success for all.*

62. Fuson, K. C., Kalchman, M., & Bransford, J. D. (2005). Mathematical understanding: An introduction. In M. S. Donovan & J. D. Bransford (Eds.), *How students learn: History, mathematics, and science in the classroom* (pp. 217–256). National Research Council, National Academies Press; Martin, G. W. (2009). The NCTM high school curriculum project: Why it matters to you. *Mathematics Teacher, 103*(3), 164–166.

63. Huinker, D. (2013). Examining dimensions of fraction operation sense. In F. Fennell & W. R. Speer (Eds.), *Defining mathematics education: Presidential yearbook selections 1926–2012. Seventy-fifth Yearbook of the National Council of Teachers of Mathematics (NCTM).* NCTM; Stylianou, D. A., & Silver, E. A. (2004). The role of visual representations in advanced mathematical problem solving: An examination of expert-novice similarities and differences. *Mathematical Thinking and Learning, 6*(4), 353–387.

64. National Mathematics Advisory Panel (NMAP). (2008). *Foundations for success: The final report of the National Mathematics Advisory Panel.* U.S. Department of Education. https://files.eric.ed.gov/fulltext/ ED500486.pdf; National Research Council. (2001). *Adding it up: Helping children learn mathematics.* National Academies Press.

65. Ashcraft, M. H. (2002). Math anxiety: Personal, educational, and cognitive consequences. *Current Directions in Psychological Science, 11*(5), 181–85; Baroody, A. J. (2006). Why children have difficulties mastering the basic number combinations. *Teaching Children Mathematics, 13*(1), 22–31. https://www .kentuckymathematics.org/docs/eerti-BaroodyTCM2006.pdf; Griffin, S. (2003). Laying the foundation for computational fluency in early childhood. *Teaching Children Mathematics, 9*(6), 306–309; Ramirez, G., Gunderson, E. A., Levine, S. C., & Beilock, S. L. (2013). Math anxiety, working memory, and math achievement in early elementary school. *Journal of Cognition and Development, 14*(2), 187–202.

66. Carpenter, T. P., Loef Franke, M., & Levi, L. (2003). *Thinking mathematically: Integrating arithmetic and algebra in elementary school.* Heinemann; Griffin, S. (2003). Laying the foundation for computational fluency in early childhood. *Teaching Children Mathematics, 9*(6), 306–309.

67. Bottoms, G., Merritt, A., Mollette, D., & Tadlock, J. (2018). *Making math matter: High-quality assignments that help students solve problems and own their learning.* SREB.

68. Boaler, J., & Staples, M. (2008). Creating mathematical futures through an equitable teaching approach: The case of Railside School. *Teachers College Record, 110*(3), 608–645; Hiebert, J., & Wearne, D. (1993). Instructional tasks, classroom discourse, and students' learning in second-grade arithmetic. *American Educational Research Journal, 30*(2), 393–425; Stein, M. K., & Lane, S. (1996). Instructional tasks and the development of student capacity to think and reason: An analysis of the relationship between teaching and learning in a reform mathematics project. *Educational Research and Evaluation, 2*(1), 50–80.

69. Hiebert, J., & Grouws, D. A. (2007). The effects of classroom mathematics teaching on students' learning. In F. K. Lester Jr. (Ed.), *Second handbook of research on mathematics teaching and learning* (pp. 371–404). National Council of Teachers of Mathematics. https://citeseerx.ist.psu.edu/viewdoc/ download?doi=10.1.1.405.3591&rep=rep1&type=pdf; National Council of Teachers of Mathematics (NCTM). (2014). *Principles to actions: Ensuring mathematical success for all;* Warshauer, H. K. (2011). *The role of productive struggle in teaching and learning middle school mathematics* (Doctoral dissertation). University of Texas at Austin. https://repositories.lib.utexas.edu/handle/2152/ETD-UT-2011-12-4527

70. Bottoms, G., Merritt, A., Molette, D., & Tadlock, J. (2018). *Making math matter: High-quality assignments that help students solve problems and own their earning.* SREB.

71. Bossé, M., Lynch-Davis, K., Adu-Gyamfi, K., & Chandler, K. (2017). Instruction and learning through formative assessments. *Mathematics Teacher, 110*(5), 372–379.

72. Reinhart, S. C. (2000). Never say anything a kid can say! *Mathematics Teaching in the Middle School, 5*(8), 478–83. https://www.nctm.org/Publications/Mathematics-Teaching-in-Middle-School/2000/Vol5/Issue8/Never-Say-Anything-a-Kid-Can-Say!/; Stein, M. K., Smith, M. S., Henningsen, M., & Silver, E. A. (2009). *Implementing standards-based mathematics instruction: A casebook for professional development* (2nd ed.). Teachers College Press.

73. National Council of Teachers of Mathematics (NCTM). (2014). *Principles to actions: Ensuring mathematical success for all.*

74. Boaler, J., & Brodie, K. (2004). The importance, nature, and impact of teacher questions. In D. E. McDougall & J. A. Ross (Eds.), *Proceedings of the 26th annual meeting of the North American chapter of the International Group for the Psychology of Mathematics Education* (Vol. 2, pp. 774–782), Ontario Institute for Studies in Education, University of Toronto; Chapin, S. H., & O'Connor, C. (2007). Academically productive talk: Supporting students' learning in mathematics. In *The learning of mathematics, sixty-ninth yearbook of the National Council of Teachers of Mathematics* (pp. 113–128). NCTM.

75. Jacobs, V. R., & Ambrose, R. C. (2008). Making the most of story problems. *Teaching Children Mathematics, 15*(5), 260–66; National Council of Teachers of Mathematics (NCTM). (2014). *Principles to actions: Ensuring mathematical success for all.* NCTM.

76. Simpson, A., Mokalled, S., Ellenburg, L., & Che, S. M. (2015). A tool for rethinking teachers' questioning. *Mathematics Teaching in the Middle School, 20*(5), 294–302.

77. Bray, W. S. (2013). How to leverage the potential of mathematical errors. *Teaching Children Mathematics, 19*(7), 424–431.

78. North Carolina End-of-Grade and End-of-Course Assessment Data, 2015–2016.

79. Wiliam, D. (2007). Keeping learning on track: Classroom assessment and the regulation of learning. In Frank K. Lester Jr. (Ed.), *Second handbook of research on mathematics teaching and learning* (pp. 1051–1098). Information Age.

80. Duckor, B., Holmberg, C., & Becker, J. R. (2017). Making moves: Formative assessment in mathematics. *Mathematics Teaching in the Middle School, 22*(6), 334–342.

81. Crespo, S. (2000). Seeing more than right and wrong answers: Prospective teachers' interpretations of students' mathematical work. *Journal of Mathematics Teacher Education, 3*(2), 155–181; Sarama, J., & Clements, D. H. (2009). "Concrete" computer manipulatives in mathematics education. *Child Development Perspectives, 3*(3), 145–150; Swan, M. (2001). Dealing with misconceptions in mathematics. In P. Gates (Ed.), *Issues in mathematics teaching* (pp. 147–165). Routledge.

82. Bottoms, G., Merritt, A., Mollette, D., & Tadlock, J. (2018). *Making math matter: High-quality assignments that help students solve problems and own their learning.* SREB.

83. National Council of Teachers of Mathematics (NCTM). (2014). *Principles to actions: Ensuring mathematical success for all.*

84. Hufferd-Ackles, K., Fuson, K. C., & Sherin, M. G. (2004). Describing levels and components of a math-talk learning community. *Journal for Research in Mathematics Education, 35*(2), 81–116; National Council of Teachers of Mathematics (NCTM). (2014). *Principles to actions: Ensuring mathematical success for all.*

85. Bottoms, G., Merritt, A., Mollette, D., & Tadlock, J. (2018). *Making math matter: High-quality assignments that help students solve problems and own their learning.* SREB.

86. Stein, M. K., Russell, J., & Smith, M. S. (2011). The role of tools in bridging research and practice in an instructional improvement effort. In W. F. Tate, K. D. King, & C. R. Anderson (Eds.), *Disrupting tradition: Research and practice pathways in mathematics education* (pp. 33–44). NCTM.

87. Townsend, C., Slavit, D., & McDuffie, A. R. (2018). Supporting all learners in productive struggle. *Mathematics Teaching in the Middle School, 23*(4), 216–224.

88. Hamilton, L., Halverson, R., Jackson, S. S., Mandinach, E., Supovitz, J. A., & Wayman, J. C. (2009). *Using student achievement data to support instructional decision making* (NCEE 2009-4067). Institute of Education Sciences, U.S. Department of Education. https://ies.ed.gov/ncee/wwc/Docs/PracticeGuide/ dddm_pg_092909.pdf

89. National Council of Teachers of Mathematics (NCTM). (2014). *Principles to actions: Ensuring mathematical success for all.*

90. Hiebert, J., Morris, A. K., Berk, D., & Jansen, A. (2007). Preparing teachers to learn from teaching. *Journal of Teacher Education, 58*(1), 47–61. https://www.researchgate.net/publication/241141383_Preparing_ Teachers_to_Learn_from_Teaching; Wiliam, D. (2011). *Embedded formative assessment.* Solution Tree.

91. Gray, K., & Koncz, A. (2017). The key attributes employers seek on students' résumés. National Association of Colleges and Employers (NACE).

92. Gewertz, C. (2018., September 15). What literacy skills do students really need for work? *Education Week, 38*(06). https://www.edweek.org/ew/articles/2018/09/26/what-literacy-skills-do-students-really-need .html

93. Berger, R. (2003). *An ethic of excellence: Building a culture of craftsmanship with students.* Heinemann; Birky, G. D., Chazan, D., & Farlow Morris, K. (2013). In search of coherence and meaning: Madison Morgan's experiences and motivations as an African American learner and teacher. *Teachers College Record, 115*(2), 1–42; Borman, G. D., Slavin, R. E., Cheung, A. C. K., Chamberlain, A. M., Madden, N. A., & Chambers, B. (2007). Final reading outcomes of the national randomized field trial of Success for All. *American Educational Research Journal, 44*(3), 701–731; Camera, L. (2016, January 13). Achievement gap between white and black students still gaping. *U.S. News & World Report.* https://www.usnews.com/news/blogs/ data-mine/2016/01/13/achievement-gap-between-white-and-black-students-still-gaping

94. National Assessment of Educational Progress (NAEP). (2019). NAEP report card: 2019 NAEP reading assessment. https://www.nationsreportcard.gov/highlights/reading/2019/

95. Clough, S., & Montgomery, S. (2015). *How ACT assessments align with state college and career readiness standards.* https://www.act.org/content/dam/act/unsecured/documents/Alignment-White-Paper.pdf

96. Amos, J. (2018, April 11). *Nation's report card shows little progress in reading and math—except on this measure.* Alliance for Excellent Education. https://all4ed.org/nations-report-card-shows-little-progress-in- reading-and-math-except-on-this-measure/

97. Wine, J., Jansen, N., & Wheeless, S. (2011). *2004/09 beginning postsecondary students longitudinal study (BPS:04/09).* Institute of Education Sciences, U.S. Department of Education. https://files.eric.ed.gov/ fulltext/ED566501.pdf

98. Moore, D. W., Bean, T. W., Birdyshaw, D., & Rycik, J. A. (1999). *Adolescent literacy: A position statement for the Commission on Adolescent Literacy of the International Reading Association.* International Reading Association, p. 3.

99. Murray, R., & Bottoms, G. (2008). *Getting students ready for college and careers: Transitional senior English.* SREB; Murray, R., Bottoms, G., Cooney, S., Feagin, C., Nohara, D., & the SREB panel for reading/language arts. (2003). *Getting students ready for college-preparatory/honors English: What middle grades students need to know and be able to do.* SREB; Common Core State Standards Initiative. (n.d.). *Common Core State Standards for English language arts & literacy.* http://www.corestandards.org/ELA-Literacy/RL/introduction- for-6-12/

100. Guthrie, J. T., Anderson, E., Alao, S., & Rinehart, J. (1999). Influences of concept-oriented reading instruction on strategy use and conceptual learning from text. *Elementary School Journal, 99*(4), 343–366.

101. Graham, S., Hebert, M., Sandbank, M., & Harris, K. R. (2016). Assessing the writing achievement of young struggling writers: Application of generalizability theory. *Learning Disability Quarterly, 39*(2), 72–82; Kamil, M. L., Borman, G. D., Dole, J., Kral, C. C., Salinger, T., & Torgesen, J. (2008). *Improving adolescent literacy: Effective classroom and intervention practices: A practice guide* (NCEE #2008-4027). National Center for Education Evaluation and Regional Assistance, Institute of Education Sciences, U.S. Department of Education.

102. Greenleaf, C. L., Litman, C., Hanson, T., Rosen, R., Boscardin, C., Herman, J., et al. (2011). Integrating literacy and science in biology: Teaching and learning impacts of reading apprenticeship professional development. *American Educational Research Journal, 48*(3), 647–717; Fang, Z., & Schleppegrell, M. J. (2010). Disciplinary literacies across content areas: Supporting secondary reading through functional language analysis. *Journal of Adolescent & Adult Literacy, 53*(7), 587–597.

103. Shanahan, T., & Shanahan, C. (2008). Teaching disciplinary literacy to adolescents: Rethinking content area literacy. *Harvard Educational Review, 78*(1), 40–59.

104. Bottoms, G., Rock, D., & Tadlock, J. (2018). *Literacy across the curricula: Literacy success stories.* SREB.

105. Kamil, M. L., Borman, G. D., Dole, J., Kral, C. C., Salinger, T., & Torgesen, J. (2008). *Improving adolescent literacy: Effective classroom and intervention practices: A practice guide* (NCEE #2008-4027). National Center for Education Evaluation and Regional Assistance, Institute of Education Sciences, U.S. Department of Education.

106. Kosanovich, M. L., Reed, D. K., & Miller, D. H. (2010). *Bringing literacy strategies into content instruction: Professional learning for secondary-level teachers.* RMC Research Corporation, Center on Instruction; Brown, R., Pressley, M., Van Meter, P., & Schuder, T. (1996). A quasi-experimental validation of transactional strategies instruction with low-achieving second-graders. *Journal of Educational Psychology, 88*(1), 18–37.

107. Kamil, M. L., Borman, G. D., Dole, J., Kral, C. C., Salinger, T., & Torgesen, J. (2008). *Improving adolescent literacy: Effective classroom and intervention practices: A practice guide* (NCEE #2008-4027). National Center for Education Evaluation and Regional Assistance, Institute of Education Sciences, U.S. Department of Education.

108. Judkins, D., St. Pierre, R., Gutmann, B., Goodson, B., von Glatz, A., Hamilton, J., et al. (2008). *A study of classroom literacy interventions and outcomes in Even Start, executive summary* (NCEE 2008–4028). National Center for Education Evaluation and Regional Assistance, Institute of Education Sciences, U.S. Department of Education. https://ies.ed.gov/pubsearch/pubsinfo.asp?pubid=NCEE20084028

109. Brown, R., Pressley, M., Van Meter, P., & Shuder, T. (1996). A quasi-experimental validation of transactional strategies instruction with low-achieving second-graders. *Journal of Educational Psychology, 88*(1), 18–37.

110. Gersten, R., Fuchs, L. S., Williams, J. P., & Baker, S. (2001). Teaching reading comprehension strategies to students with learning disabilities: A review of the research. *Review of Educational Research, 71*(2), 279–320.

111. Moss, C., Brookhart, S., & Long, B. (2011). Knowing your learning target. *Educational Leadership, 68*(6), 66–69.

112. Kamil, M. L., Borman, G. D., Dole, J., Kral, C. C., Salinger, T., & Torgesen, J. (2008). *Improving adolescent literacy: Effective classroom and intervention practices: A practice guide* (NCEE #2008-4027). National Center for Education Evaluation and Regional Assistance, Institute of Education Sciences, U.S. Department of Education.

113. Mueller, C. M., & Dweck, C. S. (1998). Praise for intelligence can undermine children's motivation and performance. *Journal of Personality and Social Psychology, 75*(1), 33–52.

114. Henderlong, J., & Lepper, M. R. (2002). The effects of praise on children's intrinsic motivation: A review and synthesis. *Psychological Bulletin, 128*(5), 774–795. doi: 10.1037/0033-2909.128.5.774

115. Leong, C. K., & Jerred, W. D. (2001). Effects of consistency and adequacy of language information on understanding elementary mathematics word problems. *Annals of Dyslexia, 51*, 277–298.

116. Duffy, G. G. (2002). The case for direct explanation of strategies. In C. C. Block & M. Pressley (Eds.), *Comprehension instruction* (pp. 28–41). Guilford; Kosanovich, M. L., Reed, D. K., & Miller, D. H. (2010). *Bringing literacy strategies into content instruction: Professional learning for secondary-level teachers.* Portsmouth, NH: RMC Research Corporation, Center on Instruction.

117. Brown, A. L., Campione, J. C., & Day, J. D. (1981). Learning to learn: On training students to learn from text. *Educational Researcher, 10*(2), 14–21.

118. Pearson, P. D., & Dole, J. A. (1987). Explicit comprehension instruction: A review of research and a new conceptualization of instruction. *Elementary School Journal, 88*(2), 151–165.

119. Duffy, G. G. (2002). The case for direct explanation of strategies. In C. C. Block & M. Pressley (Eds.), *Comprehension instruction* (pp. 28–41). Guilford.

120. Kamil, M. L., Borman, G. D., Dole, J., Kral, C. C., Salinger, T., & Torgesen, J. (2008). *Improving adolescent literacy: Effective classroom and intervention practices: A practice guide* (NCEE #2008-4027). National Center for Education Evaluation and Regional Assistance, Institute of Education Sciences, U.S. Department of Education.

121. Applebee, A. N., Langer, J. A., Nystrand, M., & Gamoran, A. (2003). Discussion-based approaches to developing understanding: Classroom instruction and student performance in middle and high school English. *American Educational Research Journal, 40*(3), 685–730; ASVAB. (2020). ASVAB Scoring. http://www.officialasvab.com/understand_res.htm

122. Langer, J. A. (2001). Beating the odds: Teaching middle and high school students to read and write well. *American Educational Research Journal, 38*(4), 837–880.

123. Kamil, M. L., Borman, G. D., Dole, J., Kral, C. C., Salinger, T., & Torgesen, J. (2008). *Improving adolescent literacy: Effective classroom and intervention practices: A practice guide* (NCEE #2008-4027). National Center for Education Evaluation and Regional Assistance, Institute of Education Sciences, U.S. Department of Education.

124. Reznitskaya, A., Anderson, R. C., McNurlen, B., Nguyen-Jahiel, K., Archodidou, A., & Kim, S. (2011). Influence of oral discussion on written argument. *Discourse Processes, 32*(2&3), 155–175; Applebee, A. N., Langer, J. A., Nystrand, M., & Gamoran, A. (2003). Discussion-based approaches to developing understanding: Classroom instruction and student performance in middle and high school English. *American Educational Research Journal, 40*(3), 685–730; ASVAB. (2020). ASVAB Scoring. http://www.officialasvab.com/understand_res.htm

125. Kamil, M. L., Borman, G. D., Dole, J., Kral, C. C., Salinger, T., & Torgesen, J. (2008). *Improving adolescent literacy: Effective classroom and intervention practices: A practice guide* (NCEE #2008-4027). National Center for Education Evaluation and Regional Assistance, Institute of Education Sciences, U.S. Department of Education.

126. Klingner, J. K., Vaughn, S., & Schumm, J. S. (1998). Collaborative strategic reading during social studies in heterogeneous fourth-grade classrooms. *Elementary School Journal, 99*(1), 3–22.

127. Black, P. J., & Wiliam, D. (1998). Assessment and classroom learning. *Assessment in Education: Principles, Policy and Practice, 5*(1), 7–74.

128. Kamil, M. L., Borman, G. D., Dole, J., Kral, C. C., Salinger, T., & Torgesen, J. (2008). *Improving adolescent literacy: Effective classroom and intervention practices: A practice guide* (NCEE #2008-4027). National Center for Education Evaluation and Regional Assistance, Institute of Education Sciences, U.S. Department of Education.

129. Black, P., Harrison, C., Lee, C., Marshall, B., & Wiliam, D. (2003). *Assessment for learning: Putting it into practice.* Maidenhead, Berkshire, UK: Open University Press; Kamil, M. L., Borman, G. D., Dole, J., Kral, C. C., Salinger, T., & Torgesen, J. (2008). *Improving adolescent literacy: Effective classroom and intervention practices: A practice guide* (NCEE #2008-4027). National Center for Education Evaluation and Regional Assistance, Institute of Education Sciences, U.S. Department of Education.

130. Webb, N. L. (1997). *Criteria for alignment of expectations and assessments in mathematics and science education* (Research Monograph No. 6). Council of Chief State School Officers.

131. Boyle-Baise, M., Hsu, M.-C., Johnson, S., Serriere, S. C., & Stewart, D. (2008). Putting reading first: Teaching social studies in elementary classrooms. *Theory & Research in Social Education, 36*(3), 233–255; Colwell, J., & Taylor, V. (2020). Peer review in online professional communities to support elementary disciplinary literacy planning. In R. Karchmer-Klein & K. E. Pytash (Eds.), *Effective practices in online teacher preparation for literacy educators* (pp. 107–127). Hershey, PA: IGI Global. doi: 10.4018/978-1-

7998-7294-8.ch028; Shanahan, C., & Shanahan, T. (2014). Does disciplinary literacy have a place in elementary school? *The Reading Teacher, 67*(8), 636–639.

132. Bottoms, G., Rock, D., & Tadlock, J. (2018). *Literacy across the curricula: Teacher success stories.* SREB. https://www.sreb.org/publication/literacy-across-curricula, p. 6.

133. Ibid., p. 18.

134. Literacy Design Collaborative and Mathematics Design Collaborative. (2014). Students step up when teachers and leaders transform classrooms. SREB, p. 24. https://www.sreb.org/sites/main/files/file-attachments/14v10_ldc_mdc_vignettes.pdf

135. Wang, J., Herman, J. L., Epstein, S., Leon, S., La Torre, D., & Bozeman, V. (2020). *Literacy Design Collaborative 2018–2019 evaluation report* (CRESST Report 867). University of California, Los Angeles, National Center for Research on Evaluation, Standards, and Student Testing (CRESST).

136. Wang, J., Herman, J. L., Epstein, S., Leon, S., La Torre, D., Chang, S., et al. (2019). *Literacy Design Collaborative 2017–2018 evaluation report for New York City Department of Education.* University of California, Los Angeles, National Center for Research on Evaluation, Standards, and Student Testing (CRESST).

137. National Assessment of Educational Progress (NAEP). (2019). *NAEP report card: Mathematics: Explore results for the 2019 NAEP mathematics assessment.* https://www.nationsreportcard.gov/mathematics/?grade=8; *NAEP report card: Reading: National average scores.* https://www.nationsreportcard.gov/reading/nation/scores/?grade=8

138. See the National Assessment of Educational Progress (NAEP), The nation's report card: Reading 2019 and math 2019.

139. Georgia Leadership Institute for School Improvement (GLISI). (2019). *The human element in improving education.* https://glisi.org/resources/the-human-element-in-improving-education/

140. Wise, A. E. (2019, April 29). Toward equality of educational opportunity: What's most promising? *KAPPAN, 100*(8), 8–13. https://kappanonline.org/equality-educational-opportunity-most-promising-wise/

141. Bottoms, G., Preston, A., & Han, L. (2004). *High school reform works—when implemented: A comparative study of high- and low-implementation schools.* SREB; Bottoms, G., Preston, A., & Han, L. (2006). *Students can't wait: High schools must turn knowledge into action.* SREB.

142. See https://www.sreb.org/readiness-courses-0.

143. Interview with district leader.

144. Ibid.

145. Rettig, M. D., & Canady, R. L. (1998, March). High failure rates in required mathematics courses: Can a modified block schedule be part of the cure? *NASSP Bulletin, (82)*596, 56–65. https://journals.sagepub.com/doi/pdf/10.1177/019263659808259611

146. Ibid.

147. See https://www.sreb.org/readiness-courses-0.

148. Bottoms, G. (2010, March 15). Best practices for a successful summer transition program. Presentation at the National Summer Learning Association, Tampa, FL; Bottoms, G. (2002). *Opening doors to the future: Preparing low-achieving middle grades students to succeed in high school.* SREB. https://eric.ed.gov/?id=ED469956

149. Bottoms, G. (2002). *Opening doors to the future: Preparing low-achieving middle grades students to succeed in high school.* SREB. https://eric.ed.gov/?id=ED469956.

150. Blankstein, A. M. (2004) *Failure is not an option: 6 principles that guide student achievement in high-performing schools.* Corwin.

151. Bottoms, G. (2010). A survey of schools in SREB's school improvement network using Success for All. Findings summarized in "Ensuring failure is not an option in middle grades and high schools" [PowerPoint presentation], SREB Summer Staff Development Conference.

152. Blankstein, A. M. (2004) *Failure is not an option: 6 principles that guide student achievement in high-performing schools.* Corwin.

153. Bottoms, G. (2002). *Opening doors to the future: Preparing low-achieving middle grades students to succeed in high school.* SREB.

154. Ibid.

155. Ibid.

156. Ibid., pp. 9–12.

157. ACT. (2019). *The condition of college and career readiness 2019.* https://www.act.org/content/dam/act/unsecured/documents/National-CCCR-2019.pdf

158. Ibid.

159. Ibid.

160. Carnevale, A. P., Smith, N., & Strohl, J. (2013). *Recovery: Job growth and education requirements through 2020.* Georgetown Public Policy Institute, Georgetown University. cew.georgetown.edu/recovery2020

161. ACT. (2019). *The condition of college and career readiness 2019.* https://www.act.org/content/dam/act/unsecured/documents/National-CCCR-2019.pdf

162. *Phi Delta Kappan.* (2019, September). Frustration in the schools: The 51st annual PDK poll of the public's attitudes toward the public schools [Special supplement], *Phi Delta Kappan, (101)*1, p. 13.

163. Bottoms, G., & Young, M. (2008). *Lost in transition: Building a better path from school to college and careers.* SREB.

164. Superintendent transition team report, Guilford County (NC) Schools, 2016–2017.

165. Bottoms, G. (2001, February). *The lost opportunity of the senior year: Making grade 12 count.* SREB.

166. SREB. (2018, Spring). High Schools That Work and Technology Centers That Work survey analysis.

167. Smialek, J. (2020, May 14). Poor Americans hit hardest by job losses amid Covid-19 lockdowns, Fed says. *New York Times.*

168. ACT. (2019). *The condition of college and career readiness.* https://www.act.org/content/act/en/research/reports/act-publications/condition-of-college-and-career-readiness-2019.html

169. SREB Commission on Community Colleges. (2015, February). *Community colleges in the South: Strengthening readiness and pathways.* Report of the SREB Commission on Community Colleges. SREB. https://www.sreb.org/publication/community-colleges-south-strengthening-readiness-and-pathways

170. Author's interviews with school leaders.

171. Bottoms, G., & Squires, J. (2017). *Readiness courses: Preparing students for college and careers.* SREB. https://www.sreb.org/sites/main/files/file-attachments/17v05_readinesscourses_preparing_final.pdf; see courses at https://www.sreb.org/readiness-courses-literacy-math.

172. *SREB's Ready for College: Three years of evidence,* J. Squire & K. Barger, SREB. https://www.sreb.org/publication/ready-college-three-years-evidence

173. Author's interviews with state leaders.

174. Author's interviews with state leaders.

175. National Center for Educational Statistics at the Institute of Educational Sciences. (2020, May). *The condition of education 2020.* U.S. Department of Education. https://nces.ed.gov/pubs2020/2020144.pdf

176. National Student Clearinghouse Research Center. (2019). High school benchmarks—2019 Progression Rates. https://nscresearchcenter.org/high-school-benchmarks-2019/

177. Ibid.

178. Ibid.

179. Damon, W. (2008). *The path to purpose: Helping our children find their calling in life*. Free Press.

180. Phi Delta Kappan national public opinion poll, September 2017.

181. SREB. (2018). High Schools That Work student survey (unpublished).

182. National Research Council & Institute of Medicine. (2004). *Engaging schools: Fostering high school students' motivation to learn*. National Academies Press, p. 220.

183. Holzer, H. J., & Lerman, R. I. (2007). *America's forgotten middle-skill jobs: Education and training requirements in the next decade and beyond*. Workforce Alliance. https://www.urban.org/sites/default/files/publication/31566/411633-America-s-Forgotten-Middle-Skill-Jobs.PDF

184. Microsoft News Center. (2011, September 7). Microsoft releases national survey findings on how to inspire the next generation of doctors, scientists, software developers and engineers. https://news.microsoft.com/2011/09/07/microsoft-releases-national-survey-findings-on-how-to-inspire-the-next-generation-of-doctors-scientists-software-developers-and-engineers/; Harris Interactive. (2011.) *STEM perceptions: Student & parent study—Parents and students weigh in on how to inspire the next generation of doctors, scientists, software developers and engineers*. Study Commissioned by the Microsoft Corporation. https://news.microsoft.com/download/archived/presskits/citizenship/docs/STEMPerceptionsReport.pdf

185. See https://www.sreb.org/middle-grades-stem for information on middle-grades STEM courses.

186. Nelson, D. E. (1998). *An evaluation of the comprehensive guidance program in Utah Public Schools*. Utah State Office of Education.

187. Bottoms, G., & Phillips, I. (2010). *Skills for a lifetime: Teaching students the habits of success*. SREB; Bingham, M., & Stryker, S. (1990). *Career choices: A guide for teens and young adults: Who am I? What do I want? How do I get it?* Academic Innovations.

188. Bottoms, G. (2012). Career pathway programs of study for success: Engaging students intellectually, emotionally, socially and behaviorally in learning. Presentation at the 26th Annual High Schools That Work Staff Development Conference, New Orleans, LA.

189. Marshall, W., & Craig, R. (2019, March 29). The dangers of skills-gap skepticism. *The Hill*. https://thehill.com/opinion/finance/436350-the-dangers-of-skills-gap-skepticism

190. Carnevale, A. P., Smith, N., & Gulish, A. (2018). *Women can't win: Despite making educational gains and pursuing high-wage majors, women still earn less than men*. Georgetown University Center on Education and the Workforce.

191. McCloy, R. A., Rottinghaus, P. J., Park, C. J., Feller, R., and Bloom, T. (2020). YouScience: mitigating the skills gap by addressing the gender imbalance in high-demand careers. *Industrial and Organizational Psychology 13*, 426–441.

192. Strahota, H. (2020, October 14). First-year earnings for the same degree and major can vary by $80,000 at different colleges, says new Georgetown University report. Georgetown University. http://cew.georgetown.edu/wp-content/uploads/GeorgetownCEW_PressRelease_CollegeMajorROI_10-14-20.pdf

193. Carnevale, A. (2018, August 20). Thinking about college? Pay attention to these 5 rules. LinkedIn. https://www.linkedin.com/pulse/thinking-college-pay-attention-5-rules-anthony-carnevale/

194. https://www.youscience.com/

195. Valant, J. (2021). We've built schools for a modern economy—but they overlook the challenges of our modern democracy. *Brown Center Chalkboard*, Brookings Institution. https://www.brookings.edu/blog/brown-center-chalkboard/2021/02/01/weve-built-schools-for-a-modern-economy-but-they-overlook-the-challenges-of-our-modern-democracy/

196. Jennings, J. (2020). *Fatigued by school reform*. Rowman & Littlefield, p. 1.

197. Snyder, T. D., de Brey, T., & Dillow, S. A. (2019). *Digest of education statistics, 2017*. Table 204.10: Number and percentage of public school students eligible for free or reduced-price lunch, by state: Selected years, 2000–01 through 2015–16. National Center for Education Statistics. https://nces.ed.gov/programs/digest/d17/tables/dt17_204.10.asp

198. Jennings, J. (2020). *Fatigued by school reform*. Rowman & Littlefield, p. 1.

199. Gould, E. (2019, March 27). Decades of rising economic inequality in the U.S.: Testimony before the U.S. House of Representatives Ways and Means Committee. Economic Policy Institute. https://docs.house.gov/meetings/WM/WM00/20190327/109167/HHRG-116-WM00-Wstate-GouldE-20190327.pdf

200. Jennings, J. (2020). *Fatigued by school reform*. Rowman & Littlefield.

201. Hanauer, N. (2019, July). Better schools won't fix America. *The Atlantic*. https://www.theatlantic.com/magazine/archive/2019/07/education-isnt-enough/590611/

202. Conant, J. B. (1959). *The American high school today*. McGraw-Hill.

203. Proefriedt, W. A. (2005, May 17). Revisiting James Bryant Conant: Realism, then and now. *Education Week*. https://www.edweek.org/leadership/opinion-revisiting-james-bryant-conant/2005/05

204. Oakes, J. (1985). *Keeping track: How schools structure inequality*. Yale University Press.

205. Ibid.

206. Oakes, J., & Saunders, M. (2008). *Beyond tracking: Multiple pathways to college, career, and civic participation*. Harvard Education Press.

207. Ibid., p. 256.

208. National Research Council. (1999). *How people learn: Brain, mind, experience, and school*. National Academies Press.

209. Bottoms, G., Preston, A., & Han, L. (2006). *Students can't wait: High schools must turn knowledge into action*. SREB; Bottoms, G., Preston, A., & Han, L. (2005). *Rigor, relevance, and relationships improve achievement in rural high schools: High school reform works when schools do the right things*. SREB; Bottoms, G., Preston, A., & Han, L. (2004). *High school reform works—when implemented: A comparative study of high- and low-implementation schools*. SREB.

210. Raudenbush, S. W., Rowan, B., & Cheong, Y. F. (1993). Higher order instructional goals in secondary schools: Class, teacher, and school influences. *American Educational Research Journal, 30*(3), 523–553; Oakes, J., Ormseth, T., Bell, R. M., & Camp, P. (1990). *Multiple inequalities: The effects of race, social class and tracking on opportunities to learn mathematics and science*. RAND Corporation. https://www.rand.org/pubs/reports/R3928.html

211. *Phi Delta Kappan*. (2019, September). The 51st annual PDK poll public of the public's attitudes toward the public schools. *Phi Delta Kappan, 101*(1), 14–15; *Phi Delta Kappan*. (2016, September). The 48th annual PDK poll public of the public's attitudes toward the public schools. *Phi Delta Kappan, 98*(1), 19; *Phi Delta Kappan*. (2017, September). The 49th annual PDK poll public of the public's attitudes toward the public schools. *Phi Delta Kappan, 99*(1), 28–29.

212. Jennings, J. (2020). *Fatigued by school reform*. Rowman & Littlefield, p. 95.

213. Ward, L. (2020, May 26). In valuing colleges, tops in prestige doesn't always mean tops in starting salaries. *Wall Street Journal*. https://www.wsj.com/articles/in-valuing-colleges-tops-in-prestige-doesnt-always-mean-tops-in-starting-salaries-11590532335

214. Tobias, S. (1994). Interest, prior knowledge, and learning. *Review of Educational Research, 64*(1), 37–54.

215. Fouad, N. A. (2007). Work and vocational psychology: Theory, research, and application. *Annual Review of Psychology, 58*, 543–564.

216. Schneider, B., & Stevenson, D. (1999). *The ambitious generation: American teenagers, motivated but directionless*. Yale University Press.

217. Castellano, M., Stringfield, S., & Stone, J. R. III. (2003). Secondary career and technical education and comprehensive school reform: Implications for research and practices. *Review of Educational Research, 73*(2), 231–272.

218. National Research Council & Institute of Medicine. (2004). *Engaging schools: Fostering high school students' motivation to learn.* National Academies Press, pp. 172–177.

219. National Research Council. (1999). *How people learn: Brain, mind, experience, and school.* National Academies Press, p. 65.

220. Ibid., p. 49.

221. Holloway, S. D. (1988). Concepts of ability and effort in Japan and the United States. *Review of Educational Research, 58*(3), 327–345.

222. National Research Council. (1999). *How people learn: Brain, mind, experience, and school.* National Academies Press, pp. 146–147.

223. Dweck, C. S. (2007). *Mindset: The new psychology of success.* Ballantine Books.

224. Clotfelter, T. C., Ladd, H. F., & Vigdor, J. L. (2008). *Teacher credentials and student achievement in high school: A cross-subject analysis with student fixed effects.* NBER Working Paper No. 13617. National Bureau of Economic Research.

225. Haycock, K. (1998). Good teaching matters: How well-qualified teachers can close the gap. *Thinking K–16, (3)*2, 7.

226. *Phi Delta Kappan.* (2020, September). The 52nd annual PDK poll public of the public's attitudes toward the public schools. *Phi Delta Kappan, 102*(1), K5.

227. Haycock, K. (1998). Good teaching matters: How well-qualified teachers can close the gap. *Thinking K–16, (3)*2, 7.

228. Darling-Hammond, L., Hyler, M. E., & Gardner, M. (2017). *Effective teacher professional development.* Learning Policy Institute. https://learningpolicyinstitute.org/sites/default/files/product-files/Effective_Teacher_Professional_Development_REPORT.pdf

229. Raudenbush, S. W., Rowan, B., & Cheong, Y. F. (1993). Higher order instructional goals in secondary schools: Class, teacher, and school influences. *American Educational Research Journal, (30)*3, 523–553.

230. Bottoms, G. (2017, July). Lessons learned: Effective professional development led to student success. Keynote presentation at the 31st Annual High Schools That Work Staff Development Conference, Southern Regional Education Board, Nashville, TN.

231. Elementary and Secondary Education Act. Public Law 89-10. Signed into law on April 11, 1965.

232. Seashore Louis, K., Leithwood, K., Wahlstrom, K. L., & Anderson, S. E. (2010). *Investigating the links to improve student learning: Executive summary of research findings.* Learning from Leadership Project. University of Minnesota Center for Applied Research and Educational Improvement and University of Toronto Ontario Institute for Studies in Education, p. 15. https://www.wallacefoundation.org/knowledge-center/Documents/Investigating-the-Links-to-Improved-Student-Learning.pdf

233. Bottoms, G., & Schmidt-Davis, J. (2010). *The three essentials: Improving schools requires district vision, support, and principal leadership.* SREB.

234. Seashore Louis, K., Leithwood, K., Wahlstrom, K. L., & Anderson, S. E. (2010). *Investigating the links to improve student learning: Executive summary of research findings.* Learning from Leadership Project. University of Minnesota Center for Applied Research and Educational Improvement and University of Toronto Ontario Institute for Studies in Education, p. 15. https://www.wallacefoundation.org/knowledge-center/Documents/Investigating-the-Links-to-Improved-Student-Learning.pdf; Bottoms, G., & Schmidt-Davis, J. (2010). *The three essentials: Improving schools requires district vision, support, and principal leadership.* SREB.

235. Seashore Louis, K., Leithwood, K., Wahlstrom, K. L., & Anderson, S. E. (2010). *Investigating the links to improve student learning: Executive summary of research findings.* Learning from Leadership Project. University of Minnesota Center for Applied Research and Educational Improvement and University of Toronto Ontario Institute for Studies in Education, p. 15. https://www.wallacefoundation.org/knowledge-center/Documents/Investigating-the-Links-to-Improved-Student-Learning.pdf

236. Ibid.

237. Bottoms, G., & Schmidt-Davis, J. (2010). *The three essentials: Improving schools requires district vision, district and state support, and principal leadership.* SREB.

Index

The letter *f* following a page locator denotes a figure.

academic readiness. *See* readiness
accountability standards for meeting bold goals, 14–15
accountability systems
  academic readiness in, 19–20
  classroom experiences, evaluating, 21–22
  data required for, 18–19
  example, 14
  meeting bold goals, 14, 18–22
  school experiences, evaluating, 21–22
  technical readiness in, 20–21
  well-designed, benefits of, 18
achievement
  PLPs and, 113–114, 119–120
  PMPs for, 102–104
  powerful CTE assignments and, 71*f*
  teacher expertise and, 187–188
achievement-aspiration gap, 162–164
achievement gaps
  literacy, 108–109
  mathematics, 92–93
  racial, 124
aspiration-achievement gap, 162–164
assessment
  of learning targets in PLPs, 115
  in literacy learning, 117–118
assessment data to plan reengagement lessons, 99
assessment evidence in powerful project assignments, 83, 85–86
assessment study group, 27, 29–31
assignment action team, 54–56
assignments, powerful. *See* powerful project assignments, designing

bold goals
  for connected learning, 13, 13*f*
  requirements for, 12–13

bold goals, achieving
  accountability standards and systems in, 14–15
  actions for, 68–69
  curriculum and course design for, 16–17
  employers, working with, 16–17
  essential actions for setting and, 14–17
  measuring progress toward, 18–22
  middle school education in, 15–16
  postsecondary institutions, working with, 16–17
  readiness standards, setting higher for, 15
  teacher accountability for, 17

career and technical education (CTE) assignments
  academic assignments, connecting to, 72–73
  achievement and, 71*f*
  engineering design process applied, 84*f*
  improving the rigor of, steps for, 89–90
  readiness and, 72, 75
  student perceptions of, AC students compared, 71*f*
career and technical education (CTE) courses
  career pathways, 32, 34
  district leadership action teams role, 52–53, 56, 61
  district study groups role, 34, 36–37, 39
  powerful assignments, implementing in, 88–89
  redesign, need for, 32, 34
career and technical education (CTE) programs
  beliefs regarding, 185
  higher-level academic studies, combining with, 26–27
  pathways to success, 185
career and technical education (CTE) teachers, supporting, 51–53
career pathway, organization, and scheduling action team, 50–54

career pathways
 district high school organization and
  scheduling study group in planning for, 36–37
 rigorous and relevant, design features of, 25–26
career pathway study group, 27–28, 31–36
career readiness
 accountability standards, setting for, 14–15
 district assessment study group on, 29–31
 gaps in, 141–144
 literacy skills for, 107–108
 math-readiness for, 93–94
 meaning of, 19
 measuring, 20
 multiple pathways in preparing for, 184–186
 valuing, accountability systems for, 14
career readiness curriculum, 24f
classroom experiences, evaluating, 21–22
college for all movement, 10, 163
college graduates, 1, 9–10. See also higher education
college readiness
 accountability standards, setting for, 14–15
 district assessment study group on, 29–31
 gaps in, 141–144
 literacy skills for, 107–108
 math-readiness for, indicators of, 93–94
 meaning of, 19
 measures for determining, 19
 multiple pathways to prepare for, 184–186
 statistics, 141
 valuing, accountability systems for, 14
college readiness curriculum, 24f
connected learning, bold goals for, 13, 13f
continuous improvement. See also distributed
 leadership teams
 action teams, focus and composition, 43–44
 four Rs of, 42
 PDSAs to achieve a culture of, 44–46
 practical steps for, 61
counseling, exploring, and advising (CEA) action
 team, 58–60, 159–162
counseling, exploring, and advising (CEA) program
 aspiration-achievement gap, addressing the,
  162–164
 bold goals for graduates, 161–162
 path to success, enabling students to find a,
  164–166, 172–174
 practical steps for implementation, 174–175
 purpose of, 159
 theory of action, 172–174
counseling, exploring, and advising (CEA) program,
 design features
 counseling and advising sessions with students
  and parents/guardians, 170–171
 counselor-led advisory systems, 165, 168–170
 curriculum-based career exploration, 166–168
 informed support for post-high school
  options, 165

counseling, exploring, and advising (CEA) program,
 design features (continued)
 interest and aptitude assessments, 171–172
 multiple pathways through high school, 165
 parents as full partners, 165, 170–171
 programs of study based on paths to success, 165
 single advisor across the school years, 165
 summary, 164–166
COVID-19, 2
curriculum
 designing to meet bold goals, 16–17
 post-school plans, misalignment between, 24
 powerful assignment action team, 54–56

data, accountability, and policy action team, 47–50
data analysis
 accountability systems, 18–19
 to plan reengagement lessons, 99
 for successful transitions, 127–129, 146–147
democracy, preparing students for 21st century, 176
distributed leadership teams
 career pathway, organization, and scheduling
  action team, 50–54
 counseling, exploring, and advising action
  team, 58–60
 data, accountability, and policy action team,
  47–50
 importance of, 42
 middle to high school transition action team,
  56–57
 perspectives, 46–47
 powerful assignment action team, 54–56
 role of, 42–43
 senior-year transition action team, 57–58
district buy-in, achieving
 district leaders, role of, 27
 example, 23–24
 study groups, essential nature of, 40–41
 study groups to engage stakeholders, 27–41
district leaders, transformative, 191–194
district study groups
 assessment group, 27, 29–31
 career pathway group, 27–28, 31–36
 essential nature of, 40–41
 high school organization and scheduling, 28,
  36–37
 participants in, 27
 purpose of, 27
 strategic planning, 28–29, 38–40
dropouts, 9

employers, working with for meeting bold goals, 16–17
employment. See also workplace
 COVID-19, effect on, 2
 a good job, meaning of, 11
 preparing high-schoolers for, 1–3
expectations, setting, 12, 180–181

family engagement, increasing, 165, 170–171, 182–183

goals, bold. *See* bold goals
a good job, meaning of, 11
growth mindset, 186–187

higher education. *See also* college readiness
    readiness standards for success, meeting, 10–11
    working with, for meeting bold goals, 16–17
high school graduates
    bold goals for, 161–162
    lower-level jobs for, 2, 11
    mathematics skills, 91–92
    percent of jobs filled by, 1
    post-school plans, curriculum misalignment, 24
    statistics, 9
high school graduation
    below readiness students, preparing for, 157
    bold goals for, 161
    recommended requirements for, 25
high school organization and scheduling study group, 28, 36–37
high school transitions
    goal for, 144
    readiness determinations, 146–148
    readiness gaps, 124–127
high school transitions, best practices for improving
    assignments, higher-level and relevant, 130
    assignments, rigorous and project-based, 131
    courses aligned with college-/career-readiness standards, 130, 131
    credit recovery, 136
    culture of connected learning, 136–137
    examples, 130
    expectations in, 130
    instructional practices engaging student teams, 130
    literacy-readiness courses, 131–133
    low-level assignments replaced with higher-level learning, 130
    math instruction, 130
    professional development, 131
    redesigned student schedules, 127, 133–135
    relearning opportunities, 135
    success option, 135–136
    time provided for extended support, 133–135
high school transitions, successful
    data analysis in, 127–129, 146–147
    district assessment study group and, 29, 30–31
    district career pathway study group and, 32–33
    practical steps for, 139
    a prepared statement of need in, 127–130
    theory of action for, 137–139

high school transition teams
    data, accountability, and policy action team, 48
    Middle to High Transition (MHT) action teams, 56–57, 126–127
    senior-year transition (SYT) action team, 57–58, 141–144

leadership teams. *See* distributed leadership teams
learning
    connected, bold goals for, 13, 13*f*
    ownership of, promoting, 115–116
listening, literacy readiness and, 111–112
literacy-based assignments
    designing, 118–119
    to improve achievement, 123
    need for, 107
    written product in, 113–114
literacy gap, 108–109
literacy practices, powerful. *See* powerful literacy practices (PLPs)
literacy readiness, 110–112, 153
literacy skills, improving across the curriculum, 109–110

math achievement gap, 92–93
mathematics practices, powerful. *See* powerful mathematics practices (PMPs)
mathematics skills, 91–92
math readiness, 93–94, 153–154
middle school education for meeting bold goals, 15–16
Middle to High Transition (MHT) action teams, 56–57, 126–127
military service, 108

parents as full partners, 165, 170–171
powerful assignment action team, 54–56
powerful assignments
    characteristics of, 73–75
    criteria for, 75, 76*f*
    example, 76–78
    support CTE teachers shift to, 86–88
powerful assignments, design and implementation
    in CTE courses, theory of action for, 88–89
    establish a CTE assignment team, 79–80
    identify knowledge and skills needed, 80
    practical steps for implementation, 89–90
    timeline, 79
powerful CTE assignments
    academic assignments, connecting to, 72–73
    achievement and, 71*f*
    engineering design process applied, 84*f*
    readiness and, 72, 75
powerful literacy-based assignment (PLBA) action team, 109–110

powerful literacy practices (PLPs)
  achievement and use of, 119–121
  embed reading instruction and strategies,
    115–116
  establish, communicate and assess learning
    targets, 115
  formative and summative assessment, 117
  impact on classroom experiences, 119–121
  scaffolding with explicit strategies, 114
  shifting instruction, 113–114
  theory of action, 121–123
  use student discourse for ownership and
    comprehension, 116–117
powerful mathematics action team, 93, 101, 104
powerful mathematics assignments (PMA), 92–93
powerful mathematics practices (PMPs)
  achievement and use of, 102–104, 113–114
  characteristics of, 95–96
  engage with assignments that matter, 97–98
  goals of, 96
  impact of, 101–104
  plan for and ensure a balanced approach, 96
  practical steps for implementation, 105–106
  professional development and coaching in,
    101–103
  student perceptions of math, changes in,
    102–104
  support the ownership of learning, 100
  teacher reflection, 100–101
  theory of action, 104–105
  use data for planning reengagement lessons,
    99
  use questioning and feedback for
    understanding, 98
powerful project assignments, designing
  brainstorm project titles, 80–81
  determine assessment evidence, 83, 85–86
  determine career role for completion, 82
  develop a description to master standards and
    complete the project, 82–83
  embed mathematics, 83
  an essential question, 81–82
  example, 87–88
  the full unit, 83, 84f
  identify essential 21st century skills for
    completion, 81
  student activities, 84f
principals, transformative, 194–196
professional development, 188–190

readiness. See also career readiness; college readiness
  academic, 19–20
  literacy, 110–112, 153
  math, 93–94, 153–154
  powerful assignments and, 72, 75
  standards for success, meeting, 10–11
  technical, 20–21

readiness gaps
  college and career, 141–144
  district assessment study group on, 30
  high school readiness, 124–127
  in high school transitions, 124–127
  marginalized and minority groups, 142
  racial, 124, 141
readiness standards, 15
reading comprehension, literacy readiness and, 110–
  111, 116–117
reading instruction, 115

school experiences, evaluating, 21–22
school leaders, transformative, 191–196
school transformation
  changing attitudes and beliefs for, 177–179
  for economic success post-graduation, 176–
    177, 183–184
  meaning of, 179
school transformation, essential elements of
  boards and leaders are allies, 191–194
  different paths to success, 184–186
  expectations vs. tracking, 180–181
  family engagement, 182–183
  growth mindset, 186–187
  principal leadership, 194–196
  student vision, 183–184
  teacher expertise, 187–188
  teacher growth, 188–190
senior-year transition (SYT) action team, 57–58,
  141–144
senior-year transition (SYT) options
  approaching readiness students, 147, 152–155
  below readiness students, 147, 155–158
  postsecondary-ready students accelerated
    option, 147–152, 151–152
speaking, literacy readiness and, 111–112
strategic planning study group, 28–29, 38–40
students
  aspiration-achievement gap, 162–164
  career choice, predictors of, 184
  connecting with, 60
  economic success, preparing for, 183–184
  valuing with high readiness standards, 15
  workplace, preparing for the, 1–3, 1f
students, marginalized and minority groups
  achievement by, 186–188, 191
  achievement-household income relation, 179
  family aspirations for, 182
  percent in schools, 178
  upward mobility for, 179
student vision, developing, 183–184
success
  academic-readiness standards for, meeting, 10–11
  different paths to, respecting, 184–186
  economic, preparing students for, 1–3, 1f,
    10–11, 16–17, 91, 107, 145, 176–177

teacher accountability, 17
teacher accountability with support, 17
teacher expertise, achievement and, 187–188
technical readiness, 20–21
transitions. *See* high school transitions; senior-year
    transition (SYT) options

unemployment, 2, 11
United States, economic competitiveness, 11

workplace. *See also* career readiness; employment
    job requirements, 10–11, 16–17
    literacy skills, need for, 107
    preparing high-schoolers for the, 1–3, 1*f*
    STEM-related skills, demand for, 91
    work from home option, 145
writing, literacy readiness and, 111

About the Author

Gene Bottoms's efforts to improve educational experiences for all children began more than 60 years ago, when he became an 8th grade teacher in Cherokee, Georgia, with only two years of college education.

The next year, he became the principal and teacher at the first of two rural elementary–middle schools. He created the first school library in both schools. He led the teachers in a reading program where students read a book of their choosing each month. This early experience developed a lifelong passion for engaging all students in developing strong literacy skills through reading and expressing their understanding orally and in writing.

Bottoms's true vision of "education for all" was planted during a 1960 summer school class at the University of Georgia, when he participated in a field trip to Clarksville, Georgia, to one of the state's two postsecondary schools that prepared students for trade and technical occupations. There he learned how career and technical teachers embedded both mathematics and literacy into their instructional strategies. From this he saw the true power of how career and technical education provided a way for students to learn academic knowledge and skills. His career shifted from the classroom when he became director of student services at South Georgia Technical College. He also worked with the Georgia Department of Education to design innovative programs to connected academics and CTE studies. In 1972, he was named director of a newly created division to improve both academic and career and technical education.

Later, Bottoms was elected president and then executive director of the American Vocational Association, where he advocated for higher-quality career and technical studies linked to higher-level academic courses for preparing students for multiple career and postsecondary options. This placed him in a key position to help shape the federal legislation for reauthorizing vocational education in 1984—The Carl D. Perkins Vocational and Technical Education Act.

Once the Perkins Act was passed, Bottoms returned to Georgia, where he began his 30-plus year tenure with the Southern Regional Education Board. There he led a high school improvement network called High Schools That Work, to improve high schools across the Southeastern states and beyond by championing the connecting of higher-quality CTE studies with rigorous academic coursework. In 2010, Bottoms launched a multistate initiative to develop advanced career courses to do for CTE what advanced placement curricula did for academics.

He has authored or coauthored more than 200 books, articles, reports, and editorials including several SREB Commission Reports: *A New Mission for the Middle Grades: Preparing Students for a Changing World*, *The Next Generation of School Accountability: A Blueprint for Raising High School Achievement and Graduation Rates*, and *Credentials for All: An Imperative for SREB States*. He holds doctorate and master's degrees in guidance and counseling from the University of Georgia.

This book is a continuation of a journey Bottoms began more than six decades ago. Throughout that journey, he was informed by research, policymakers, and practitioners. He remains dedicated to maximizing the potential of CTE to help more students—students of color, students who have grown up in poverty, students in rural areas and small towns—have a real chance to succeed in college, careers, and their adult lives. Bottoms hopes this book will inspire current and future district and school leaders in creating accelerated learning experiences for all students in our public middle and high schools.

Related ASCD Resources

At the time of publication, the following resources were available (ASCD stock numbers in parentheses).

Design Thinking for School Leaders: Five Roles and Mindsets That Ignite Positive Change by Alyssa Gallagher and Kami Thordarson (#118022)

Engineering Essentials for STEM Instruction: How do I infuse real-world problem solving into science, technology, and math? (ASCD Arias) by Pamela Truesdell (#SF114048)

Fighting for Change in Your School: How to Avoid Fads and Focus on Substance by Harvey Alvy (#117007)

Leading Change Together: Developing Educator Capacity Within Schools and Systems by Eleanor Drago-Severson and Jessica Blum-DeStefano (# 117027)

Leading High-Performance School Systems: Lessons from the World's Best by Marc Tucker (#118055)

Lesson Imaging in Math and Science: Anticipating Student Ideas and Questions for Deeper STEM Learning by Michelle Stephan, David Pugalee, Julie Cline, and Chris Cline (#117008)

STEM Leadership: How do I create a STEM culture in my school? (ASCD Arias) by Traci Buckner and Brian Boyd (#SF114081)

Ten Steps to Managing Change in Schools: How do we take initiatives from goals to actions? (ASCD Arias) by Jeffrey Benson (#SF115072)

What Makes a World-Class School and How We Can Get There by James H. Stronge with Xianxuan Xu (#117078)

Download resources from a professional learning platform with hundreds of research-based best practices and tools for your classroom at http://myteachsource.ascd.org/

For more information, send an email to member@ascd.org; call 1-800-933-2723 or 703-578-9600; send a fax to 703-575-5400; or write to Information Services, ASCD, 1703 N. Beauregard St., Alexandria, VA 22311-1714 USA.

THE WHOLE CHILD

The ASCD Whole Child approach is an effort to transition from a focus on narrowly defined academic achievement to one that promotes the long-term development and success of all children. Through this approach, ASCD supports educators, families, community members, and policymakers as they move from a vision about educating the whole child to sustainable, collaborative actions.

Tomorrow's High School relates to the **challenged** tenet.
*For more about the ASCD Whole Child approach, visit **www.ascd.org/wholechild.***

WHOLE CHILD
TENETS

1 HEALTHY
Each student enters school healthy and learns about and practices a healthy lifestyle.

2 SAFE
Each student learns in an environment that is physically and emotionally safe for students and adults.

3 ENGAGED
Each student is actively engaged in learning and is connected to the school and broader community.

4 SUPPORTED
Each student has access to personalized learning and is supported by qualified, caring adults.

5 CHALLENGED
Each student is challenged academically and prepared for success in college or further study and for employment and participation in a global environment.

Become an ASCD member today!
Go to www.ascd.org/joinascd
or call toll-free: 800-933-ASCD (2723)

CPSIA information can be obtained
at www.ICGtesting.com
Printed in the USA
LVHW050047221222
735709LV00005B/356